Missing
Missing Without Trace in Ireland

Barry Cummins

Gill & Macmillan

For everyone who has been lost

Gill & Macmillan Ltd
Hume Avenue, Park West, Dublin 12
with associated companies throughout the world
www.gillmacmillan.ie
© Barry Cummins 2003
0 7171 3290 0

Design and print origination by Carole Lynch
Printed by ColourBooks Ltd, Dublin

This book is typeset in Goudy 10.5 on 14.5pt.

*The paper used in this book comes from the wood pulp of
managed forests. For every tree felled, at least one tree
is planted, thereby renewing natural resources.*

A CIP catalogue record for this book is available
from the British Library.

7 9 11 12 10 8

Contents

❧⟡❧

Acknowledgments vii

Introduction 1

1. Annie McCarrick 23

2. Jo Jo Dullard 50

3. Fiona Pender 78

4. Ciara Breen 102

5. Fiona Sinnott 122

6. Operation Trace 142

7. Mary Boyle 186

8. Philip Cairns 210

9. Ireland's Missing 234

Acknowledgments

<figure>⋖⋗∘⋖⋗</figure>

This book would not have been possible without the kind assistance of many families of missing people. These families kindly gave me their time and hospitality, and shared many painful memories. I am conscious that missing people have become something of a 'commodity', with certain journalists wildly speculating about what might have happened to them, without thinking of the effect such insensitive reporting may have on the relatives of those missing people. This book deals with a number of missing people who have been murdered; in other cases the families of the missing people are not in a position to state categorically what they believe happened, and they still hold out hope that their loved ones may yet walk through the front door. To every one of the families of the missing people featured in this book I offer my profound thanks for your time and your trust.

In particular I say thank you to Nancy and John McCarrick, whose only daughter, Annie, was abducted and murdered in Ireland in 1993. I also thank Mary and Martin Phelan and Kathleen and Séamus Bergin. Mary and Kathleen's sister Jo Jo Dullard was abducted and murdered in 1995; Mary continues to campaign vigorously for more action to be taken by the Gardaí and the state to find missing people; through the Jo Jo Dullard Memorial Trust she has ensured that missing people will never be forgotten. I thank Josephine Pender, whose daughter Fiona was abducted and murdered in 1996 while seven months pregnant.

Josephine's remarkable fortitude in the face of a number of tragedies should be a source of inspiration to all. I thank Bernadette Breen, whose only child, Ciara, was abducted and murdered in 1997. Bernadette's remarkable bravery is matched only by her love for her missing child. I also express profound thanks to Caroline and Diane Sinnott, whose younger sister Fiona disappeared in 1998. Thank you for your time and trust.

Two families have been devastated by the loss of a child in unexplained circumstances. I thank Ann and Charlie Boyle, whose daughter Mary disappeared in 1977; your hospitality and openness will not be forgotten. I thank also Alice and Philip Cairns, whose young son Philip was abducted while walking to school in 1986, for their kindness and the many hours spent discussing the most painful of subjects. I thank also Collette McCann, whose sister Eva Brennan disappeared in 1993.

In deference to a request from her family, one missing woman is not referred to by name in this book. I would also like to thank that family for their time.

Many members of the Garda Síochána gave invaluable assistance in the research on each of the missing persons cases featured in this book. Ultimately the Gardaí were talking about investigations that have failed so far to reach a conclusion. Their frustrations at failing to solve each missing person case, and in some cases to catch murderers, were clearly evident during our conversations, briefings, and formal interviews.

In particular I thank Superintendent John Farrelly of the Garda Press Office for his continuous assistance during my research. I also thank Garda Damien Hogan of the Garda Press Office for his invaluable help in obtaining background information. Thank you to all the team at the Garda Press Office for dealing so efficiently with my queries.

I thank Assistant Commissioner Tony Hickey, who oversaw the establishment of Operation Trace in 1998, which sought to establish whether there were links between any of the cases of missing women in Leinster. I thank also Superintendent Jerry O'Connell (retired), who headed Operation Trace. I thank the gardaí who worked as part of the Operation Trace team: Alan Bailey, Pat Treacy, Mark Kerrigan, Maura Walsh, and Marianne Cusack.

I thank the following retired and serving gardaí, all of whom gave of their time without hesitation: Chief Superintendent Martin Donnellan, Chief Superintendent John O'Brien, Superintendent Tony Brislane, Superintendent John McFadden, Superintendent Tony Sourke, Superintendent Bill McMunn (retired), Superintendent Michael Duffy (retired), Superintendent Gerry Murray (retired), Inspector John Dunleavy, Detective-Sergeant Declan Goode, Detective-Sergeant Tom Doyle, Detective-Sergeant Con Nolan, Detective-Sergeant Pat Campbell, Detective-Sergeant Joe Molloy, Detective-Sergeant Gary Kavanagh, Detective Sergeant Aidan Murray (retired), Detective-Sergeant Mick Dalton, Sergeant Seán Leydon, Detective-Garda Aubrey Steedman, Detective-Garda Mary Fallon, Detective-Garda Val Smith (retired), Detective-Garda Noel Lynagh (retired), and Detective-Garda John Harrington (retired).

There are other gardaí who, because of the nature of the information they imparted, cannot be named. Thank you to each one of you for your time and trust.

I thank also the many other people who gave of their time during the writing of this book. In relation to my research into the disappearance of Annie McCarrick I thank her former boy-friend Dermot Ryan, her friend Geraldine Delaney, and her former college lecturer Father Mícheál Mac Gréil. I thank also Jo Jo Dullard's friend Mary Cullinane, and also the photographer Edward Cody. I thank John McGuinness TD, who campaigns alongside Jo Jo's sister Mary for the establishment of a specialist Garda National Missing Persons Unit. I thank also Fiona Pender's friend Emer Condron, who continues to campaign to raise awareness about missing people. I thank Ciara Breen's former tutor Rosaleen Bishop and the journalists Eoin McGarvey in Co. Donegal and David Tucker in Co. Wexford.

I thank all the staff at Gill and Macmillan, especially the commissioning editor, Fergal Tobin, for giving me the opportunity to write this book.

I thank my friends in journalism, both in crime reporting and beyond, for their interest and support, especially my colleagues at the Four Courts and in Today FM. I thank also my former boss Barry Flynn for giving me my first break in journalism, and the staff of St Mark's Community School in Tallaght.

On a personal level I would like to thank my parents, Patricia O'Neill and Barry Cummins, and my brother Mark for their constant support and interest. Finally, I especially thank Grace for all her enthusiasm, guidance and suggestions, and without whom I could not have completed this book.

Introduction

❦

Between March 1993 and July 1998 six young women aged between seventeen and twenty-six disappeared without a trace in Ireland. It is feared that all six women were abducted and murdered. Despite intensive Garda investigations, massive media coverage and public appeals, the bodies of the six women have not been found. Their disappearance has brought untold anguish to their families and shocked a country unused to such unexplained and seemingly random violence. And, of course, there is the disturbing reality that the killers responsible have not been caught. There live among us killers who have gone to extraordinary lengths to conceal their crimes, who have not left an identifiable crime scene behind, who have somehow hidden the bodies of their defenceless victims.

Four of the families of the missing women accept the terrible fact that their loved ones have been murdered. A fifth family fear that the same fate befell their loved one but still hold out a glimmer of hope that she may be alive. The sixth family maintain that any speculation about their missing teenager being murdered is simply that—speculation.

The trauma of the families of the six women has been laid bare in the glare of the media. Hundreds of buildings and thousands of acres of land have been painstakingly searched; suspects have been arrested and questioned; but still the mystery of the disappearance of the women remains. We will never know the emotional and physical pain they suffered in the hours or minutes after they were last seen alive. The recovery of the bodies of the missing women is crucial for the distraught families, who long for some kind of closure; it might also help prevent similar murders being committed in the future. Wherever the missing women now lie, there is evidence to link the killer or killers to each individual crime. Recovering the bodies is a must for the Gardaí, who know that some of the most heinous crimes to be committed in Ireland remain unexplained, undetected, and unsolved.

This book confronts the disturbing fact that a number of Ireland's most evil murderers have not been caught. In each of the cases of young women believed to have been abducted and murdered in Leinster, suspects have been identified by the Gardaí. In three of the cases prime suspects have been identified, yet no charges have been brought. Without the bodies of the women being discovered, and without the exact crime scenes being found, the job of bringing a case before the courts is an almost impossible one. Yet each of these cases remains an active one for the detectives involved.

The first of the six women to disappear was an American woman, Annie McCarrick, who was twenty-six when she was abducted and murdered somewhere near the Wicklow Mountains in March 1993. Her disappearance devastated her parents, John and Nancy McCarrick, who are now divorced. Annie was an only child, and the fact that her body has never been found has caused great distress for her parents, who live in Long Island, New York. Growing up in an Irish-American community, Annie developed a passion for Ireland. When she was nineteen she arrived in Dublin for the first time and fell in love with Irish culture and the Irish people. She lived in Ireland for three years while she studied in Dublin and Maynooth. She developed serious relationships with two men during that time, and had a wide circle of friends. By Christmas 1992 she was back in New York and trying to decide what she wanted to do with her life. She was thinking of becoming a teacher, and she decided, once and for all, that she was going to go back to Ireland to see if she could settle down and make her life here. She arrived in Dublin in January 1993. Less than three months later she was abducted and murdered, after heading out for a walk in Enniskerry, Co. Wicklow. Her body has never been found, and her killer has never been caught.

The second woman to disappear in similar chilling circumstances was the 21-year-old Co. Kilkenny woman Jo Jo Dullard. Late at night on 9 November 1995 she was trying to hitch a lift home in Moone, Co. Kildare, when her killer stopped to offer her a lift. She had already hitched lifts from Naas to Kilcullen, and then from Kilcullen to Moone, but she was still more than forty miles from her home in Callan, Co. Kilkenny. Whoever stopped to offer her a lift at about 11:40 p.m. managed to conceal his murderous intentions. Jo Jo Dullard's body has never been found, leading to one of her sisters, Mary Phelan, publicly criticising the failure of the Gardaí to conduct an extensive search within a twenty-mile radius of where she was last seen. Mary has also spearheaded a campaign for the establishment of a specialist Garda National Missing Persons Unit. Jo Jo's disappearance has traumatised her three sisters and brother and her nieces and nephews. There are a number of suspects for this abduction and murder, but without Jo Jo's body being found the killer or killers remain at large.

In August 1996 25-year-old Fiona Pender, who at the time was seven months pregnant, was lured out of her flat in Tullamore by someone she knew. At some unknown place in the midlands she was murdered, and her body was concealed. Her violent death was the second tragedy to hit the Pender family: her younger brother, Mark, was killed in a motorbike accident in June 1995; but the murder of Fiona Pender and her unborn baby was not the last tragedy to befall the Penders. In March 2000 Fiona's father, Seán Pender, took his own life at the family home in Connolly Park, Tullamore.

The abduction and murder of Fiona Pender differ from those of Annie McCarrick and Jo Jo Dullard, in that the Gardaí believe Fiona knew her attacker. While Annie McCarrick and Jo Jo Dullard were both out walking or standing on the roadside when they were attacked by their killers, Fiona Pender was last seen at home in her flat in Church Street, Tullamore. There was no sign of a struggle or disturbance; the most credible hypothesis is that Fiona either left the flat in the company of her would-be killer or left to meet that person by arrangement. A prime suspect has been identified, but no charges have been brought.

The fourth woman to disappear was technically a child when she was abducted and murdered. Ciara Breen was a few weeks short of her eighteenth birthday when she sneaked out of her bedroom window in Dundalk in the early hours of the morning in February 1997. Whoever she was going to meet, and wherever she was going, she didn't want her mother to know about it. The Gardaí believe she was going to meet an older man, and that this is the person who is responsible for her abduction and murder. A prime suspect has been identified and has been questioned at length, but he denies that he even knew Ciara. Her murder has devastated her mother, who has lost her only child in the most callous of circumstances. Whoever killed Ciara Breen has taken not only Bernadette Breen's only child but her best friend, her whole life.

A year after Ciara Breen's murder another teenager disappeared in sinister circumstances, this time at the other end of Leinster. Fiona Sinnott was nineteen and the proud mother of eleven-month-old Emma Rose when she vanished from her home in Broadway, Co. Wexford, in February 1998. She is the only one of the six missing women who has left behind a child. A number of people have been questioned about her suspected abduction, but no charges have been brought. A major operation leading to the draining of a lake in the locality also led nowhere. A prime suspect has been identified, but, as in the other cases, without a crime scene, or a witness, or a body, a prosecution is unlikely.

The sixth woman to vanish in the Leinster area within the five years between 1993 and 1998 disappeared in circumstances that have instilled fear throughout the country. In deference to a specific request from this woman's family, she is not referred to by name in this book. She was just eighteen when, on a Tuesday afternoon in July 1998, she vanished from the front gate of her home at Roseberry, near Droichead Nua, Co. Kildare. She was within yards of her front door, having walked home along the side of the road from Droichead Nua, when something happened that prevented her making it into the safety of her home. Unlike the previous five missing women cases, this time the Garda response was immediate, with detectives combing the area for clues within hours of the disappearance. In the five other cases the alarm was not raised for hours or even days, and for more than a week in the case of Fiona Sinnott.

Despite an intensive search of bogland and forest in Cos. Kildare and Wicklow, and raids on the homes of a number of criminals, nothing was found to show exactly what had happened to the young woman, who came from a loving family and was looking forward to studying to become a teacher. Whatever happened that afternoon in 1998, a heartbreaking mystery remains for the young woman's family. This case was hampered for a number of months when a Co. Fermanagh man made a number of hoax phone calls claiming he had information about the disappearance. In a separate aspect of the case, it was not until almost two years later that it emerged that one of the country's most dangerous men, who is now serving a fifteen-year prison sentence for a random attack on another woman, was working in the area at the time. This man has been questioned in prison by detectives but has denied any knowledge of any of the missing women. Detectives fear that whoever is responsible for the disappearance of other missing women—particularly of Annie McCarrick and Jo Jo Dullard—may be responsible for the Droichead Nua case too.

Indeed it is such speculation that led in September 1998 to the establishment of a special Garda initiative—Operation Trace—to explore the possibility that the cases of any of the six missing women might be linked. A six-member team analysed the movements of more than seven thousand convicted or suspected sex offenders who had lived or travelled in Ireland since the early 1980s. Using a computer program that they nicknamed OVID (for Offenders, Victims and Incidents Data-base), they compiled and analysed information on all known offenders, all known victims, and all violent incidents known to have occurred in the previous two decades. It was a massive task, with every scrap of information being logged in the hope that a previously unseen link might be established between any of the cases. From the Operation Trace headquarters at Naas, Co. Kildare, detectives would co-ordinate the arrests of nine men and women in connection with the investigations, but no charges were brought.

Despite the massive amount of information collected, no clear links could be established between any of the missing women. Members of the Operation Trace team were always conscious that they were only analysing information relating to known sex offenders and that there were many other offenders who had not yet been caught and who might be responsible for one or more of the disappearances. Indeed in the years since Operation Trace was set up a number of violent men who had never before come to the attention of the Gardaí have been caught for some of the most shocking crimes Ireland has known. These offenders are usually married men with children, who somehow have been able to keep their evil and violent tendencies hidden from even their closest family members. Detectives remain convinced that more of these men of seemingly unblemished character will be caught in the future.

There are so many questions and so few concrete answers. Are the men who killed some of Ireland's missing women family men? Do their parents or wives or children suspect them? Are they men with no previous convictions, having never come to the attention of the Gardaí? Are they local people who know the area around the site of each disappearance? Or are they living a vagrant life, travelling around Ireland or beyond, evading detection? Have some of them already taken their secret to their grave? Or are they in prison serving sentences for other crimes, and remaining for ever silent about their evil deeds?

Detectives investigating many unsolved missing and murder cases will often state publicly that somebody knows something that could help solve the crime. A perfect example of the truth of this belief was seen at the Central Criminal Court in October 2002 when John Crerar, a former army sergeant and father of five from Co. Kildare with no previous convictions, was convicted of the murder of 23-year-old Phyllis Murphy, who was raped and murdered in December 1979. For twenty-three years John Crerar evaded capture for one of Ireland's oldest unsolved crimes, but he was finally caught after two crucial developments. The first came when advances in forensic science finally identified semen taken from Phyllis Murphy's body as being Crerar's. The second was that one man's conscience finally got the better of him.

From December 1979 until July 1999 a former workmate of John Crerar's, Paddy Bolger, gave Crerar an alibi for the night Phyllis Murphy was abducted and murdered. He said Crerar had been working alongside him as a security guard at the Black and Decker plant in Kildare throughout the night of 22 December 1979. It was only when detectives put it to Bolger in July 1999 that they had scientific evidence to suggest that Crerar was the murderer that Paddy Bolger suddenly admitted that he was lying, and had been lying for twenty years. Lies like these have protected other murderers, and may continue to protect some of Ireland's most evil killers. Paddy Bolger did not think his colleague could have been the vicious killer who took the life of Phyllis Murphy; by the time his suspicions began to form, the lie was already established, and for almost twenty years he kept his mouth shut.

The successful prosecution of John Crerar is vital in considering the difficulties faced by detectives investigating the murders of missing women in Leinster. For twenty-seven days Phyllis Murphy's naked body lay undiscovered in a wooded area near the Wicklow Gap. Despite the length of time it took to find her remains, the forces of nature conspired eventually to put her killer behind bars. During the four weeks that her body lay hidden by ferns in a dense forested area, freezing temperatures preserved her body and in turn the valuable evidence that twenty-three years later would lead to John Crerar being jailed for the murder. Within hours of the body being discovered a sheet of snow lay across the eastern part of Ireland. If the body had still been lying in the forest, the blanket of snow would most probably have concealed it from view. As it was, the recovery of Phyllis Murphy's body was a source of comfort to her grieving family, who already knew in their hearts that something terrible had happened to her.

From the point of view of the Garda investigation, the recovery of Phyllis Murphy's body was crucial. In 1979, because of the small amount of the sample recovered from the body, the type of scientific analysis available could not establish the DNA profile of the killer to be matched with any of the many local men who volunteered a blood sample. In March 1980 John Crerar volunteered a blood sample at a Garda station. However, it would be another nineteen years before advances in DNA technology enabled forensic scientists to match his blood with the swabs taken from Phyllis Murphy's body. It was thanks to the foresight of a number of gardaí, including Christy Sheridan (now retired), who stored the swabs in a Garda safe 'just in case,' that a 23-year murder mystery was eventually solved.

The investigation into the murder of Phyllis Murphy is a perfect example of how crucial it is to have a body or a crime scene when investigating a murder. For the four weeks before the body was found in January 1980 Phyllis Murphy was classified as a missing person. From the circumstances of her disappearance while she was travelling home from Droichead Nua to Kildare for Christmas it was clear that something terrible had happened. Yet for those four weeks she was in the same category that Annie McCarrick would be fourteen years later, and later Jo Jo Dullard and the other missing women. It was only when her body was found that any real progress could be made in catching Phyllis Murphy's killer.

Another of Ireland's most violent men was not known to Gardaí when Operation Trace was set up. Larry Murphy, a 36-year-old father of two from Baltinglass, Co. Wicklow, is now serving a fifteen-year prison sentence for one of the most horrific crimes to be committed in Ireland. Whether or not he has any relevant information relating to any missing women, the circumstances of his shocking crime in February 2000 provide solid evidence that cold and calculating would-be killers live among us.

Just before midnight on 11 February 2000, Ken Jones and Trevor Moody were hunting in a secluded forest area of Kilranelagh in west Co. Wicklow. It was a quiet night, and both men thought there was no-one else for miles. Suddenly they heard a piercing scream, followed by the sound of a car revving up. Almost as quickly, the two hunters saw a car approaching them. As it sped past, both men got a look at the driver of the car—and they both recognised him. It was Larry Murphy from Woodside, a small community a few miles away in Baltinglass. Just then the two men saw the naked woman. She was stumbling towards them, her face bloodied. As they spotted her, she too saw them. Still trying to comprehend what was going on, the two men approached the woman and—not knowing what else to say—asked her if she was all right. She recoiled in terror: in her terrified state she thought they were with her abductor, who over the previous three hours had severely beaten, repeatedly raped and then tried to kill her.

The woman screamed repeatedly, her cries echoing in the secluded forest. Having put down their guns, the two men managed to convince her that they were not going to harm her. They covered her with one of their jackets, brought her to their car, and set off for the Garda station in Baltinglass, where they were met by three gardaí. They told them the identity of the man who fled the forest. The woman told them her name and—despite the agony of a fractured nose and the physical injuries resulting from a multiple rape—began telling a harrowing story of what she had endured. It began to dawn on the gardaí that the two hunters had just saved the woman's life. Detectives investigating the abductions and suspected murders of a number of women in Leinster were alerted.

Thirteen months later, on 11 May 2001, Larry Murphy was jailed for fifteen years after admitting four charges of rape and one charge each of kidnapping and attempted murder. A packed courtroom heard the shocking details of how he had attacked the 28-year-old woman in a secluded car park in Carlow shortly after she left the nearby business premises she ran. He punched her in the face, fracturing her nose, and forced her to remove her bra, which he used to tie her hands behind her back. He used a headband of a GAA team to gag her mouth and then put her in the boot of his car. He drove nine miles to Beaconstown, near Athy, Co. Kildare, where he raped her. He then forced her back into the boot and drove fourteen miles to Kilranelagh, Co. Wicklow, where he repeatedly raped her again.

It was in Kilranelagh that, while being forced back into the boot of the car, the woman managed to free her hands and tried to spray Murphy in the face with an aerosol she had found in the boot. But the spray didn't work, and then events took an even more sinister turn. Murphy produced a black plastic bag and put it over the woman's head and pulled it tightly around her neck. It was at this point that Ken Jones and Trevor Moody arrived on the scene. Seeing the two men approaching, Murphy fled the scene, leaving his victim lying on the ground. He drove to his home a few miles away and, having drunk a large amount of whiskey, looked in on his two children, who were fast asleep, and then got into bed beside his wife. He was arrested the next day.

On the day on which he pleaded guilty to rape and attempted murder, Murphy fainted in the Central Criminal Court. As barristers stepped over the unconscious would-be murderer, it was left to two prison officers to lift him from the carpeted floor of the Central Criminal Court.

It is a sobering fact that before Larry Murphy abducted and attempted to murder his victim in February 2000 he had never come to the attention of the Gardaí. To all intents and purposes the self-employed carpenter was a dedicated family man and a loving husband. His main passion was hunting, through which he became familiar with the forested land of west Wicklow. Detectives investigating the disappearance of missing women in the Leinster area over the previous decade had never come across Larry Murphy before his sinister attack on the Carlow woman. It gave their investigation a fresh impetus, and they began looking into the background of this would-be killer. They were conscious that Murphy lived only five miles from where Jo Jo Dullard was abducted and murdered, and it was also established that he was working in Droichead Nua in July 1998, when the teenage girl disappeared. His car was searched for any trace of the missing women; but despite their initial optimism, the Gardaí could find no concrete evidence that Murphy had abducted any women before February 2000. If he had succeeded in killing his victim in February 2000, it is not known what he planned to do with her body. He has never given any explanation or motive for his attack on the woman, whom he did not know. His wife and two children have since left Co. Wicklow, and only his close family ever visit him in the high-security Arbour Hill Prison in Dublin.

The depraved nature of the crime for which Larry Murphy was jailed gives us an insight into the mind of a potential killer who chooses his victims at random. When Murphy approached his victim at the car park in Carlow he had immediately disarmed her by punching her in the face, fracturing her nose. He then used the woman's own clothing to tie her up. He subjected her to a horrific and prolonged sexual attack, then used a plastic bag to try to suffocate her. When he set out to abduct, rape and kill, he was confident and calculating. If he had succeeded in murdering his victim and her body was never discovered, or not discovered until years later, we would never have known of the horrific ordeal she had suffered.

It is believed that three of the six missing women whose cases formed part of Operation Trace were attacked by people who lived in the general locality of each crime. These three cases, in which the victim was last seen alive at her home, are not believed to be linked to those of any of the other missing women. The first of these cases is that of Fiona Pender, last seen alive at her flat in Tullamore in August 1996; Ciara Breen was last seen alive in her home at Bachelor's Walk, Dundalk, in February 1997; and Fiona Sinnott was last seen alive at her home at Broadway, Co. Wexford, in February 1998. The investigations into each of these disappearances have resulted in suspects being identified. A man from the midlands with a previous history of violence has been questioned about the murder of Fiona Pender and her unborn baby. A Dundalk man who gardaí believe was in a relationship with Ciara Breen has been arrested and questioned about her murder, but no charges have so far been brought. And in Co. Wexford a man with a history of violence against women has been earmarked as a suspect in the disappearance of Fiona Sinnott.

The Gardaí have been frustrated at the rate of progress in these three cases, in which prime suspects have been identified but without enough evidence to bring them to court. The difference between these cases and the solving of the Phyllis Murphy murder is stark. It was only with the discovery of Phyllis Murphy's body that the crime was solved. On the one hand, detectives believe this applies also to the cases of these three missing women, barring the unlikely event of a confession, or any of the killers striking again. But in more recent times there is privately an increasing air of optimism among many detectives that charges may still be brought in the absence of a body. Indeed, though it is very rare, there are a number of examples of prosecutions for murder without the victim's body being found. In November 1977 a 24-year-old Co. Armagh man, Liam Townson, was jailed for life by the Special Criminal Court after being convicted of the murder of Captain Robert Nairac of the SAS, whose body has never been found. Soon after Nairac's disappearance, in May 1977, gardaí discovered the scene where he had been shot dead, near Ravensdale, Co. Louth, and Townson was convicted largely on his own confession. The state successfully argued in court that circumstantial evidence, and an admission from the accused, could be accepted as evidence of death and of murder. During the investigation gardaí had discovered bloodstains and trampled grass near a bridge at Ravensdale, where it is believed Nairac was shot dead. The IRA claimed responsibility for the killing, and republican sources have since suggested that the body was disposed of in a manner in which it would never be found, by putting it through a cutting machine. Liam Townson served thirteen years in Port Laoise Prison before being released under licence in 1990. His conviction is one example of a confession made while under arrest being crucial in securing a murder conviction in the absence of a body. While a confession is indeed an important plank of such a prosecution case, it is not always essential in bringing charges against suspects.

A more recent example also involved a cross-border investigation. Gerard McGinley was murdered at his home at Enniskillen, Co. Fermanagh, in August 2000 by his wife, Julie McGinley, and her lover, Michael Monaghan, who then disposed of the body across the border in Co. Leitrim. Police in the North, investigating what was at first a missing person case, soon concentrated on McGinley's home as a possible crime scene. Through the use of chemicals they established that a bedroom had been redecorated to cover up evidence of the murder. Julie McGinley and Michael

Monaghan were charged with murder before Gerard McGinley's body was found. It was not until June 2001, ten months after his violent death, that it was discovered by a girl walking in a wood at Ballinamore, Co. Leitrim. Both Julie McGinley and Michael Monaghan are now serving life sentences for murder.

In May 2002 a man from Co. Laois was charged with the murder of a fifteen-year-old Co. Tyrone schoolgirl, Arlene Arkinson, whose body has never been found. This followed almost eight years of investigative work in a number of countries. The body is believed to be buried in the Republic, most probably in Co. Donegal. Arlene was last seen alive on 14 August 1994, having travelled across the border from her home in Castlederg, Co. Tyrone, to a disco in the Co. Donegal seaside resort of Bundoran. She never returned home. Gardaí and Northern police believe her body may lie in the Pettigo area of south-east Co. Donegal, south of Lough Derg and close to the border. Despite a number of extensive searches, no trace has been found. The evidence to be brought in the prosecution case against the man does not contain details of a crime scene.

While Arlene Arkinson is one of the youngest missing people in Ireland, there are two cases of younger long-term missing children who are not the victims of parental abduction. The disappearance of seven-year-old Mary Boyle in March 1977 and the abduction of thirteen-year-old Philip Cairns in October 1986 have baffled the detectives who have investigated them for decades, as well as causing untold anguish to the parents and the brothers and sisters of the missing children.

Mary Boyle was last seen walking near her grandparents' home near Ballyshannon, Co. Donegal, on a bright afternoon in March 1977. For more than a quarter of a century her disappearance has devastated her parents, Ann and Charlie Boyle, her twin sister,

Ann, and her older brother, Patrick. There is still no firm evidence of an abduction, yet numerous searches of lakes and surrounding bogland have failed to yield any results. Whether it was through an accident or through a violent act, what happened to Mary Boyle, and where she lies, remain a terrible mystery.

A more sinister cloud hangs over the case of the second of Ireland's long-term missing children, Philip Cairns, who was just thirteen when someone snatched him from the roadside as he walked to school in Rathfarnham, Co. Dublin, in October 1986. He was walking along a busy road at lunchtime when he vanished, after an unknown abductor swooped in a matter of seconds. A week after his disappearance, his schoolbag was left in a laneway close to his home, left there either by the abductor or by someone who found it after the crime and therefore has crucial information that could help the Gardaí solve this tragic case. Philip's parents, Alice and Philip Cairns, and his four sisters and brother accept the disturbing fact that Philip was abducted from the roadside. But that is the only definite thing about this child abduction. Whatever happened to Philip, wherever he was taken and whatever emotional or physical pain he later suffered, are a mystery known only to his abductor.

While it seems likely that Philip Cairns was murdered by his abductor, in the absence of a crime scene or the discovery of his body he is still officially missing, and indeed his parents still hold out hope that such a terrible fate did not befall their son.

Every parent's worst nightmare has been visited on the Boyle and Cairns families, whose lives have been turned upside down. As well as dealing with Ireland's missing women who are believed to have been murdered, this book also examines the cases of these two missing children—a girl last seen eating a packet of sweets near her grandparents' house in Co. Donegal, and a boy violently abducted as he walked to school along a busy Co. Dublin road.

It has long been feared by many gardaí that one or more people might be travelling to Ireland to commit violent crimes, such as abductions and murders, and then leaving the jurisdiction. Experienced gardaí are mindful of the two convicted English serial killers who brought terror to Ireland in 1976, committing two heinous murders before they were caught in Co. Galway. John Shaw and Geoffrey Evans were two long-term criminals who started their criminal life by committing small-time robberies but later made an evil pact to rape and murder one woman every week. This depraved union saw the pair abduct and murder their first victim near Brittas Bay, Co. Wicklow, in August 1976. Elizabeth Plunkett was a 23-year-old Dublin woman whom they abducted from the roadside and then raped and strangled in a wooded area nearby. They then tied a lawnmower to her body and rowed out to sea, where they threw her weighted body overboard. It would be weeks before her body was recovered from the sea. Shaw and Evans went on to commit a spate of robberies over the next few weeks, as gardaí in Co. Wicklow investigated the case of the missing Elizabeth Plunkett. In September 1976 they committed their second rape and murder when they abducted 23-year-old Mary Duffy from the roadside at Castlebar, Co. Mayo. She was tied up and driven to Ballynahinch, Co. Galway, where the horrific assault continued. She was then suffocated, and the two murderers took her body to Lough Inagh, where they stole a boat, rowed out onto the lake, and threw the body overboard, weighted down with a large block.

Shaw and Evans were captured at Barna, Co. Galway, before they could kill a third woman. They are now Ireland's longest-serving prisoners. Any temporary release granted to John Shaw or Geoffrey Evans will evoke strong protest whenever such a prospect appears.

In more recent times Ireland was shocked by the chilling actions of Michael Bambrick, who killed his wife, Patricia McGauley, at their home in Dublin in September 1991 and then, in July 1992, killed another woman, Mary Cummins, also at his home. Both women were classified as missing from the time of their disappearance until the truth caught up with Bambrick when his young daughter bravely began to tell gardaí how her daddy had killed her two pets, and other terrible things he was doing. They soon established a link between Bambrick and Mary Cummins, whom he had met only on the day he killed her. Soon after his arrest he claimed he had killed both women during bondage sex sessions that had gone wrong. He dismembered their bodies and disposed of them in an old drain close to Balgaddy Dump in west Co. Dublin. It was not until May 1994, when he was finally caught and admitted killing the two women, that their remains were found. In 1996 Bambrick was jailed for eighteen years on two charges of manslaughter; he is now in Arbour Hill Prison, Dublin. The Gardaí have him earmarked as a suspect for unsolved crimes in the late 1980s and early 90s.

The term 'serial killer' can often be bandied about, causing unnecessary fear in a community. This book examines the evidence supporting the belief that at least one serial killer is responsible for one or more of the missing persons cases it describes. The most likely cases are those of Annie McCarrick, Jo Jo Dullard, and the missing Droichead Nua woman. But these are not the only cases where random killers may have struck. Coupled with these three cases where women were apparently snatched from the roadside there have been a number of chilling murders of women where bodies have eventually been found but no killer has yet been caught.

Antoinette Smith was last seen alive in Rathfarnham, Co. Dublin, on 12 July 1987. A 27-year-old mother of two, she had just returned from a David Bowie concert in Slane, Co. Meath. She got into a taxi with two men in Westmorland Street, Dublin, and they travelled to Rathfarnham. Those two men have never come forward. Antoinette Smith's body was found nearly nine months later on 3 April 1988 at the Feather Bed, near Glencree in the Dublin Mountains. She had been strangled, and a bag had been placed over her head. Her body had then been buried in a turf bank that later subsided, leading to its discovery. From the evidence gathered so far it is the firm belief of a number of gardaí that two men were involved in the killing. A number of men were questioned as part of the investigation, but no charges were brought. The murder caused terrible anguish for Antoinette's estranged husband and her two children, who are now adults. The abduction and murder have also weighed heavily on the minds of gardaí, who, under the law, could not compel people to give a blood sample as part of the investigation.

Four years after the murder of Antoinette Smith, another mother of two was strangled and her body was also buried in the Dublin Mountains. Patricia O'Doherty, a thirty-year-old prison officer, was last seen alive on 23 December 1991. That day she had been making preparations for Christmas, travelling to the shopping centre at the Square, Tallaght, to buy Santa hats for her two children. At some point later that night she left her home at Allenton Lawns, Tallaght, and was not seen again. When he did not see her the next day—Christmas Eve—her husband, Paddy Doherty, assumed she had gone to work at Mountjoy Prison. It was not until Christmas Day that she was reported missing. The case remained that of a missing person until the following June, when a man out cutting turf near the Lemass Cross at Killakee in the Dublin Mountains made the terrible discovery. Patricia Doherty's body was found in a bog drain within a mile of where Antoinette

Smith's body had been hidden in July 1987; the key to her front door was found close by. No-one has ever been arrested in connection with the murder of Patricia Doherty.

There is a third recent case of a missing woman who was abducted and murdered and whose killer remains at large. In June 1994 a man was visiting his son who was cutting turf at Pim's Lane near Portarlington, Co. Laois, when in a bog drain he discovered the body of 34-year-old Marie Kilmartin, who had been missing from her home in Port Laoise since the previous December. Whoever murdered her had placed a concrete block over her chest to submerge her body in the water. As with the previous discovery of the bodies of Antoinette Smith and Patricia Doherty, the scene of the discovery of Marie Kilmartin's body was one that severely affected the most hardened detectives. She was still wearing the heavy coat and boots she was last seen wearing as she entered her house at the Stradbally Road in Port Laoise on 16 December 1993. Some time shortly after she was last seen she was lured out of her house by a phone call made to her home from a nearby call box. She was strangled and her body was later left at the bog near Portarlington. Two men from Co. Laois were arrested within days of the discovery of the body; both were released without charge. There is a prime suspect for the horrific murder of Marie Kilmartin, who remains at large.

Not only are there three unsolved murders where missing women are now officially classed as murdered but there are other cases of women who are still missing—outside the six Operation Trace cases—whose families now fear they also have been murdered. One such case is that of Eva Brennan, who was thirty-nine when she was last seen storming out of her parents' house in Terenure, Dublin, in July 1993 after a trivial dispute about what they were going to have for Sunday lunch. Her family assumed she had gone home to her own apartment in nearby Rathgar. It is now believed that she may indeed have made it home to her apartment but decided to go back out, perhaps for a walk. Her handbag and keys have never been found. She had previously had bouts of depression, and one line of inquiry remains that she may have chosen to go away somewhere by herself. However, Eva Brennan's case has privately been looked at by detectives investigating the case of other missing women. She disappeared less than four months after the abduction and murder of Annie McCarrick, who was also last seen in south Co. Dublin; she was also last seen just a few miles from where Antoinette Smith was last seen alive six years before. Eva Brennan's family fear that she was abducted while walking along the roadside and now lies buried in the Dublin Mountains.

The discovery of the bodies of Antoinette Smith, Patricia Doherty and Marie Kilmartin reclassified their cases from that of missing women to murdered women. While the official status of the cases that formed part of Operation Trace is that of missing women, the devastated families of four of those women accept that their loved ones have been murdered. And, including the fears of Eva Brennan's family that she was also the victim of a violent attack, there exists the distinct possibility that the murderers of at least eight women in Leinster have not been caught. There is also the continuing search for the person who abducted Philip Cairns. Some of the most evil people in Ireland remain at large.

The searches for the missing people who are believed to have been the victims of violent crime have been exhaustive. Detectives have followed thousands of lines of inquiry, dug up acres of land, employed infra-red machines to detect soil movements, used sniffer dogs, and questioned a number of suspects. Yet, despite prime suspects being identified in many of the cases, no charges have been brought, and the bodies of many of Ireland's murder victims have not been found. The failure to find the remains of those believed murdered is a cause of constant anguish to their families and of constant frustration to detectives.

With the co-operation of the families concerned, this book examines the cases of five of the missing women that formed the basis of Operation Trace. It also examines the two oldest cases of Ireland's missing children who are not the victims of parental abduction. In being so selective I am conscious that the great majority of missing persons are not the victims of crime, though the anguish felt by their families is no less acute. To this end I also look at the developments in honouring the memory of all missing people, and at the sterling work of some of the families of missing people to keep their loved ones on the media and political agenda. I consider what more can be done from an investigative and humanitarian point of view by the Gardaí and the state, not only to find Ireland's missing but to honour their memory.

More than 1,800 people are reported missing in Ireland every year—the equivalent of five people being reported missing every day. But only a small number, between five and fifteen, remain unaccounted for at the end of each year. Of this number there are some people who will never come home, and whose bodies may never be found, people who have most probably met a violent death and have disappeared without a trace.

1

Annie McCarrick

❧❀❧

In March 1993, 26-year-old Annie McCarrick was abducted and murdered in the Wicklow Mountains. A native of Long Island, New York, she had left her home in Sandymount, Dublin, late on the afternoon of Friday 26 March. She travelled to nearby Ranelagh, where she got on a bus heading for Enniskerry, the picturesque village in north Co. Wicklow, just east of the Wicklow Mountains. This was the last definite sighting of Annie McCarrick. Some hours later a woman matching her description was seen by members of the staff in Johnnie Fox's Pub, just north of Enniskerry, in the company of a man in his twenties. Annie McCarrick was known to have visited this pub before, where she loved to listen to bands playing Irish and country music.

Despite numerous appeals for information, the woman matching Annie McCarrick's description has never been found. Perhaps crucially, the man spotted with that unidentified woman has never come forward. Was it Annie and the man who would later murder her? The investigation into Annie McCarrick's disappearance was privately classified as a murder investigation almost immediately. The fact that she was probably murdered by a man who has attacked or murdered other women has caused immense frustration for gardaí, who admit they never got a break in the case.

Annie McCarrick's disappearance was totally out of character. She was no stranger to Ireland, having lived in Dublin for three years while studying in Dublin and Maynooth. Her murder, and the fact that her body has not been found, has caused unimaginable distress for her parents, John and Nancy McCarrick, who have lost their only child. They are now divorced and deal with their pain separately.

In January 1993 Annie McCarrick left New York for the last time to travel to Dublin. She wanted to see, once and for all, whether she would settle down and make her home in Ireland. Three months later she would be abducted and murdered.

Just after three o'clock on the afternoon of Friday 26 March 1993, Annie McCarrick pulled the door shut on her apartment in Sandymount. It was a dry, fresh day, and she was planning a walk in Enniskerry. Earlier that day she had phoned her friend Anne O'Dwyer in Rathgar, asking her if she would like to join her for a stroll in the foothills of the Wicklow Mountains. Anne had hurt her foot and told Annie she wouldn't be able for the trip. Annie wished her friend a speedy recovery and decided to head for Enniskerry by herself. It was a day off: she wasn't due back in work in Café Java in Leeson Street until the next day. She had arranged for two friends to call over the following evening for dinner, and she might meet another old college friend for a drink on Sunday. Today she was at a loose end, and it was just the weather for a walk in a part of Ireland she had grown to know and love. She put on her favourite tweed coat, grabbed her handbag, and headed out the door.

As Annie McCarrick left her apartment at St Catherine's Court in Sandymount, a plumber, Bernard Sheeran, was working at a nearby apartment. He spotted her leaving her home and heading down the road. She was also seen by Bruno Borza, who ran the local chip shop: he saw her heading down Newgrove Avenue towards the terminus of the number 18 bus. This would bring her over to Ranelagh, where she would get a number 44 to Enniskerry. By now, Annie had the knack of Dublin transport.

She saw a number 18 at the terminus but was still about a hundred yards away when the bus began to leave. She ran towards it, trying to catch the driver's attention. He spotted her, and slowed down to let her on. She paid the fare to bring her to Ranelagh. Within hours she would be abducted and murdered.

Annie McCarrick loved Ireland. By March 1993 she had spent many years travelling back and forth between Dublin and New York. She first arrived in Ireland for a week's holiday at Christmas 1987, when she was twenty, as part of a group led by her cousin Danny Casey, who taught Irish studies at the State University of New York. She instantly fell in love with the country and the people. Her great-grandfather and grandmother on her mother's side had left Ireland many decades previously. On her father's side there were also strong links with Ireland. Annie grew up among many Irish-American influences on Long Island, New York. Two Irish people who were friends of the family lived with the McCarricks for a time, and many members of a local order of nuns who knew the McCarricks were originally from Ireland.

When Annie McCarrick arrived in Ireland for the first time she felt as if she was coming home. She lived in Ireland for three years while she studied at St Patrick's Training College in Drumcondra, Dublin, and later at St Patrick's College, Maynooth. In between her studies in Ireland she returned to her home in New York in 1990 to continue her studies there for a year. But she missed Ireland, she had made so many friends. By Christmas 1992 she had decided that she wanted to return to Ireland. She discussed the matter with her parents, telling them she wanted to see once and for all if she wanted to make her life in Ireland, to see if she could settle here. They didn't want to see their only child leave America again, but they knew Annie was restless and had her heart set on returning to Ireland. On 6 January 1993 they kissed their daughter goodbye for the last time. Annie stepped on board a plane at JFK airport and left for Dublin. They would never see their daughter again.

Annie McCarrick spent the first eighteen years of her life in the leafy suburbs of Bayport on the south shore of Long Island, New York. Bayport had become famous as the setting for the fictional exploits of the Hardy Boys, in which the teenage detectives Frank and Joe Hardy solved numerous crimes. Bayport is an hour's drive from JFK Airport and an hour and a half south-east of Manhattan. It is a prosperous town, with wide, clean streets and large detached houses with low walls. Just south of Bayport is the Atlantic Ocean, where Annie spent many happy hours standing on the shore looking across at the lights on the islands south of Bayport.

Annie McCarrick's parents are both New Yorkers. From the mid-1960s until the mid-90s they lived together in Bayport, raising one daughter, Annie Bridget McCarrick. They divorced in the wake of Annie's abduction and murder; both still live on Long Island, but at separate ends. John is suffering considerable ill-health. Nancy told me that Annie had a very happy childhood here in the quiet streets of Bayport.

Annie was born in March 1967 at Bay Shore, just a few miles from here. When Annie was about fourteen months we moved into our first house at Delores Court, which is just a few hundred yards from here. When she was twelve the three of us moved to Bayview Avenue. Annie was living there right up until she went to Ireland. For her primary, middle and high school Annie went to the local school for the towns of Bayport and Bluepoint. I worked as a secretary in the school, and her father was a teacher. This is the area where Annie spent the first eighteen years of her life. She had so many friends. It was wonderful.

It was from their home at Bayview Avenue that, on an evening in late March 1993, Nancy McCarrick rushed to JFK Airport to get a flight to Dublin. A phone call from Hilary Brady, a friend of Annie's in Dublin, had set alarm bells ringing in the minds of John and Nancy. Nobody had seen Annie in Dublin for more than three days. She hadn't turned up for work, and wasn't to be found in her apartment. Nancy remembers that they knew immediately something was terribly wrong.

Annie's friend Hilary had phoned on the previous Saturday to say he was trying to reach Annie in Dublin and had forgotten her phone number. He said there was no answer from her apartment and they were meant to meet for dinner. We thought nothing of it, but it was a couple of days later that Hilary phoned again. He still hadn't spoken to Annie. But now alarm bells started to ring. Hilary had gone to where Annie worked on Leeson Street and discovered she hadn't turned up for work. Her flatmates who had returned to Dublin after the weekend hadn't seen her either. When he phoned that second time, Hilary said to me, 'No-one has seen Annie.' I just knew something was wrong. Within four hours I was at JFK Airport and on a flight to Dublin.

Nancy McCarrick arrived in Dublin the next morning. Hilary Brady met her at the airport. They travelled to the Garda station in Irishtown, where Nancy McCarrick formally reported her daughter missing. John McCarrick arrived over shortly afterwards. The McCarricks still hoped that there might be some news of Annie at any moment. They didn't know it then, but they would be staying in Ireland for the next two months. By the time they left Ireland broken-hearted in May 1993, they would be faced with the terrible realisation that their daughter would not be coming home.

When Annie McCarrick was formally reported missing, the Gardaí in Irishtown had a difficult job in trying to piece together her last known movements. The fact that she was going about her normal routine made the job even more difficult. The Gardaí had no crime scene. There was no scream, there were no personal belongings found on the roadside. In tracing all Annie's known friends, detectives were quickly able to establish that she had intended travelling to Enniskerry; but had she made it there? One detective noted that the last positive sighting is very helpful in this regard.

We knew that Annie had got on the number 18 bus from Sandymount. We knew that she would have intended getting off in Ranelagh to connect with the 44 to Enniskerry. But we had to consider every possibility, like whether she fell asleep on the 18 and ended up across Dublin city, miles from her intended destination, or whether she felt unwell and got off the bus before Ranelagh. These were all things we had to consider; but then we got a positive sighting from a former workmate of Annie's that put her on a number 44 in Ranelagh. All the indications are that she was going to Enniskerry.

Just before four o'clock on the afternoon of Friday 26 March 1993, Annie McCarrick joined the queue at the bus stop in Ranelagh, opposite the Ulster Bank. She had walked around from Chelmsford Road after getting off the number 18. She was wearing her dark tweed jacket, a pair of jeans, and oxblood-coloured boots. She carried her tan-coloured shoulder bag. Also waiting for a bus was Éimear O'Grady, who was ahead of Annie in the queue. She recognised Annie from their time working together in the Courtyard Restaurant in Donnybrook the previous month.

The number 44 arrived, and Éimear got on. She sat downstairs, because she was only going a short distance to her home at nearby Milltown Court. She saw Annie get on the bus after her and go upstairs. This is something that happens thousands of times on public transport every day—one person recognising another. Little did she know it, but Éimear's sighting of Annie going upstairs on the bus was to be of immense importance and led to the Gardaí concentrating the bulk of their subsequent investigation on the Wicklow Mountains. Éimear O'Grady got off the bus a short time later, unaware that she was now the last person to positively identify Annie McCarrick. Within hours, Annie would be murdered.

The positive sighting of Annie on the number 44 bus gave the Gardaí encouragement that they might be able to trace her movements after she got on the bus. However, all their inquiries to establish where she went after that led nowhere. The driver, Paddy Donnelly, couldn't remember Annie being on the bus. None of the passengers who came forward could remember her getting off the bus at the terminus in the centre of Enniskerry, or at any stop before that. One detective remembered the frustration felt by the Garda team.

Annie was a striking-looking girl, and she stood out because of her accent. She was tall, and when she disappeared she was wearing a distinctive jacket and cowboy-type boots. And yet nobody saw anything. We knew from Éimear O'Grady that Annie had got on the number 44 bus, and this would correspond with her telling her friend Anne that she was planning to go to Enniskerry. But after that we don't have any positive sighting of her. We know she had to get off the bus somewhere between where Éimear got off the bus at Milltown and the last stop at Enniskerry. All our instincts say Enniskerry. But there is no-one to positively identify her there.

Three miles east of Enniskerry is the seaside town of Bray; to the west lie the Dublin Mountains and hundreds of acres of forest. Less than a mile south are the Powerscourt Estate and Gardens— a popular venue for visitors. If Annie McCarrick did get the bus all the way to Enniskerry, she would have got off in the centre of the village, which is shaped like a triangle, with three converging roads and a monument in the centre. If she did get the number 44 to Enniskerry she would have arrived there before five o'clock. As day began to turn to dusk there would still have been at least a good hour of daylight left on that March evening. Did she decide to wander south towards Powerscourt waterfall? This would have been a logical journey for a young woman out enjoying the Co. Wicklow countryside. It would bring her along a fairly busy road, which heads on towards the Great Sugar Loaf. But this is speculation. No-one has ever reported seeing Annie McCarrick heading out of Enniskerry towards Powerscourt. Even more frustrating, no-one has ever reported a positive sighting of Annie in Enniskerry.

As the Gardaí appealed for information, a woman came forward to say she had served someone matching Annie's description at the post office in Enniskerry that Friday evening; she thought she had sold the woman three stamps for postcards. This would be in keeping with Annie's habit of staying in regular touch with her friends and family by post. Unfortunately, there was no closed-circuit television tape of Annie in the post office. This is the closest the Gardaí have come to placing Annie McCarrick in Enniskerry.

As the search entered its second week, a conference was held among detectives attached to Irishtown, Enniskerry and Bray Garda Stations. It was decided that a further appeal would be made for information. A photograph of Annie was circulated to television and newspapers. And then a man came forward with information that would shed new light on Annie's disappearance.

Sam Doran was working as a doorman at Johnnie Fox's pub on the night of Friday 26 March. He phoned the Gardaí to say he recognised the woman featured on the missing person posters: she had been to Johnnie Fox's that night. Another doorman, Paul O'Reilly, also told the Gardaí that a woman matching her description had been in the back lounge of the pub at about 9:30 that evening. It was a busy night, and the Jolly Ploughmen were playing into the early hours. Sam Doran was able to recall that the woman was in the company of a young man. He remembered telling the couple that there was a £2 cover charge for the lounge; the young man had paid for both of them, saying something like 'I'll take care of that.'

If Annie McCarrick did get to Enniskerry by five o'clock that evening, and if she was the woman seen in the pub four hours later, where was she in the meantime? How did she get to Johnnie Fox's pub? She was known to be a keen walker and could definitely have walked the four miles in that time. If so, did she just meet the mysterious man at Johnnie Fox's, or had she arranged to meet him? Did she hitch a lift, or did she bump into someone she knew, someone who has never come forward? The Gardaí had, and continue to have, many such questions.

Assuming that the woman identified in the pub by Sam Doran and Paul O'Reilly was Annie McCarrick, detectives now had a description of a man they would like to question. He was described as being in his mid-twenties, clean-shaven, of average build, with dark-brown hair. But despite repeated appeals for information, neither the woman nor the man has ever come forward. One detective believes this is significant.

> For one person to remain silent is not uncommon, but for two people not to come forward is highly unusual. If they were entirely innocent, surely one, if not both, would have come forward, even years later. It made us think that perhaps the woman was actually Annie, and the man in question was the man who would later attack her. It's still a valid theory; but it doesn't really get us any further. If it was Annie, nobody could identify the man she was with. Nobody saw them leave the pub.

There was another American woman in Johnnie Fox's pub that night, who looked somewhat like Annie McCarrick; but this woman was with her mother. Detectives who would later work as part of Operation Trace would revisit the description of the man seen in Johnnie Fox's. One detective believes this unidentified man could hold the answer.

> If you consider the description of this fellow—clean-shaven, in his mid-twenties, and with dark-brown hair—it actually matches a man who is the closest we have really come to in recent years in relation to a suspected serial killer. This man only came to our attention years later for a horrific attack on a young woman in Co. Wicklow. During the attack this man, who was in his mid-thirties by this time, tried to kill his

victim. He had never come to our attention before. We suspect he has attacked other women. It would make you wonder if he was the man in Johnnie Fox's. But in other ways, the description of a clean-shaven man in his twenties with brown hair is one which matches thousands of men. But we haven't ruled this man out. He was always clean-shaven; he was always charming. And underneath it, he's one of the most violent men I've ever encountered. And we definitely believe he has attacked women before.

Within days of Nancy McCarrick arriving in Dublin in March 1993, her husband followed. Her brother, Tim Dungate, also travelled from New York, as did her brother-in-law John Covell, who was married to Nancy's sister Maureen. The four of them met gardaí to see how the investigation was going. Nancy remembers that they seemed at a loss to explain what might have happened.

It was just beyond their comprehension. Annie wasn't the first woman to go missing in Ireland, but she was the first of a number of women to disappear over a short number of years. But back then the Gardaí just couldn't explain it. It was new to them. I remember suggesting that Annie might have responded to a particular ad for someone to work with animals. The ad was in relation to a place on the way from Dublin to Enniskerry. I remember asking if they had questioned this man, and a garda said, 'Oh, Mrs McCarrick, you don't think Annie responded to the ad, and the man thought to himself that he'd keep her; no such thing could happen.' It was just beyond their experience. Now it's different, they know that there are people capable of these terrible deeds. Gardaí worked extremely hard on Annie's case, but it was so new to them.

Though the disappearance of Annie McCarrick is still officially classified as a missing person case, every detective who worked on it knows it is a murder inquiry, and was so from very early on. As detectives began to consider where Annie's body might have been buried, they were conscious of the unsolved murders of two women whose bodies had been left less than a mile apart in the Dublin Mountains in 1987 and 1991.

In July 1987, Antoinette Smith, a mother of two from Clondalkin, Dublin, was abducted and murdered. She had attended a David Bowie concert at Slane, Co. Meath, and was last seen getting a taxi with two men in Westmorland Street, Dublin, to go to Rathfarnham. The taxi driver dropped his three passengers close to Rathfarnham in the early hours of the morning. Antoinette's body was found in April 1988 in a bog at the Feather Bed at Killakee in the Dublin Mountains. She had been strangled, and a plastic bag had been placed over her head. The Gardaí are satisfied that she was murdered by two attackers. At Christmas 1991 Patricia Doherty, a prison officer and mother of two from Co. Kerry was abducted and murdered. She also was strangled. Her body was found in June 1992 just three miles from her home in Tallaght at Glassamucky Borders, Killakee, less than a mile from where Antoinette Smith's body had been found four years before. It was found by ramblers after dry weather caused the turf bank where she was buried to subside. No-one has ever been charged in relation to these horrific murders, which have devastated two families. One detective says that the Gardaí feared that Annie McCarrick had suffered a similar fate.

If you look at the similarities in both those cases, both Antoinette Smith and Patricia Doherty were strangled and their bodies buried in relatively close proximity in the Dublin

Mountains. We have particular information to suggest two men may be responsible for the murder of Antoinette Smith. Neither of those terrible murders has been solved as yet. So, the persons responsible for those separate murders are still out there—killers who know the Dublin Mountains; killers who knew where they could work undetected as they sought to hide their crimes by burying the bodies. In searching for Annie we were conscious of those murders; but it was only years later, when Operation Trace came on stream, that all these cases were really looked at for links. One thing that cannot be denied: whoever murdered Antoinette Smith is still out there, and whoever murdered Patricia Doherty is still out there. It's often speculated whether the person who killed Annie killed other women later on. But we must also consider if the person who killed Annie had killed before.

The Gardaí were also conscious of the murder of a nineteen-year-old woman, Patricia Furlong, strangled at Glencullen, Co. Dublin, in July 1982. Glencullen is just two miles north of Enniskerry and very close to Johnnie Fox's pub. A Dublin disc-jockey, Vincent Connell, was convicted of the murder in December 1991, but his conviction was quashed by the Court of Criminal Appeal in April 1995. Connell, who was later convicted of assaulting a number of former girl-friends, died in 1998 while continuing to protest his innocence.

As the Gardaí pieced together the movements of Annie McCarrick in the twenty-four hours before her disappearance, there was nothing to suggest that she had planned to disappear. She was going about her normal everyday life. Though her body has not been found, everyone involved knows she was abducted and killed. Back in New York, Nancy McCarrick confirmed to me that she knows Annie was murdered.

It was so hard for me to leave Ireland and return to New York in May 1993. But I just had to. There was no news—nothing. We knew early on that Annie had been murdered. But you always wonder if she'll return. You do that for ever: your head tells you otherwise, but you still wonder. Logically, I know she'll never come home. I know she was killed. But sometimes it just hits you again. It might be a birthday, or Christmas, but sometimes it can be a smell, or when someone says something nice, that I think of Annie. And then it hits me all over again. Some of the detail of the months after Annie's disappearance is a bit muddled. But the pain never ends.

Annie McCarrick had been sharing an apartment at St Catherine's Court in Sandymount for a few weeks before she disappeared. Her two flatmates were Jill Twomey and Ida Walsh. They had met Annie when she responded to an ad about sharing the apartment. They instantly took a liking to her and offered her a room in the apartment. They last saw her just before nine o'clock on the morning of the day she disappeared; she was sitting up in bed knitting, and Jill and Ida were heading out. They were going down the country for the weekend, and the three wished each other a happy weekend before Jill and Ida pulled the front door shut.

Annie later left the apartment to walk the short distance to Quinnsworth in Sandymount. She bought ingredients to make up some desserts for Café Java, where she was due back at work the next day. The receipt for the ingredients shows that she paid for the goods at 11:02 a.m. She then went to the AIB branch in Sandymount; she wanted to change her account from the Clondalkin to the Sandymount branch. When she arrived in Dublin in January 1993 she had stayed with her friends Hilary and Philip Brady at their home at Cherrywood Avenue, Clondalkin.

She was also storing a car she had at the Brady home, but sh
now settled into her apartment in Sandymount. The clos
circuit television tape of Annie in the AIB branch in Sandymount
shows her going about her normal life. There is nothing out of the
ordinary. After leaving the bank she walked back to her apartment,
where she later phoned Anne O'Dwyer to see if she wanted to join
her for a walk in Enniskerry. She also phoned Hilary Brady to
arrange that he and his fiancée, Rita Fortune, come over for dinner
the following evening. She didn't leave the apartment again until
around 3:15 p.m., when she left to jump on the number 18 bus for
Ranelagh.

Annie had been friendly with the Brady family for many years.
Soon after she arrived in Ireland in 1988 to begin her studies at St
Patrick's Training College in Drumcondra she began going out with
Philip Brady. This was one of two serious relationships she had
while she studied in Ireland. She later met Dermot Ryan, a fellow
sociology student at St Patrick's College, Maynooth, and they
dated for about two years. After Annie and Philip Brady broke up
they remained on friendly terms, and Annie kept in regular contact with the Brady family, including Philip's brother Hilary and
his fiancée. On the day she disappeared she was looking forward to
preparing dinner the following evening for Hilary and Rita.

Hilary Brady was concerned almost immediately about Annie.
It was around eight o'clock on the evening of Saturday 27 March
1993, and he and Rita were standing outside Annie's apartment.
He was ringing the doorbell, but there was no response. This was
not like Annie: if she had to cancel the dinner engagement, surely
she would have phoned. The apartment was in darkness. Hilary
couldn't remember Annie's phone number. He still had her home
number in New York from many years before. It would be the
afternoon in New York, and John or Nancy would definitely have

had 1-

nber. 'Nancy, I'm standing outside Annie's

1, but I don't have her phone number,' he

e him the number, and they had a brief chat.

er, but there was no answer. It was now dark.

, went for a drink in a nearby pub and tried again later. There was still no answer. The couple decided there wasn't much else they could do at that hour of the night, so they headed home.

The next day Hilary called into Café Java in Leeson Street. What he was told only increased his concern. Annie had not turned up for work. She had been due in the day before, and had not phoned to say she wouldn't be in. It was quickly established that the last time anyone had seen her in work was about three o'clock on the Thursday afternoon. Hilary phoned Annie's flatmates, who had arrived home from the country. She wasn't in the apartment. The ingredients she had bought were still in a plastic bag on the kitchen table. Hilary Brady made another phone call to John and Nancy McCarrick in New York. 'No-one's seen Annie. She hasn't been to work. She's not at home.'

Annie McCarrick was a confident woman, chatty and friendly. She made many friends in Ireland from the time she first arrived in 1987. For Annie McCarrick to decide to go for a walk alone in the foothills of the Dublin-Wicklow Mountains was the act of a confident and resourceful woman. When she arrived back in Ireland in January 1993 her work papers weren't in order, but she just couldn't wait to get back to Ireland, to her friends. When one job fell through because of problems with her work visa, she wasn't too bothered: she just began looking for another job. On 17 March 1993—nine days before she was murdered—she joined thousands of people in O'Connell Street, Dublin, where she celebrated St Patrick's Day. She missed her family back in New York, but she was where she wanted to be.

No-one has ever been arrested for the abduction and murder of Annie McCarrick. There is no prime suspect. A number of men have been interviewed at length, but no-one has ever been detained for questioning. One detective told me how three years after the abduction they thought they might have been on the verge of a breakthrough.

I remember it was in early 1996. Gardaí in Blanchardstown in west Dublin were investigating the rape and murder of Marilyn Rynn, who was attacked as she was walking home following a Christmas party. During that investigation an extensive trawl was undertaken to establish who Marilyn had been in contact with in the hours before her death. And out of the blue, it hit us. One of the men who had been in Marilyn's company, just hours before her terrible death, had also known Annie McCarrick. He had met Annie a number of times in the Sandymount area. Alarm bells started going off. Could we be about to get a break in Annie's case? Could this be it? But it wasn't: it was just a total coincidence. Another man, David Lawler, who was not known to Marilyn Rynn, was caught and convicted for her murder. The other man who knew both Marilyn and Annie was out of the loop. It was just a bizarre coincidence.

The Garda investigation extended to the Continent, where a former employer of Annie's was travelling at the time. He had no information with which to help the Gardaí. Within weeks of Annie's disappearance, John McCarrick decided to hire a private investigator to help find his daughter. The investigator, Brian McCarthy, had been recommended by an official at the US Embassy in Dublin. However, he also failed to turn up any solid leads. Detective-Inspector (now Chief Superintendent) Martin Donnellan said the search for Annie was exhaustive.

> We carried out massive searches on foot, inch-by-inch physical searches. We chased up leads right around the country, such as when a lorry driver came forward to say he gave a woman matching Annie's description a lift from Mount Juliet in Kilkenny to Waterford. There were other reported sightings in Cork. Any person who we knew had a history of sexual assaults was looked at. A pet cemetery in Enniskerry was also searched, and indeed there were numerous searches throughout north Co. Wicklow. Right from the start, Annie's case was treated like a murder investigation. A retired superintendent from Scotland Yard came over at John McCarrick's request, and he reviewed the file. He was satisfied with the scope of our investigation. But, at the end of the day, Annie is still out there somewhere.

In June 1997 new information was given to detectives about suspicious activity seen near Enniskerry on the day Annie McCarrick had vanished four years before. A decision was taken that a pet cemetery near Enniskerry should be searched. The search, involving twenty gardaí, began on the morning of Monday 16 June. Gardaí from the Forensic Science and Ballistics sections were on hand to provide guidance on the unpalatable but crucial job of searching through the graves. The information given to the Gardaí consisted of a report of a large box being buried at the pet cemetery shortly after Annie McCarrick had disappeared. As word spread of the search, two men contacted the Gardaí. They told detectives they had buried a greyhound in the cemetery in late March 1993. The men's story was borne out when the remains of the dog were unearthed a short time later. By one o'clock the following afternoon, the search of the pet cemetery was completed. There were no new leads.

Annie McCarrick wanted to be a teacher. When she arrived again in Ireland in January 1993 she planned to get any job to tide her over and then to begin studying for the higher diploma in education, which would allow her to teach in secondary schools. When she started her studies in 1988 she went to St Patrick's Training College in Drumcondra. As part of her studies she worked as a junior assistant teacher at Our Lady of Victories National School in Ballymun. She absolutely loved it: she loved the interaction with the children, who were in turn fascinated by Annie's tales of New York. She later studied at St Patrick's College, Maynooth, entering in the second year of a course in which she studied sociology and English. It was here she met Geraldine Delaney, a fellow-student, who is now a teacher in a secondary school in Palmerstown, Co. Dublin, the kind of job that Annie McCarrick would have happily ended up doing, and that she should be doing now. Geraldine Delaney has many fond memories of Annie McCarrick.

Annie was an only child, and so was I, so we had a particular bond. Annie was what you'd call a real Celtic woman. She wore lovely cloaks and knitwear. And she was such a reliable person—even to the extent that when we studied in the reading room in the Arts Block in Maynooth, if Annie took a break she'd write on a note the time she had left. She'd leave the note on top of her books. She was that reliable, that pre-dictable. I also visited her in New York after she finished her studies here. We would have great chats about everything. On the night before Annie disappeared, the Thursday, we had a chat on the phone. She was really looking forward to her mother, Nancy, coming over to visit her the following week, and she had made plans for what they would do together. We said we might meet up for a drink on the Sunday night. Annie was to call me. She never did.

Back in New York, Nancy McCarrick told me how she was looking forward to that coming visit to Annie in Dublin when she got the phone call to say her daughter was missing. During a subsequent search of Annie's apartment in Sandymount, gardaí found theatre tickets that Annie had bought in anticipation of her mother's visit. During the time Annie was living in Ireland, Nancy would visit her every Easter, staying for about a week or ten days. Nancy and Annie were very close, much like sisters. Nancy told me a simple story that shows how resilient and confident her daughter was.

It was the summer of 1989, and Annie was in Germany. She was there with her college friends from Maynooth. They all went to work there for the summer, and they had jobs already arranged in a pickle factory near Hamburg. But when Annie went to start work there she was told that she couldn't work with her friends in the factory, because she didn't have a European passport. She didn't have the right permit to let her work there. Undeterred, Annie went down to the local fruit market, and within minutes she had found a job with a stall-holder. I remember she phoned me and she was joking, saying, 'I'm lifting all these wooden crates; wait till you see the muscles I've developed.'

Annie McCarrick was a self-confident woman who saw the best in people. One of her lecturers at Maynooth was Father Mícheál Mac Gréil, who taught her sociology for one year.

Annie was a most trusting person, someone without guile. She was a fine young person, and she had a deep love for Ireland. She was an outgoing person, always in good humour, always enthusiastic. To think that someone might have breached Annie's trust, and hurt her, is so sad. To think that some violent person may have let the whole country down, it is truly awful.

Nancy McCarrick does not blame Ireland or Irish people for her daughter's murder. There are many examples of young Irish men and women travelling to America on student or work visas and becoming the victims of murder, while the abduction and murder of Annie McCarrick is but one of a small number of violent attacks that American citizens have suffered in Ireland. Annie loved the way of life in Ireland, the culture, the music, the people. Some time late on 26 March 1993 some violent person shattered that view of Ireland. But Nancy McCarrick bears no ill-will towards the country and people with whom Annie chose to live.

When I left Ireland in May 1993 without any news of Annie, I was just devastated. I managed to return to Ireland in August of that year for about a week. I didn't go back there for a long time after that. John and I later divorced. I feel as close to Annie here in New York as when I would visit Ireland. It was another eight years after Annie disappeared that I went back to Ireland. I went over in 2001, and I met a number of gardaí, including the Assistant Commissioner, Tony Hickey, who briefed me on their investigations into whether a serial killer might be involved in Annie's case. Despite the reason for my return there, I was very happy to visit Ireland. I don't blame Ireland at all. Even now, Dublin is a much safer place than parts of New York. There is just no comparison.

I asked Nancy about her feelings towards the person who murdered Annie. She paused, thought carefully, and after a few moments replied:

> I feel that if in any way Annie's death was not what the person intended to happen, or if it was accidental, and if that person responsible was not to harm anyone else, I would have no interest in seeing any person punished. I just want Annie back. I want her home.

John McCarrick has also been devastated at the loss of Annie. He now lives in Mattituck, a town on the north-eastern fork of Long Island. He did everything he could possibly do to find his daughter: he made numerous appeals on radio and television; he hired both a private investigator and a retired English police officer to review the Garda investigation; he offered a $150,000 reward for information leading to the recovery of Annie's remains. The loss of his only child shattered him. He now suffers considerable ill-health and spends much of his time in hospital. Despite this, his message to the person responsible for killing his daughter is as clear today as it was in 1993: 'Whoever is responsible better realise that I'm not giving up. Whoever murdered my daughter had best realise I'm not going away.' Before his health deteriorated he brought an Irish film crew to Bayport to show them where Annie grew up. He brought them along Bayview Avenue, down Delores Court, and down to the beach from where the popular Fire Island is visible across the bay. During the summers when Annie was a teenager, she and her father used to stand on the beach and look at the glistening lights across the bay, where groups of young people would party into the early hours. With tears streaming down his face, he told the film crew that if he could have one wish, he would like nothing else than to be standing on the same beach with Annie by his side just like the old times, with them both listening to the sound of the water and looking across the bay.

Hundreds of acres of woodland and bogland have been searched in an attempt to find Annie McCarrick's remains. The search of the pet cemetery in Enniskerry, four years after her disappearance, is but one example of many searches that have been made for her some years after her disappearance. Another tip-off, that Annie would be found in a well in Co. Wicklow, was also investigated but led nowhere. Other information led to a search of Crone Wood, three miles south-west of Enniskerry, which also yielded nothing. Every lead must be followed up; every anonymous tip-off must be investigated. One detective told me you never know when a break will come.

Look at the investigation into the murder of Phyllis Murphy, who was murdered in 1979. It was over twenty years later before a breakthrough was made in that investigation. Now I know the circumstances were different, in that there was a body found in that case, but in any case that you are investigating you never know when the break will come. You never know when that crucial bit of information will come in. It might be someone coming in to tell us they gave a false alibi for someone on the day in question and they want to make amends for the lie. It does happen.

Looking at the time that elapsed before Annie McCarrick was reported missing, the killer had at least forty-eight hours to cover his tracks. While it is a remote possibility that he may have driven Annie back towards Dublin, this is thought to be unlikely, for the simple reason that there would not be as many places in which to conceal a body. The feeling of detectives involved in the case is that Annie is buried in the Dublin or Wicklow Mountains. The Gardaí are conscious that there are miles and miles of bogland in which her remains may lie. This is the type of terrain in which Antoinette Smith's body was found in 1988 and Patricia Doherty's body was found in 1992. Did the killer travel west of Enniskerry and Glencullen towards the mountains at Glendoo, or Tibradden, or Kippure? Did he go south-west towards Powerscourt Mountain or Djouce Mountain? And what about the forested land that extends for twenty miles along the Wicklow Way from just south of Rathfarnham to deep within mid Co. Wicklow, close to Roundwood? These are all possible places where Annie's remains may lie. This seems the most likely explanation; but without a witness, or a confession, or a chance discovery, it may never be proved.

By the time Operation Trace came to analyse Annie McCarrick's case—together with those of five other missing women in the Leinster area—one extremely violent man had not yet come to the attention of the Gardaí. The violent acts carried out by Larry Murphy on the night of 11 February 2000 shocked the most hardened detectives. He kidnapped a woman in Carlow and brought her in the boot of his car to an isolated spot near Athy, Co. Kildare, where he raped her. He then brought her to an isolated woodland area at Kilranelagh, Co. Wicklow, were he attempted to murder her by putting a plastic bag over her head. The place where Larry Murphy tried to kill his victim and the village of Enniskerry, from where Annie McCarrick is believed to have disappeared, are on opposite sides of Co. Wicklow. Between the two places there lies more than ten miles of dense woodland and mountainous terrain. Murphy knew the back roads of the Wicklow Mountains and had hunted in the area of west Wicklow. He would have an intimate knowledge of many of the remote woodland areas in Co. Wicklow. However, when detectives from Operation Trace went to Arbour Hill Prison to speak to him about Annie McCarrick, he simply told them he knew nothing and politely ended the conversation.

Annie McCarrick touched the lives of many people in her twenty-six years. Apart from her devastated parents, she is survived by many aunts, uncles and cousins on both the McCarrick side and the Dungate side. And she left behind many friends in Ireland, people who knew her in college and in work. The two men with whom she had serious relationships later met their future partners and have settled down. Both have their own private memories of Annie. In private conversations with those close to her, Annie would talk of settling down and of one day having a family. Dermot Ryan, who went out with Annie for over two years, later met an Italian woman at Maynooth, whom he since married. He was nineteen when he started going out with Annie, who was a year older than him. He told me he often dreams about her.

I last saw Annie over two years before she disappeared. We broke up towards the end of 1990, and I didn't see her after that. I remember I visited her over in Long Island that summer, after she returned there for a while to study there. I stayed with her for about four months, and we had a really nice time. But eventually I had to come home, and Annie was staying there for the moment. She drove me to JFK Airport from her home, and she wanted me to make a commitment to our relationship, but I didn't: I wanted to come home and think clearly. I remember she had $5 on her, and she bought me one of those toys, a little 'snow-shaker', as a memory of New York—you know, you shake it and snow falls over Manhattan. I remember

I left her and I went into the toilet at the airport and I cried. I never saw Annie again. I later phoned her and we spoke for an hour, but I never saw her again. I was living in Italy with my fiancée when I got the news over two years later that Annie was missing. I'm married now and have my own family. I still dream about Annie.

Dermot Ryan remembers Annie as a gentle, sweet young woman who was often more romantic than practical.

When I was going out with Annie and we were both studying at Maynooth, she was actually renting a cottage in Ballyboden in south Dublin. She was sharing this cottage with another woman, and it was out in the wilds. It took about two hours to get from there to Maynooth, but Annie wouldn't live anywhere else: she just loved that cottage. Annie had a romantic view of Ireland that most Irish people would find corny, but she just loved this country. She had the most beautiful warm voice, and she would never snub anyone. It's just so sad.

Detective-Garda Val Smith retired from Irishtown Garda Station in November 2002. Just before this he looked once more over the file that consumed so much of his time over the previous nine-and-a-half years: file C31/24/93, missing woman: Annie McCarrick. Val tells me this is the only case that he ever got personal about.

What is frustrating is that we never got a run for our money on it. The last sighting of Annie on the bus in Ranelagh heading towards Enniskerry opens up so many possibilities, so many avenues of inquiry. We never made an arrest in this case. We questioned a number of men at length about their movements around the time of Annie's disappearance, but we just never got that break. This case affected all the gardaí who worked on it. It was exhaustive. If it affects gardaí, God only knows how it affects Annie's parents and family and friends. If Annie's body was found, that would at least be one thing: that would be something. I served here in Irishtown for thirty years, and this is the biggest unsolved case we've had. I would dearly love to be called out of retirement one day to give evidence in this case.

Nancy McCarrick told me of a clear memory she has of her only child. In the present circumstances it paints a particularly poignant picture.

Annie was such a romantic, she was such an emotional person. I remember she was in Manhattan one time and she phoned me. 'Mom,' she said, 'I'm at the opera. I'm at *La Bohème*; there's standing room only. Mom, I'm having the most wonderful time, it is so beautiful, and I am crying my eyes out.'

For Nancy and John McCarrick there is no closure, no ending. Nancy told me that she does not know how she has coped.

I really don't know; it's really difficult to say. Time helps a lot, but I'm always wondering. I'd give anything to know where my daughter is. But I don't have a choice: I just have to go on. My brother Tim lives just next door to me, and I mind his little boy three days a week. I'm kept occupied and happy in that regard, but you never know when it's going to hit you. Sometimes the terrible realisation just hits you. I miss her so much. I would just love to have my daughter back. I want Annie's body found.

2

Jo Jo Dullard

Late on the night of Thursday 9 November 1995, 21-year-old Josephine (Jo Jo) Dullard was abducted in Co. Kildare and murdered. She was half way home when her killer or killers struck. It was a cold winter's night in the village of Moone when, just after half past eleven, Jo Jo accepted her third lift that night. After spending the day in Dublin she had missed the bus that would bring her directly home to Callan, Co. Kilkenny. Instead she had got a bus from Dublin to Naas, Co. Kildare, and started hitching. She got lifts from Naas to Kilcullen, and from there to Moone. By the time she got to Moone she still had more than forty miles to go.

At 11:37 p.m. she entered the public phone box in Moone, just yards from the busy road. She phoned her friend Mary Cullinane, telling her where she was. She was now thinking of trying to hitch a lift ten miles to Carlow, where she could stay with a friend. During the short, stilted conversation she was looking out of the phone box, trying to flag down passing motorists. Suddenly she dropped the phone and ran out to the side of the road: a car had stopped. Jo Jo ran back to the box, told Mary she'd got a lift, and hung up.

At some point during the next few hours, Jo Jo Dullard was murdered. There are a number of different suspects whom the Gardaí believe may be responsible for the killing. These include a man who gave the Gardaí false information about his movements that night and a man from Co. Wicklow now in prison for a horrific attack on a woman. Two members of a criminal gang of travellers are also earmarked as suspects.

Jo Jo's disappearance has caused immense pain for her sisters Mary, Nora, and Kathleen, her brother, Tom, and her nieces and nephews. The failure to find her remains has led her sister Mary to launch a national campaign for the establishment of a specialist Missing Persons Unit and also the establishment of a National Missing Persons Remembrance Day. Whoever killed Jo Jo Dullard will never be allowed forget their evil deed.

On Thursday 9 November 1995 Jo Jo Dullard had collected her last dole payment in Harold's Cross, Dublin, and had spent the afternoon looking around the shops and having a few drinks with friends at the Bruxelles pub off Grafton Street. It was the end of an era in her life. Having spent more than two years living and working in Dublin, she had recently moved home to Callan, where she had got a flat in the centre of town and now had full-time work at a pub and restaurant there. The collection of her last dole payment was the last of the loose ends to tie up in Dublin.

Jo Jo woke just as the bus was coming into Naas. She was still almost sixty miles from home. She began to hitch, hoping she might be lucky enough to find someone driving as far as Kilkenny or even Callan; a more realistic prospect might be finding a motorist heading towards Carlow. Jo Jo had a friend there who would put her up if she could only make it that far. It was already dark as she began thumbing, standing on the busy road. It was a cold night, and she was wearing a black cotton jacket, a shirt, blue jeans, and boots. One motorist stopped; he was heading for Kilcullen, five miles down the road. Again it was a step in the right direction, so Jo Jo got in. She had hitched lifts many times before in Co. Kilkenny and was aware of the dangers of taking lifts from strangers. However, it is clear that, later that night, she accepted a lift from some person who she did not suspect was a violent man.

It was now after eleven o'clock, and Jo Jo was standing in Kilcullen, twenty miles from Carlow and forty-five miles from Callan. She had only put out her hand to start hitching a lift again when another car stopped. This driver was also heading in the direction of Jo Jo's ultimate destination but not going the whole way. He said he could bring her as far as Moone. Jo Jo got in, knowing that this lift would get her to within ten miles of Carlow and closer to a bed for the night.

It was 11:35 p.m. when this motorist dropped Jo Jo off at Moone, Co. Kildare. The village was quiet but for the distant sound of people having their last drinks in a nearby pub. Jo Jo decided to phone her friend Mary Cullinane to let her know where she was. The man who left her in Moone had dropped her close to a public phone box. At 11:37 p.m. she stepped into the phone box and made the call. 'Hi, Mary. I'm in Moone. I missed the bus,' she said. They had a general chat for three minutes, while Jo Jo kept an eye out for any cars heading south. Suddenly she said, 'Hold on.' She dropped the phone, left the phone box, and returned a few seconds later. 'I have a lift. See you, Mary.' She left the phone box and walked towards a nearby car. She would not be seen again.

Jo Jo Dullard was the youngest of five children. She never knew her father, John Dullard: he died when his wife, Nora, was pregnant with Jo Jo in 1973. Nora died in 1983, when Jo Jo was nine, leaving just Jo Jo and her sister Kathleen, still living at home at Newtown, near Callan. The responsibility for raising Jo Jo fell on Kathleen, who was only ten years older. Soon afterwards Kathleen married her sweetheart, Séamus Bergin, and they brought Jo Jo to live with them at Ahenure, on a quiet road just outside Callan. It is here that Jo Jo lived with Kathleen and Séamus until her mid-teens. As I spoke to Kathleen about her memories of Jo Jo, the constant pain caused by her disappearance was all too evident. Even with happy memories, tears welled up in her eyes.

> I was only nineteen when Mam died, and it was just Jo Jo and me in the cottage in Newtown. I was quite nervous with just the two of us in the cottage, but we always felt safe in Mammy's room. I was going out with Séamus, and we got married in 1985 and had our first child, Aisling, in 1986. We decided to move up here to Ahenure, and Jo Jo came with us. She was about fourteen at the time. Myself and Séamus were just starting out, and we later had three more children. Our children were very close to Jo Jo: she was more like a sister to them than an auntie. She lived with us until she was about sixteen. I would do it all again in a second if I could. None of us can believe that Jo Jo is gone now; there's an emptiness in our hearts that we just can't fill.

It was Kathleen Bergin who first reported to the Gardaí the fact that her sister was missing, less than twenty-four hours after Jo Jo had vanished. Yet despite the fact that she had disappeared from the side of a road on a dark night, Kathleen remembers an initial lack of urgency from the Gardaí that she found distressing.

> Jo Jo was meant to be at work at Dawson's pub in Callan on the Friday evening. I remember I got a call from the manager, Tom.

He said Mary Cullinane—Jo Jo's friend—was with him, and Jo Jo hadn't arrived for work. Mary then told me about the phone call from Moone. Immediately I knew this was serious. I called a friend of Jo Jo's in Carlow, but she hadn't seen her. I contacted the Gardaí in Callan, and the officer told me Jo Jo was twenty-one and might have decided to go back to Dublin. I called the Gardaí three times, but I got the same type of response. Eventually I called in to the Garda station. I went up to a garda and said, 'If there was a bank robbed you'd be out there with checkpoints.' In the years since, many gardaí have worked very hard on Jo Jo's case, but that initial response was so wrong.

It was the following Monday, more than three days after Jo Jo Dullard's abduction and murder, that the search and appeal for information began in earnest. One senior garda in the Kilkenny division later revealed that he wasn't even aware of Jo Jo's disappearance until the Monday. Vital days were lost during which suspicious activity, such as unusual digging, went undetected. The search, when it did begin, was extensive; but the feeling of many, including certain gardaí, is that it was all too late. One detective who later worked on the case believes the delay may have given the killer time to cover his tracks.

There is a feeling among some detectives that the person or persons responsible for killing Jo Jo may have actually been questioned at some stage during the investigation. I mean the investigation was massive, and it stands to reason that we may well have spoken to the killer during our search. Over eight hundred statements were later taken, and two thousand questionnaires were completed. A number of men who drove through Moone that night were detected. Some of them gave misleading or evasive answers. We even tracked people down in France and the USA who had driven through Moone that night, but we ruled them out. But the fact that the case lay dormant for the first few days gave the person responsible time to compose themselves, to concoct a story, to practise it, maybe even to start believing their own lies. Also, the killer had a clear seventy-two hours to conceal Jo Jo's body. There are a number of theories about where Jo Jo's body may lie. But, given the time the killer had, even a particular theory put forward that she is buried at a certain location in Co. Kerry is a distinct possibility.

Jo Jo's sister Mary Phelan and her husband, Martin Phelan, believe the answer to what happened to Jo Jo lies close to where she disappeared in Moone. When I met them at their farmhouse at Grange, between Callan and Kilkenny, they told me they are aware of the identity of a particular person who detectives confirmed made contradictory statements when first questioned and who was identified as a suspect.

The strain of years of campaigning is evident on both their faces. Before Jo Jo vanished, Mary and Martin Phelan were farmers, tending to cows and sheep on their ninety-acre farm. They were also parents, rearing their two children. Imelda was eight and Melvin was five when their aunt Jo Jo was taken from them. Since November 1995 Mary and Martin Phelan have spent most of every day planning, pressuring, fund-raising, phoning, faxing and pleading with the power-holders in society for help in finding Jo Jo. Mary told me of the shock she felt when a garda told her they knew more than they were saying.

This senior garda told me that they thought they knew where Jo Jo might be buried. It's a section of private land. The garda also told me that a man had made contradictory statements. We later hired a private detective, who approached this man on the pretext of seeking directions to a golf course. All the detective could tell us was that he got a very uneasy feeling about the man. He also said the man had a deep scratch on his face. It could be something, or it could be nothing, but all we want is for this private land to be searched. Surely if someone makes two different statements there is at least grounds for serious suspicion.

The Phelans have long campaigned for all land within a twenty-mile radius of Moone to be combed thoroughly for clues to Jo Jo's whereabouts. This search would extend over both public and private land in Cos. Kildare and Wicklow. Mary and Martin Phelan have met successive Ministers for Justice and the Garda Commissioner to argue their point. The lands remain unsearched. One senior officer who reviewed the case strenuously denies that the Gardaí were in any way reluctant to follow this line of inquiry.

Yes, this man did make two different statements about what he did and where he was on the night Jo Jo disappeared. We now know he was in Moone at around the time Jo Jo was. He had earlier been over in Co. Offaly and was heading home. There were certain discrepancies in his statements. He told us he had been genuinely mistaken in his first statement and was sorry, that it wasn't malicious. You need more than that to get a search warrant. That's the law we work under.

It was at the Phelans' home in Grange that Jo Jo lived from the age of sixteen, having moved from Kathleen and Séamus Bergin's house in Callan. For months after Jo Jo's disappearance Mary couldn't face going into Jo Jo's old bedroom, or looking at her old schoolbooks, or clothes, or posters. Eventually the precious keep-sakes were gathered up and put away for safe keeping.

When the Gardaí began their investigation into the dis-appearance of Jo Jo Dullard, a number of people came forward with information that suggests she may have accepted not three but four lifts that November night. Detectives had quickly traced the two motorists who had given her lifts from Naas to Kilcullen and from Kilcullen to Moone. But a number of people were now reporting seeing a woman hitching a lift in Castledermot, Co. Kildare, five miles south of Moone, at about 11:55 p.m. This time would correspond with Jo Jo getting a lift in Moone at about 11:40 p.m. Four people reported seeing a woman matching Jo Jo's description in Castledermot that night; two of those witnesses saw the unidentified young woman thumbing a lift on the Carlow side of the town, near the Schoolhouse restaurant.

This new information threw a different light on the investi-gation, one that remains to this day. If the woman in Castledermot was Jo Jo Dullard, whoever gave her a lift from Moone to Castledermot has never come forward. Why is this? Did the same person circle back to Castledermot and offer her a further lift and then attack her? If the person is entirely innocent, why do they remain silent? Do they know the identity of the person who gave Jo Jo the fourth lift, or did they spot anything that might be of use to the Gardaí? One detective agreed that the person may have crucial information.

We must assume first that the woman hitching in Castledermot is Jo Jo. Certainly, the timing is right: it's just before midnight. And whoever that woman was, she has never been located. And not one but four people saw this unidentified woman in the town. Neither the woman nor whoever picked her up have ever been located. That mystery driver could be the breaking of this case.

In February 1997, fifteen months after the disappearance of Jo Jo Dullard, the Gardaí released new information that raised the distinct possibility that Jo Jo might have been taken against her will a further fifty miles south, as far as Co. Waterford. The news came after a taxi driver contacted the Gardaí with a deeply disturbing story that raised the possibility that Jo Jo might have been attacked by not one but two men. He gave a story that he had kept to himself for over a year. At about 1:20 a.m. on the morning of 10 November 1995 he was driving along the main road at Kilmacow, three miles north of Waterford, when he saw a red car with English number-plates parked at the side of the road. One man was urinating beside the car. Suddenly he saw a woman running from the left-hand rear door of the car towards the front. She had bare feet, and seemed distressed. Within seconds a second man appeared, also from the back of the car. He followed the woman, grabbed her by the hair, and got her in a bear hug; he then dragged her back to the car. It then took off in the direction of Waterford. The taxi driver had seen all this happen in a matter of seconds as he drove past the car; yet it would be more than a year before he reported it. A senior officer who has worked on Jo Jo Dullard's case from the beginning believes this reported sighting may yet yield results.

The report by the taxi driver opens up a number of lines of inquiry. It is more than disappointing that the man waited over a year to come forward. I think he was advised by someone close to him that it was none of his concern and that he should keep out of it, but he eventually came forward, and better late than never. We have our suspicions as to who the two men were. The car was described as a red-coloured Ford Sierra Sapphire or Ford Grenada, with English registration plates. Despite the foreign registration, we believe the two men in the car were Irish. But it just makes you think. If it was Jo Jo who was spotted by the taxi driver, she was taken over fifty miles from where she made the phone call in Moone.

In February 2000, more than four years after Jo Jo Dullard disappeared, 35-year-old Larry Murphy, a self-employed carpenter and father of two, abducted a woman in Carlow. He disarmed her by punching her in the face, fracturing her nose. He bound and gagged the terrified woman, who he placed in the boot of his car, then drove her first to an isolated spot at Beaconstown, Athy, and then to a forest at Kilranelagh, near Baltinglass, Co. Wicklow. At both places he subjected the woman to prolonged sexual assaults. He then attempted to murder her by putting a bag over her head. Two men stumbled upon Murphy and his victim, and Murphy fled. He was arrested the following day, and once the full picture of his terrible crime was established, detectives from Operation Trace were immediately alerted. They were conscious that the route Murphy had travelled that night, with his victim in the boot of his car, was very close to both Moone and Castledermot. In driving her from Athy to Kilranelagh he had crossed over the N9 road close to where Jo Jo Dullard had been hitching a lift in November 1995. Murphy had never come to the attention of the Gardaí before he repeatedly raped and attempted to murder the woman in February 2000. After he had been sentenced to fifteen years' imprisonment, two senior gardaí went to meet him in prison. He politely told them he had no information about any missing women.

A total of nine people, including a number of women, were formally arrested for questioning by detectives from Operation Trace investigating a number of crimes, including the murder of Jo Jo Dullard. Two of the men who were questioned are members of a criminal gang from the Waterford area. They are believed to have been socialising in Dublin on the Thursday afternoon and evening. Detectives suspect they were travelling through Moone and Castledermot later that night. One garda explained that it is very difficult to bring this any further right now.

> Basically, these two fellows are travelling criminals. Many of the answers they gave us are evasive, but that could be because they don't want to reveal a totally separate crime they may have been involved in. But we received certain information that outlined in very clear detail an allegation that these two men had abducted Jo Jo and had killed her. The two men deny any knowledge of Jo Jo. We need a witness, or we need a confession, or we need a body. We are definitely watching these men.

Three weeks before Jo Jo Dullard disappeared she travelled to England to have an abortion. This private information was published in a number of newspapers, which quoted an unnamed Garda source as suggesting that she might have been depressed at the time of her disappearance. Jo Jo's family believe this information was deliberately leaked to a journalist by a garda, who had been given the information in confidence. Whatever way the information made its way to the press, it has caused untold distress to Jo Jo's family and anger among many gardaí. Mary Phelan says the whole episode left a sour taste in her dealings with gardaí.

> Jo Jo's brother and sisters were the only ones to know this information. And we were just trying to do everything we

could to find our sister. So, we told the Gardaí this fact in total confidence. The reporter who later wrote the story told me a garda had told him the information, and the suggestion was that Jo Jo might have been depressed and had gone away by herself, which is crazy. That was so hurtful. That information was private, and it hurts that some garda leaked it. I think it might have been done because I was giving out about the Gardaí so publicly.

A detective close to the case agrees that Jo Jo's trip to England shortly before her disappearance has absolutely nothing to do with what happened to her.

I don't know if it was through stupidity or malice that the information was leaked. I know it wouldn't have come from her family, but it was never proven that a garda had done it. There's also a question about whether such matters should be reported by the media anyway. But whatever the source of the leak, every detective who worked on this case knows Jo Jo did not choose to disappear. Her family know that, everyone knows that. It was a dark, cold night along a busy road in Co. Kildare. Jo Jo just wanted to get home, and some killer was lurking in a car.

Back in Callan, Kathleen Bergin told me that Jo Jo had been thinking of not going to Dublin at all that fateful Thursday.

Jo Jo had to get to Harold's Cross at some stage to get her last dole payment. She had just got a new job in Callan and so had to get to Dublin to tie up loose ends whenever she got a chance. She was actually meant to go earlier in the week, but she had to cover in work for a girl who was sick. The day before she went I told her that if she didn't go to Dublin next day we could meet for a coffee in Callan town. But Jo Jo went to Dublin, and I never saw her before she went.

Jo Jo Dullard lived in Dublin for two years. She and her friend Mary Cullinane both arrived in Dublin from Co. Kilkenny with dreams of becoming beauticians. Both young women signed up for a beauty course in Crumlin, but they found that the cost of books and materials was just too great; so they dropped out and got jobs working in pubs in Dublin. If they made enough money they could always go back to the course. Jo Jo got a job at the Red Parrot in Dorset Street, where members of the staff remember her as a courteous young woman who was a hard worker. She and Mary Cullinane first lived in Dolphin's Barn for about a year then later moved to Phibsborough, and then to Rialto. Another friend of theirs, called Claire, who now lives in Boston, also lived with them for a time.

It was during her time in Dublin that Jo Jo met her only long-term boy-friend. Mike was an American who was travelling around the world. He found himself in Dublin and loved it so much he decided to stay longer than intended. He met Jo Jo Dullard, and they soon began going out. Kathleen Bergin remembers that Jo Jo was very excited when she first brought Mike down to Co. Kilkenny.

She phoned me one time and she told me she was coming down to see us that weekend. Then she said, 'Do you mind if I bring a friend?' They both came down, and we met Mike. He really was a nice chap. We all went out for a pint. I know that Jo Jo was very keen on Mike. When they broke up I know Jo Jo was really upset. When we saw her with Mike we couldn't believe how grown up she was: we all felt so proud of her. Jo Jo had a hard life, with Mam dying when Jo Jo was so young and Dad dying just before Jo Jo was born. Going up to live in Dublin is never an easy thing for a young girl to do, but Jo Jo was so brave, so grown up.

By the time Jo Jo disappeared, Mike had left Ireland to continue his travels on the Continent. The Gardaí would later track him down in Spain, after a farmer made a discovery that detectives hoped might be a development in the case. In the summer of 1996 a farmer found a watch in a dyke on the Carlow side of Castledermot, seven miles from the phone box in Moone. The farmer thought nothing of his find until he saw a fresh appeal for information on Jo Jo Dullard's disappearance in late 1996. He contacted the Gardaí, who immediately set about trying to establish whether the watch was Jo Jo's. Detectives learnt that her former boy-friend, Mike, had given her a watch. They found him in Spain, where they asked him if he could identify the watch, but he couldn't. He later wrote to Kathleen and Séamus Bergin to say how sorry he was to hear of Jo Jo's disappearance.

In June 1997, arising out of crossed wires and inexperience, it was reported that the body of Jo Jo Dullard had been found in the River Shannon. These untrue reports were broadcast only once on radio before being dropped, but they caused distress and confusion to Jo Jo's family and the community. The mistake arose after a body was discovered in the Shannon at Bush Island, near Ennis. The body, which was later identified as that of a man who had gone missing in the west, could not be identified for a number of days. An initial examination suggested that a pair of Wrangler jeans and trainers might offer a good indication of the identity of the person. One senior garda told another that it could be Jo Jo

Dullard, and as the information was passed on, somebody wrongly picked up the idea that it actually was her, and this was reported on radio. One broadcaster who read the misleading report later sent a letter of apology to Jo Jo Dullard's family.

In the weeks immediately after Jo Jo Dullard's disappearance the Gardaí had to sift through thousands of questionnaires and investigate hundreds of reported sightings. One senior garda says the search for the missing woman was extensive.

A Garda sub-aqua team searched thirty-six miles of the River Barrow, which is just a few miles west of Castledermot and Moone. All the roads from Moone to Carlow were searched inch by inch for clues. Woodland and forests were searched. For twelve months, forest, woods and bogs were searched every weekend. Over two thousand witness statements were taken, and detectives made inquiries as far as America and Australia. This investigation is very much still open.

Shortly after Jo Jo Dullard's disappearance, the Gardaí established one particular line of inquiry that they first thought might lead them to her. Gardaí in Kilkenny remembered that the night after her disappearance, and before the alarm was raised, two English men had been arrested for breaking into a phone box in the town, apparently looking for money. The two men were released, and they left the country. But detectives would later be alerted to the incident at Kilmacow, outside Waterford, where two men in a car with English number-plates were seen in the company of a woman who was barefoot and in obvious distress. They tracked the men down to Portsmouth. At first neither man could account for his movements. One detective told me that the Gardaí thought they had two serious suspects.

64

These two men used to travel over by ferry from Fishguard to Rosslare and then travel around the country breaking into coin boxes in small villages. Although it was fairly minor-scale crime, they could make up to seven or eight thousand pounds over a week, and then head home on the ferry. We finally caught up with these fellows, and they couldn't tell us where they had been on the night of Jo Jo's disappearance. We took their car and we pulled it apart, checking it for any evidence of Jo Jo having been in it, or any crime having been committed. We knew they had been travelling around the country and were involved in petty crime, and of course that can often be a precursor to much more serious, violent crime. For three months we thought we might have our men, but then we found that they were effectively in the clear. We established that on the night Jo Jo disappeared they had checked in to a bed and breakfast in Cork under the alias of Cunningham. An extensive check of phone records showed that they had actually called home to England at 12:20 a.m. on 10 November 1995. So these two could not have been in Moone or Castledermot only half an hour before, and were not the two men seen bundling an unidentified woman into a car outside Waterford city later that night. They weren't able to clear themselves; it was actually gardaí who eventually established their alibi for them.

From the time Jo Jo Dullard was dropped off in Moone, and once she left the phone box only minutes later, a sinister mystery began. The closely knit community in Moone has suffered in the knowledge that some person who drove through their village that night was a murderer, a person out looking for a woman to kill. It is a distressing thought for local people, who know that the killer could very well have picked on any woman out on the road by the phone box that night.

A lasting memory to Jo Jo Dullard, in the form of a memorial stone, now lies by the phone box from where she told her friend Mary that she'd 'just got a lift.' However, the installing of the stone was not an easy task. There were objections from some local people, who thought the village was being unfairly characterised in relation to Jo Jo Dullard's disappearance. Jo Jo's family and friends decided to take matters into their own hands. One of those involved was John McGuinness TD, who campaigns in Dáil Éireann for more action to be taken to find missing people. He described to me the covert operation that saw the memorial stone erected in Moone.

Mary and Martin Phelan came to me one day in 1998 and told me they wanted to put up some kind of memorial to Jo Jo in Moone. I had known them for about two years before, since they first came and basically demanded that I do something to help find Jo Jo. One thing that we could at least do was put up a memorial in Moone. The vast majority of people in Moone were supportive of the idea, but one or two people were not so keen. There was a real fear that there might be an objection if planning permission was sought. A memorial stone had been carved in Co. Kerry and was brought up to my office in Kilkenny, and we decided we would erect it ourselves. At around five o'clock one morning, myself, my brother Declan, Martin Phelan and his brother Gerard loaded the stone up into a jeep and we headed off for Moone with the cement mixed in the back. Before it was bright we had cemented the stone against the wall beside the phone box. To this day, that memorial stone has not been touched. It is a fitting tribute to Jo Jo, which has been accepted by the people of Moone.

The memorial stone reads: *Jo Jo Dullard, missing since 9 November 1995. What happened to her? Where is Jo Jo now?* Local people, and motorists passing through the village, often stop, lay flowers, and reflect on the enormity of the unexplained death of Jo Jo Dullard.

On 22 November 1998, Moone became the scene of the first Mass for missing people. Members of the families of many missing people attended the service at the Church of the Blessed Trinity. It was an emotional evening, with many families who thought they suffered alone meeting other families who suffer the same loss. The Mass was organised by the Jo Jo Dullard Memorial Trust, which was set up by Mary Phelan. In May 2002, in another landmark in Mary Phelan's campaign for missing people, President Mary McAleese unveiled the National Monument to Missing People in the grounds of Kilkenny Castle.

Martin Phelan has watched his wife campaign on behalf of her sister from the day Jo Jo was reported missing. He has supported her every step of the way. Sometimes he has taken matters into his own hands. It was through his impassioned initiative that John McGuinness became a close associate of the Jo Jo Dullard Memorial Trust. It happened one day, about a year after Jo Jo's disappearance, when John McGuinness was Mayor of Kilkenny and Martin Phelan thought to himself, 'Enough is enough.' He marched into the mayor's office and got McGuinness's undivided attention by standing up on a glass table. For fifteen precarious minutes he spoke frantically at McGuinness from the top of the table and told him why the people of Kilkenny and the representatives of Kilkenny should be outraged that one of their own could go missing, be murdered and not be found. John McGuinness had heard enough. He committed himself to fighting for the Phelans. This promise has culminated in a trip to the United States by John McGuinness and Mary and Martin Phelan as part of their campaign for the establishment of a specialist Missing Persons Unit. They hope to learn from the FBI what types of investigative tools are available, be they psychological profiling techniques or advanced equipment that could aid the Gardaí by detecting soil movements. Martin Phelan says that they have to keep fighting for Jo Jo, whatever way they can.

> It's just not right that someone can go missing like that and not be found. Irish people are going missing, are being murdered. And we have none of them solved. After all, Ireland is only an island. More has to be done. We think a Missing Persons Unit has to be put in place, where young police officers know exactly what to do when someone goes missing, where time isn't wasted, where dogs and helicopters are sent out immediately.

Operation Trace examined a number of possible explanations for who may have murdered Jo Jo Dullard. One that is still being investigated is a report that two members of a criminal gang from the south-east of the country were responsible. Despite searches in a number of locations in Leinster and Munster, nothing was found.

Another report from a member of the public led to a search of woodland near Clonmel, Co. Tipperary, in April 1999. A couple out collecting holly in November 1995 said they had seen two men and a woman in the forest. The woman appeared to be unwell or under duress. The couple did not report the sighting at the time and forgot about it, but more recent publicity about missing women brought it back to them. Detectives believed they might be on to something. The woodland is about fifteen miles from the reported sighting of two men and a distressed woman at Kilmacow on the night of Jo Jo Dullard's abduction. The witnesses were able to point out a specific area where they saw the two men and the dis-tressed woman. However, an extensive search revealed nothing.

Nine people were arrested by the Gardaí investigating the dis-appearance of Jo Jo Dullard. A number of those were also ques-tioned about other crimes in the Leinster area. Those arrested included two men who were living in the Waterford area at the time of Jo Jo Dullard's disappearance and who were living in the Co. Louth area when seventeen-year-old Ciara Breen disappeared from her home in Dundalk in February 1997. No charges were brought, but a number of individuals are still suspects in relation to the abduction and murder of Jo Jo Dullard.

The Gardaí conducted an extensive trawl through Jo Jo Dullard's life in an effort to establish whether the person who gave her a lift had, by fluke, actually known her. One line of inquiry that was eventually ruled out as a coincidence was that Jo Jo was known to socialise in a particular pub where a now convicted murderer also drank. David Lawler is serving a life sentence for the rape and murder of Marilyn Rynn, who he attacked as she walked home along an isolated pathway in Blanchardstown, Co. Dublin, in December 1995, just over a month after Jo Jo Dullard's dis-appearance. Lawler worked for Telecom Éireann as a van driver and would have had the opportunity to travel around the country alone. Detectives established that Lawlor and Jo Jo Dullard had frequented the same pub. One detective told me that further investigations revealed that it was just a coincidence.

We established that David Lawler had never met with or spoken to Jo Jo in the pub. It was purely a coincidence that they drank in the same pub. They had been there at different times. I suppose if Jo Jo disappeared in Dublin, close to or near her home, we would have been even more suspicious initially.

But a receipt from an ATM machine put David Lawler in Dublin that night, and he didn't have access to a vehicle at that time. Certainly he was looked at purely because of his murderous activity only a month after Jo Jo's disappearance, and the fact they had been in the same pub fuelled our initial speculation, but Jo Jo's abduction and murder was different from Marilyn Rynn's. Jo Jo was standing on a lonely road in Moone, miles and miles from Dublin and miles and miles from home. Whoever the killer is, it was a chance encounter.

On Christmas Day in 1995 Mary and Martin Phelan rose early. Despite the trauma of Jo Jo's disappearance six weeks before, Santa had to arrive in some way for Imelda and Melvin, then eight and five years old. The Phelans sat at the kitchen table and ate tea and toast. The four of them then put on their coats and went to meet Martin's brother Gerard. They travelled towards Moone, where they spent all day searching for Jo Jo. They continued searching hedges, drains and roadsides until it got dark, but they found nothing. Mary will never forget that Christmas Day.

We set off early for Moone; we couldn't just sit at home while Jo Jo was still out there. We started from the phone box once again and searched wherever we could. I remember thinking as we searched the roadside that the man who is responsible for murdering my sister would be sitting down having his Christmas turkey, sitting with his family, maybe sitting by a cosy fire. And here we were continuing to search for Jo Jo. It's just not right.

Shortly after Jo Jo Dullard went missing, Mary and Kathleen searched her flat at Green Street, Callan. They found a list that Jo

Jo had made of people she would be buying Christmas presents for. There was her only brother, Tom, and his family in Kildare, and closer to home in Co. Kilkenny her sister Nora, her sister Kathleen and her family, and Mary and her family. Then there were her many friends in Callan.

Kathleen Bergin told me of many fond memories she has of her little sister.

Jo Jo was sometimes a little tom-boy when she was growing up. She'd play in the fields and swim in the river; she'd climb trees, and play soccer. Then she became a teenager, and she was into music. She loved George Michael, Michael Jackson and A-Ha and had posters of them all in her bedroom. Jo Jo loved animals, and she had a cocker spaniel; she called him Freeway, after the dog in the TV show 'Hart to Hart'. She got the dog just six months after Mam died, and she really loved him. When she grew up Jo Jo was still deciding what to do with her life. She was only twenty-one when she disappeared. She was working in a restaurant and a pub. She said she might go back to the beautician's course some day, but she was also talking about being an air stewardess. She had so much ahead of her.

Kathleen's husband, Séamus Bergin, told me that more needs to be done to find missing women in Leinster.

There are five or six who have gone missing in very suspicious circumstances. Surely to God something should be found by now. It's hard to believe that nothing has been found. It would make you wonder if there is some kind of planning or organisation involved. It is so scary. There are some gardaí who have worked very hard on these cases, but their hands seem to be tied. I think that if gardaí believe certain people have information but are not giving that information to detectives, then gardaí should have the power to prosecute them. Something more needs to be done. There are people who know, or at least strongly suspect, what happened to Jo Jo. Life isn't the same without Jo Jo; she should be here with us now. It feels like a nightmare that never ends.

A detective who worked on Jo Jo Dullard's disappearance agrees that the circumstances of her abduction and murder fit the profile of a serial killer.

Jo Jo disappeared two-and-a-half years after the disappearance of Annie McCarrick over the far side of Co. Wicklow. And then there was the disappearance of Eva Brennan, who may have been abducted as she was walking along a quiet road in south Dublin in July 1993. We definitely think that Annie McCarrick might have accepted a lift from a seemingly charming man. We know for a fact that Jo Jo was seeking a lift in Moone the night she disappeared. Whoever stopped for her in Moone was able to trick her or lull her into a false sense of security. Whatever happened, it wasn't a crime of passion. Jo Jo didn't know her killer, or killers. Whoever's responsible may very well have struck before, or have struck again afterwards. They may strike again, if they are not dead or in prison for something else.

Detectives have spent many hours teasing out different explanations of how Jo Jo Dullard was not immediately suspicious of the occupant or occupants of the car that she stepped into in Moone. One report made to the Gardaí early in the investigation was by a woman who said she saw a woman matching Jo Jo Dullard's description about to get into a car in Moone. She had not come forward earlier because she was away on holiday and was unaware of the significance of what she had seen. She said she saw this woman walking towards a dark-coloured car, possibly a Toyota Carina, which had stopped about fifty yards from the phone box. One of the rear doors was open. The Gardaí studied this reported sighting carefully. The make of car was vigorously pursued by detectives. It did not lead anywhere but continues to be a line of inquiry.

This sighting raised the possibility that Jo Jo might have got into the back seat of a car. This would suggest in turn that the front passenger seat was occupied. Was it possible that the front-seat passenger was a woman? This might have lulled Jo Jo into thinking she was safe in the car. Or was it occupied by a man who, like the driver, appeared to be normal? Or was Jo Jo immediately suspicious of the occupant or occupants but, before she could get away, was pulled into the car? Might this be the car that was later spotted fifty miles south near Waterford, where a barefoot woman was seen trying to escape from two men? All these ideas are credible, some of them more so than others. But they remain just speculation.

Jo Jo Dullard's home town of Callan, eight miles south-west of Kilkenny, has been the scene of two separate killings in recent years. In May 1999 Marie Hennessy, a mother of three, was beaten to death by her husband, Patrick Hennessy, who repeatedly struck her with a car jack. He attacked her on the side of the road, days after he was suspended from his job as manager of the local Social Welfare office. He had been embezzling money and had been trying to conceal this from his wife. He was later jailed for eight years for manslaughter, a sentence severely criticised as too lenient by Marie Hennessy's family. In November 2001 two-year old

Robyn Leahy was stabbed to death in Callan by her father, George McCloin, who then killed himself. He had travelled to Callan from Dublin and first attacked Robyn's mother, Lorraine, with whom he had previously split up, before killing their daughter. Both these incidents traumatised a closely knit community already reeling from the abduction and murder of Jo Jo Dullard.

Jo Jo Dullard was the second of six women to disappear in sinister circumstances in Leinster between 1993 and 1998. Within months of her disappearance her sister Mary, having failed to get satisfactory answers from certain gardaí in relation to her sister's case, was calling for the reintroduction of the Murder Squad. This specialist team of detectives had operated in the 1970s and 80s, travelling around the country, offering assistance to local gardaí dealing with any particularly complex murder investigation. In the light of the disappearance of four more young women, Mary began calling for the establishment of a specialist Missing Persons Unit. Such a unit would be able to get to the scene of a disappearance quickly, without any needless delay in deciding which Garda division had jurisdiction over the investigation. Valuable scientific evidence might also be salvaged, and psychological profiling of suspects might also prove fruitful.

The Jo Jo Dullard Memorial Trust was set up in 1998 by Mary and Martin Phelan with the assistance of John McGuinness. An honorary patron is the former President of Ireland, Mary Robinson. It is often through the persistence of the trust that the issue of missing people has remained on the political and media agenda. The beliefs of members of the trust have often clashed with the opinion of certain gardaí. An internal Garda document described the group as tending towards a radical interpretation of the situation ... listing 84 people as missing since 1990 ... this would include fishermen lost at sea, and 'presumed drowned' cases ... the general perception of their literature is distorted ... However in their particular circumstances they should be given as much leeway as possible.

This clash of opinions relates to the fact that many missing people have chosen to go missing. The Jo Jo Dullard Memorial Trust does not differentiate between the families of missing people who have been murdered and the families of those missing people who have not been the victims of violence. To the trust, every missing person leaves behind a heartbroken family, every case is tragic.

When Jo Jo Dullard disappeared she was wearing a black zip-up cotton jacket, light-blue jeans, and black boots with two-inch square heels. She had two weeks' dole money in her possession. No items of the clothing she was wearing have ever been found. There was no sign of a struggle along the roadside in Moone. Jo Jo Dullard's lonely death is in total contrast to the warmth and comfort of her extended family in Cos. Kildare and Kilkenny. In Co. Kildare her brother Tom and his family, including five of Jo Jo's nieces and nephews, grieve for her. In Co. Kilkenny her three sisters also grieve for their baby sister. Her sister Nora misses the little sister she nicknamed Jodie and often tells her other sisters that Jo Jo is with their Mam now and is safe. At the Bergin home in Callan, Kathleen and Séamus showed me dozens of photographs of Jo Jo growing up: playing with her dog, Freeway, grinning with her three sisters on the porch, making her first Holy Communion, lounging in a chair. This is where Jo Jo was safe; this is where she should be.

Just up the road in Grange, Mary Phelan told me her special memory about the night Jo Jo went to her debs' dance.

I will never forget that night. Jo Jo had bought a lovely dress, and she was getting ready here. She had her hair all up in curls. I gave her a ring and a bracelet that had been given to me. I remember walking away from her for a moment and I looked back, and do you know, I'll never forget how she looked. It was amazing: she looked just like Mum. I was looking at Mum. When Jo Jo was ready to head out she came and gave me a big hug, and she said to me, 'I'll never forget you for this.'

On 26 May 2002 a National Monument for Missing People was unveiled in the grounds of Kilkenny Castle. The steel monument, featuring the hand-prints of members of the families of missing people, is in a quiet part of the castle grounds, surrounded on three sides by flowers and bushes. A number of families did not attend the unveiling: they are not in a position to grieve openly with others. But a large number of families did attend, including those of Jo Jo Dullard, Fiona Pender, Ciara Breen, and Fiona Sinnott. President Mary McAleese unveiled the monument and was escorted around to meet the families by Mary Phelan. As Jo Jo's sister made a speech thanking everyone who had made the day special, she broke down. Mary Phelan has been at the forefront of the tireless campaign for the monument and the establishment of a Missing Persons Day. But she, and all Jo Jo Dullard's family, would dearly love one thing: to have Jo Jo's remains returned to them.

Mary Phelan also firmly believes that the person who murdered her sister will kill again.

The person who killed Jo Jo will definitely strike again. Give him time and he will. This person has got to be caught and brought in. This person has to be caught to save the life of whoever the next victim is. And we have to find Jo Jo to put her with Mum and Dad. They're buried together in Kilkenny city, and that's where Jo Jo should be resting. We have to give her a Christian burial.

3

Fiona Pender

❤❥

Fiona Pender, a 25-year-old model and hairdresser, was seven months pregnant when she was abducted and murdered in August 1996. Her killer also set in train a series of events that, four years later, would end in Fiona's father taking his own life.

The Pender family, from Connolly Park, Tullamore, has suffered unimaginable pain. Before Fiona's abduction and murder they had already lost a loved one. Fiona's younger brother Mark was killed in June 1995 when his motorbike hit a lorry near Killeigh, just south of Tullamore. Today the surviving members of the family are Fiona's mother, Josephine, and her other younger brother, John. Josephine believes she knows the identity of the person who may have murdered her daughter.

Josephine Pender does not believe that Fiona was the victim of a serial killer, a view shared by many of the gardaí who worked on the case. In April 1997 three women and two men were arrested and questioned. All five were released without charge twelve hours later. The last person known to have seen Fiona Pender was her boyfriend, John Thompson. He said goodbye to her at about six o'clock on the morning of Friday 23 August 1996. Fiona, who was suffering from a bout of heartburn, was still in bed as he left their ground-floor flat in Church Street, Tullamore. He had a busy day's work ahead at his family's farm at Grange, Co. Laois, about eight miles away.

The next evening John Thompson received a phone call at the farm in Grange. It was Fiona's mother, Josephine. 'Where's Fiona?' she asked. 'I've been around to the flat. She's not there.' 'I thought she was with you,' he replied. 'I'll be in to you shortly.' Later that night John Thompson and Fiona's mother and father and her thirteen-year-old brother walked into Tullamore Garda Station. Fiona had not been seen for more than thirty-six hours. It is most probable that she was already dead.

The last time Josephine Pender saw her only daughter was at seven o'clock on the evening of Thursday 22 August 1996. The two had spent much of the day together, making two trips to the Bridge Shopping Centre in Tullamore. Fiona was in good form. Her baby was due in just over two months' time. John was working long hours at his father's farm. Fiona was on the look-out for a new home for themselves and the new baby. The flat in Church Street was too small, a bed-sitter with a kitchen in one part of the large room. Fiona had decided that once the baby was born she was going to take it home to her mother's house, where they could both rest for a few weeks, hoping that within a short time she and John and the baby would have a nice place of their own.

On that last day that Josephine and Fiona would spend together they met at Dunne's Stores at the Bridge Centre, a few minutes' walk from Church Street. They did a bit of shopping and then decided to head back to the Pender family home at Connolly Park, about ten minutes' walk away. It was raining, so they got a taxi. Fiona's father was in the house, getting himself ready for a fishing trip. Tired after the walk around the shops, Fiona sat down and cradled her tummy. She picked up a copy of *Hello* and began flicking through it. She found a photograph of the singer Eric Clapton on a fishing trip catching a salmon; she showed it to her father, getting his own fishing gear together, and they laughed. The expectant mother was just hours away from being abducted and murdered.

Fiona Pender was the eldest of the three children of Seán and Josephine Pender. The second was Mark, two years younger than his sister; John is the youngest. He was thirteen when his only sister vanished and sixteen when his father took his own life. But the first tragedy to hit the Pender family occurred when John was only twelve, when his older brother was killed in a motorcycle accident.

Mark Pender loved motorcycles. The one he was riding that day in June 1995 was a limited-edition Fireblade. It was a sunny day, and he and a friend had just stopped for ice cream and petrol in Killeigh, south of Tullamore. After finishing their ice cream they got back on the bike and headed for Tullamore. A few moments later the bike hit a grass verge and swerved into the path of an oncoming lorry. The passenger escaped with minor injuries, but Mark Pender died. He was twenty-one years old and the proud father of three-year-old Dean. Mark and Dean's mother, Gillian, were due to be married the following May. A week after Mark's death an insurance agent—unaware of Mark's death—called to say that the couple had been given approval for a mortgage.

Fiona Pender took the death of her younger brother very badly. With only two years between them, Fiona and Mark were close. Fiona shared his interest in motorbikes; she even bought her own, but she got rid of it after Mark's death. It was through her interest in motorbikes that she had met John Thompson, a farmer from

Grange in north Co. Laois. It was Mark who introduced her to John, who he knew from working with motorbikes, fixing them up. Fiona and John hit it off immediately. They started going out in October 1993, they went on a date to Birr, and the relationship continued up to the time Fiona vanished almost three years later.

After Mark's death there were nights when Fiona could be found at his grave in Durrow, just outside Tullamore. It was in Durrow that Mark and Gillian were to be married. As Fiona spoke to her brother at his graveside she promised she would be a great aunt and would always look out for Dean, now that Mark was gone.

The sitting-room in the Pender home in Tullamore is cosy and welcoming. The room is dominated by photographs and paintings. Most of the photographs are of Fiona, who modelled for magazines. The four paintings are by Seán Pender, a talented artist. There are two landscapes and a painting of boats tied up by a snowy pier; the fourth is an adaptation of the Mona Lisa. They were mostly painted in 1998—two years after Fiona's disappearance, and two years before Seán would end his own life.

It was in this room that Fiona Pender sat with her mother and father on the afternoon of Thursday 22 August 1996. While they were still suffering the loss of Mark, there was a lot to look forward to. Mark's son, Dean, was three years old. He and Gillian were living close by, and the Penders could visit Dean whenever they wanted. Now Dean would have a new cousin, and Seán and Josephine would have a second grandchild.

Fiona's baby was due on 22 October 1996. There was great excitement. If it was a girl, Fiona said she was going to call it Emma, or perhaps Laura. If she had a boy she said she'd know immediately whether or not to call him Mark. The future looked bright. It would be a bit of a strain to find a new house or flat for herself and

John and the baby; but the baby appeared to be perfectly healthy, and that was the main thing. Fiona had been through a scare in the first three months: she was told she was in danger of having a miscarriage. But she came through it.

As Josephine and myself sat in the room that had held such excitement in August 1996, she recounted, with clarity, what was to be the last day she would spend with her only daughter.

> Well, we sat here after coming back from the Bridge Centre earlier that day. It had been raining, but it eased off a bit. We had a chat and a laugh here, and we had a bit of lunch. Seán was getting ready to go off fishing. I said to Fiona that I needed to get a new pair of trousers for John; school was starting back in a couple of weeks. Fiona said she could get a few more things for the baby as well, so we decided to head back up to the Bridge Shopping Centre. I remember clearly I bought the baby a little grey track suit, and we got Fiona a pair of shoes that she'd be able to wear after the baby was born. And Fiona got some things for the baby: she got nappy wipes, and gripe water, and Sudocrem. Those things were still in the bag unpacked when gardaí later searched her flat. My son John joined us, and the three of us walked Fiona back to her flat at Church Street. We walked into the flat with her. It was around seven o'clock. I gave her a kiss. I remember clearly, as myself and John walked across the road I waved back at her. And that's the last memory I have of Fiona: her little face at the door.

The flat in Church Street where Fiona Pender was last seen is in the centre of Tullamore. It's a three-minute walk to the Garda station, and the Bridge Shopping Centre is even closer. The flat is on the ground floor of a large converted building that houses twelve self-contained bed-sitters. Standing at the front door you can see that there are only two routes that Fiona and her killer could have taken. Coming out of the flat, turning left brings you towards the town centre, while turning right brings you to a roundabout that leads on to the roads towards Port Laoise and Portarlington. Church Street is a busy street, with pubs, restaurants, and flats. Despite this, no-one has ever come forward to say they saw Fiona leave her flat. There was no evidence of any violent attack in the flat; no evidence that an intruder broke in; no evidence of any type of disturbance. There was no evidence that she was placed in anything before being brought from the flat. It is believed, therefore, that she left the flat after someone coaxed her outside. She probably got into a vehicle with someone she knew. It most probably headed to the right, towards one of the roads leading to Co. Laois; this would be the quieter route. But this is just speculation, based on probabilities, not certainties. There is no eye-witness that we know of.

Having said goodbye to Fiona in the flat in Tullamore, John Thompson arrived at his family's farm in Killeigh early on the morning of Friday 23 August. He had a lot of work to do. It was a busy time for him, with a baby on the way. John and Fiona had lived in London for four months in late 1995 and early 1996. They had tried to find a place so they could stay a bit longer in London, but it didn't work out. John was now working long hours at the farm owned by his father, Archie Thompson, who had played a large part in raising his family because of his wife's ill-health. John was his only son, and during August 1996 they were at silage. During this busy time, and while Fiona was resting in Tullamore in preparation for the baby's arrival, John was working in Grange from early to late. He would need to take time off once the baby was born; right now, he had to work. He had no time to contact Fiona or to check on her that Friday. He thought she was with her mother.

In Tullamore, Josephine Pender went out to the shops on the Friday afternoon. She bought cabbage plants for Seán to sow in the garden. She walked down Church Street and knocked on Fiona's door. There was no answer. The blinds were still closed. Josephine headed home. It was not unusual, at the weekend, for a day or so to go by with Fiona and her mother not meeting or talking on the phone. Josephine remembered that a few of Fiona's friends were home from America that weekend; perhaps Fiona was with them.

The next day, Saturday, Josephine and John went to evening Mass. They walked down to Fiona's flat to say hello. Again it was in darkness. The blinds were closed, and there was no answer. This was very unusual; something wasn't right. They walked the ten minutes home to Connolly Park, and Josephine rang John Thompson in Grange. 'Where's Fiona?' she asked. 'She's not at the flat.' 'I thought she was with you,' he replied. 'I'll be in to you shortly.' Josephine remembers that later that night they searched all around Tullamore for Fiona.

John Thompson came in, and I went with him to the flat at Church Street. I didn't see any kind of disturbance. The stuff Fiona bought for the baby on the previous Thursday was still there. But Fiona was nowhere to be seen. We went to the graveyard in Durrow: Fiona used to go and visit Mark's grave there late at night, but she hadn't been doing that for a good few months. She wasn't there. We then checked the hospital and her friends' houses, but she wasn't anywhere to be found. I said I wanted to go to the barracks, so myself and John Thompson and Seán and my son John went to the Garda station. I told the garda there that Fiona was missing. I remember the garda didn't take us too seriously. He said something like she was twenty-five and an adult. But I knew something was wrong. She was seven months pregnant.

Though the Gardaí were informed on the Saturday night that Fiona was missing, it was the following Monday before a public appeal was made. One detective involved in the subsequent investigation believes vital hours were lost, but this was perhaps unavoidable.

Hindsight is a great thing. But you have to understand, back then there was no similar type disappearance. Okay, Jo Jo Dullard was abducted the previous November in Kildare, but the circumstances were different. In Jo Jo's case it was obvious almost from the start that she was the victim of a crime. But in Fiona's case there was no crime suspected at the start, and I mean the first few hours. There was no crime scene, no disturbance at her flat, no cry for help, no sound of a screeching vehicle. We had a missing pregnant woman who had been very upset when she lost her little brother the year before. And remember, her friends were home from America. If we had had a sniff or a hint of some violent attack on Fiona, things would have been different. But there was nothing immediately suspicious. And that's what I believe her killer wanted. They gained those first few valuable hours. Here we had a heavily pregnant woman, who was effectively on her own in her flat for a large part of each day. The last reported sighting was on a Friday morning, and the first report to the Gardaí was on the Saturday night. And it's the next day before a full missing person search is organised. Valuable hours were lost. If only we had been on it from the Friday!

One of the pictures of Fiona that hangs in her mother's sitting-room is a black-and-white photograph of Fiona modelling a wedding outfit. It was taken for a women's magazine, but this photograph tells a hidden story. Fiona Pender had a dream of making a happy life as a mother and wife. She wanted to get married, and she wanted herself and John to find a nice house and have a family. As she looked forward to the birth of their first child, Fiona's thoughts would often turn to getting engaged and getting married.

Many of the photographs of Fiona that her mother now treasures are posed shots. Fiona had been modelling since her late teens; she modelled dresses, hats, jackets, and casual wear. She did wedding fairs and other modelling events and had built up a large portfolio. It had started when a friend of hers, Emer Condron, set up her own agency in Tullamore. Emer did modelling work herself, and she soon got Fiona involved. As well as her modelling work Fiona was also a talented hairdresser. She had left the Sacred Heart Secondary School in Tullamore after doing her Inter Cert and became an apprentice with Kassard's hairdressers in Tullamore.

By Monday 26 August it was clear to the Gardaí in Tullamore that Fiona Pender was not in any of the places that she might reasonably be expected to be. A heavily pregnant woman was missing. It was now more than seventy-two hours since John Thompson said goodbye to Fiona as he left for work the previous Friday. At the time of Fiona's disappearance, Superintendent Gerry Murray, who by then had thirty-six years' experience, was the senior officer at Tullamore Garda Station.

On the Monday I sent two gardaí up to Josephine Pender in Connolly Park and got her agreement for a nationwide public appeal for information on Fiona's whereabouts. The case was on the news that lunch-time. We immediately took possession of the flat Fiona shared with John Thompson. We combed that flat, looking for any indication of where Fiona might have gone, but we found nothing. We began an extensive search of land in the greater Tullamore area. We searched all the local lakes. We went up to the Bord na Móna site and we searched silt ponds up there. And the Tullamore river, which runs at the back of the flat, where Fiona was last seen—well, we searched that inch by inch. We searched it from the back of the flat right down to where it flows to Rahan. When we found nothing I got the sub-aqua divers in a second time. We went over it, but again there was nothing. We searched the canal, and a local reservoir, all unsuccessfully. We checked out all Fiona's friends. One of her friends had left for Spain, and we tracked her down, but Fiona hadn't been in contact. We had no crime scene, no body. No expense was spared in this search. We spent more money on searching for Fiona than we did on a couple of murder cases that we solved.

As gardaí in Tullamore began an extensive search of all surrounding public land for any trace of Fiona, her family travelled about twelve miles south on a hunch. After Mark Pender's death in June the previous year, the Penders had buried his biker gear and the bike at a spot in the Slieve Bloom Mountains close to Clonaslee, Co. Laois. Perhaps Fiona had travelled there. It was just a hunch, but at a time of desperation every possibility had to be investigated. However, there was no trace of Fiona.

Gardaí privately admit they believe the Penders may have

been looking in the right direction when they headed towards the Slieve Bloom Mountains. There are vast areas of mountainous terrain that are densely forested, and other parts where steep inclines give way to deep gorges. The mountains extend west for almost twenty miles from their eastern tip near Rosenallis, Co. Laois, past the Ridge of Capard and Wolftrap Mountain, down to the south-west tip of Co. Offaly. While the Gardaí have also never ruled out the possibility that after killing Fiona Pender the murderer may have taken her to private farmland in an effort to hide her body, one detective who worked in the Laois-Offaly Division for more than thirty years believes the Slieve Bloom Mountains may hold the answer.

> If the killer brought Fiona to private land, be it farmland or whatever, there would always be the chance that someone else would have spotted him digging the ground, or using machinery at an odd time, or whatever. We never had any reports of such activity that we didn't check out fully. Also, if you bury a body on open ground there is a strong chance that, with soil move-ment and the like, that the ground will sink and suspicions will be aroused.
>
> There are two other possibilities that we always considered and until she is found will be strong contenders. Co. Offaly is so flat, and there is so much bogland, the answer may lie there; or look south to the Slieve Blooms. There are areas of that mountainside that contain gorges and areas almost totally inaccessible. There are parts of that mountain that mightn't see a human for ten or fifteen years.

Inspector John Dunleavy told me that the search for Fiona extended across acres of land in a number of counties.

The summer of 1996 had been very dry, which meant a vehicle might have travelled in further over what might be normally wet, marshy terrain. So we searched deep into remote areas of woodland, and bogland. We used metal-detectors and spent weeks walking in the Slieve Blooms. We just put people in the mountains for days on end and gave them areas to search thoroughly. We found bodies of animals. We searched large private estates in Offaly, and we did thorough searches of scrubland south of Tullamore. We also carried out searches in three other counties, but there was no sign of Fiona.

At the back of the minds of many detectives as they began their intensive search was another murder in the midlands, three years before, in which a woman was abducted and murdered. While the murder of 34-year-old Marie Kilmartin from Port Laoise is not connected to the disappearance of Fiona Pender, the Gardaí were conscious that her body lay hidden for six months before it was discovered in June 1994 in a bog drain at Pim's Lane, Borness, near Mountmellick. Detectives searching for Fiona were conscious, therefore, that one killer had previously used bogland around the Laois-Offaly border to conceal a body.

The circumstances of Marie Kilmartin's death are deeply disturbing. Her body had been placed in a secluded spot close to the Mountmellick–Portarlington road. It had been covered with water at one point, but the water had subsided. She was still wearing the tweed coat and blue suit she had on when she disappeared in December 1993. A concrete block had been placed on her upper body and head. The body had also been hidden by dense undergrowth. The state pathologist, Dr John Harbison, would later conclude that Marie Kilmartin probably died from manual strangulation.

Though her killer made attempts to conceal her body, it was found six months after her disappearance. One detective says the Gardaí initially hoped they could find Fiona as quickly.

We checked out as much an area of land as we could. We would love to bring some closure for Fiona's family. We would dearly love to find Fiona. We've established to our satisfaction that Fiona's and Marie's cases are not related. So there are two evil people out there. If we could at least find Fiona for her family, that would be something.

Josephine Pender told me she knew a few months after Fiona disappeared that she had been murdered.

One date that stuck with us during that time was the twenty-second of October 1996. That was the date that Fiona's baby was due. We had spoken about that date many times. She was so much looking forward to the birth. After she disappeared, the Gardaí contacted the maternity hospitals all around the country, and they checked in England as well. That day—the twenty-second—was very difficult. It still is. It's a special day. But in the weeks and months after that, it began to hit us that Fiona wasn't coming home.

The search for Fiona Pender was the largest Garda investigation ever undertaken in the Tullamore area. The Gardaí even considered the possibility that Fiona might have been buried under the grave of her brother Mark at Durrow graveyard; but a preliminary search of the area ruled out that possibility. A search through Fiona's belongings in the flat led the Gardaí to establish that Fiona was probably wearing a blue T-shirt, white leggings and a knee-length pink-and-black waterproof jacket when she left her flat.

Hundreds of people were interviewed, and hundreds of questionnaires were completed—at the railway station, at bike rallies, at discos, and in shops and pubs. As people wanted to do everything they could to help, the Gardaí were not short of reported sightings. Each of these was investigated, and ruled out. There were some reports that Fiona was seen around the town on the Friday afternoon, but it was not her. One woman was adamant that she had seen Fiona in Dunne's Stores that Friday afternoon, but when the supermarket receipt rolls were checked it was established that the witness had seen her not on the Friday but on the Thursday afternoon. There was also a report of a man dressed in biker gear seen speaking to Fiona in the shopping centre that Friday afternoon. Again, it wasn't Fiona. But each possible lead had to be investigated.

This was a case in which the Gardaí were inundated but where that crucial piece of information was missing. Nobody could establish Fiona Pender coming out of her flat, either alone or with one or more people. Retired Detective-Sergeant Mick Dalton, who worked in Tullamore for more than thirty years, remembers one occasion in late 1996 when the Gardaí thought Fiona might have been found safe and well.

One time, in the Garda station, we got a call from an Irishman who was over in London. He told us that he had been in a pub in London and had got talking to a woman. This woman said she was from Tullamore. She said she was just after having a baby. He described her as a young woman with blond hair. Initially it sounded like Fiona. We asked this fellow if he could tell us anything more about the woman. He remembered that she had sung a Patsy Cline song in the pub. Suddenly one garda in the station said that that sounded like a different young woman from the area who hadn't been seen around. And sure enough, we checked it out and it wasn't Fiona but another young Tullamore woman who had left the town to have her baby in England. Her baby had been born around the same time, and she looked fairly like Fiona. It was certainly quite a coincidence. Sadly, it wasn't Fiona.

One area the Gardaí investigated thoroughly was the possibility that Fiona might have travelled to London, to the area in which she and John Thompson had lived for four months in late 1995 and early 1996. They had decided to go to England in the wake of Mark Pender's death. It was a quiet time on the farm for John, and Fiona's aunt Bernie could put them up in London.

London was a totally new experience for Fiona. She had never been out of Ireland before. The couple got jobs in the Hilton Hotel in Croydon, and during their free time they went to all the tourist attractions. It was a carefree and exciting time. They even thought of settling in London, but they didn't have enough money, and after four months they came home to Tullamore. They first moved into a small flat in Clonminch Road; a short time later they found the flat in Church Street. Fiona sold all her bike gear and bought a young bull to be reared for her on the Thompson farm in Killeigh. Coming from the town, she didn't know much about farming, but she wanted to learn more from John.

In the early part of 1997 the Gardaí continued a detailed study of the hundreds of statements and questionnaires that had been completed by members of the public. They outlined the movements of hundreds of people and vehicles in the days during which Fiona Pender was believed to have been abducted and murdered. When the statements of a number of people were cross-checked an issue arose about the movements of a particular vehicle around the time of Fiona's disappearance. A conference was held, and a decision to question a number of people again was taken.

Early on the morning of Thursday 24 April 1997 three women and two men were arrested at a number of places in Cos. Laois and Offaly. Each was told they were being held under section 4 of the Criminal Justice Act, which allowed for their detention for a maximum of twelve hours. The five people were taken to Tullamore Garda station, where they were held in separate rooms, to be questioned by specialist detectives who had arrived from Dublin. The five people under arrest were asked probing questions about their knowledge of the movements of people and vehicles around the time of Fiona Pender's disappearance. Throughout the day there was no word from the Gardaí about whether anyone was going to be charged or not; then at seven o'clock that evening it was announced that all five people had been released without charge. Gardaí drove the five people, who were described as being shaken by the events of the previous twelve hours, back to their homes.

In Connolly Park a phone call was received from a garda telling the Penders that all five people had been released without charge. Josephine Pender's voice broke as she remembered that day.

When those people were arrested I answered the phone that morning and took the call from the Gardaí. I remember telling Seán. He was sitting on the couch when I told him that they had arrested five people. Seán just aged in front of me. A friend of Fiona's, Emer Condron, came around and stayed with us the whole day. That day was so long! We were just waiting, hoping something positive was going to happen. And then we get the call to say they're all being released. I told Seán. He just went downhill from there.

Seán Pender took his own life on 31 March 2000. He had become unwell in the wake of his daughter's disappearance. He died a short time after reading a newspaper article about a claim made in relation to a number of missing women. The Gardaí have confirmed that the claims made in the article are untrue. Josephine Pender told me the story was horrible.

> Even people who read the story who are not directly involved said they were reduced to tears by it. It was just terrible. Seán read it. My husband cried for his children every night. From the time Fiona went missing he was hurting. He looked like a man with cancer: he was fading away, he looked so weak. We looked for help for him, but back then we didn't know the people that I know now. Seán just became so sick as a result of what happened to our family. He went so low he couldn't take any more. I felt like killing myself sometimes too. I'll never know how Seán got the strength to do it. We had a wake here in the house, and Seán looked so much younger when he was laid out. He's at peace now. He was not at peace when he was alive. I've no doubt he's in Heaven. He suffered too much hell on earth.
>
> Whoever murdered Fiona and her baby is also responsible for my husband's death. And they denied my grandson, Dean, a granddad, and an aunt, and a cousin.

Josephine Pender and her remaining son, John, have a large extended family who comfort them. Josephine has one sister and two brothers, while her late husband is survived by five sisters and a brother. Josephine and Seán Pender were married in Durrow, where Seán and Mark are now buried.

Seán and I were married for thirty years. Our son Mark was to be married in the same church. Maybe Fiona would have been wed there too. Now John and I visit the graveyard at the church to visit Seán and Mark and to think of Fiona and the baby.

There is one man, living in the midlands, who is a prime suspect for the abduction and murder of Fiona Pender. Detectives are aware of an incident some years before Fiona Pender disappeared in which this man attacked a woman by putting his hands around her neck and choking her during an argument. The woman never made a complaint to the Gardaí. The man who carried out that attack was spoken to at length by gardaí about his movements at the time Fiona Pender disappeared. But they know that one previous attack on someone is merely an indication of the potential for violence, not proof of responsibility for murder. One detective thought they might have caught their man.

We had this man in for questioning. He wasn't under arrest; he was there voluntarily. And we were talking, and we had our suspicions about him. I said something to him about it being terrible that there was no closure for the family, that Fiona was out there somewhere. This man put his face in his hands. He began to sob. I looked at the other garda with me. We were both thinking the same thing: we thought we were about to crack this thing. Then this man wiped his eyes with his arm and suddenly sat up straight and said, 'I can't tell you anything. You won't get me.' Who knows if he had any information? We would still have our suspicions, but that's all they are: suspicions.

Josephine Pender says she is 99 per cent sure she knows who is responsible for Fiona's disappearance.

I never believed there was a serial killer involved in Fiona's case. The circumstances of Fiona's disappearance are different from some of the other missing women. I went out to see the person I believe is responsible a few times, and I asked him directly, 'Where is Fiona?' I bumped into him at a shop in Tullamore town, and he just came down and sat beside me. Fiona's murder is not linked to the other missing women.

In April 1997, nine months after Fiona's disappearance, another unrelated murder was uncovered close to Fiona Pender's flat in Church Street. Seán Brennan, who was also living in Church Street, shot dead his former partner Bernie Sherry near Portarlington and put her body in the boot of his car. The body was found close to Brennan's flat in Tullamore. The disappearance of Fiona Pender and the murder of Bernie Sherry affected many people in a town that has witnessed relatively few murders.

In 1994, five or six young women in Tullamore who were around Fiona's age decided to head to the United States. They are still there, having settled in the general New York area. These are the women who were home on a visit to Tullamore in August 1996. At first Josephine Pender thought Fiona might have been out socialising with them; but Fiona never got a chance to meet them. The women still keep in contact with Josephine. Many of Fiona Pender's friends from her work as a hairdresser and model are now married or in relationships and have children. Many still live in the Tullamore area and keep in regular contact.

Fiona's best friend, apart from her mother, was Emer Condron, who ran a modelling agency in Tullamore for ten years. She first got to know Fiona when she approached her to ask if she was interested in modelling work. Fiona was delighted to be asked.

I always thought that Fiona was beautiful, and she was very confident; and when I asked her to do some work for me she was thrilled. She entered into the Miss Offaly competition to qualify for Miss Ireland, but she didn't reach the height requirement. Fiona had an openness to care for people, and she didn't want a big fancy life-style, just a secure home for herself and her baby. She stopped modelling after Mark died in June 1995. She and Mark were very close, and she just loved her little brother John to pieces. I sold my modelling business in the summer of 1996, when Fiona was pregnant and looking forward to a happier life. We were planning to set up a mobile wedding unit to cater for hair and beauty at the bride's home.

On the weekend in August 1996 on which Fiona Pender disappeared, Emer Condron had called to the flat in Church Street a number of times but didn't knock, because the blinds were drawn. She assumed that Fiona was resting, and she didn't want to disturb her. It wasn't until just before ten o'clock on the evening of Saturday 24 August that she realised something was terribly wrong.

Fiona's boy-friend, John, knocked on the door, and Fiona's mother, Josie, was with him in the jeep. They were looking for Fiona, and John asked me if I knew where she was. I was never so scared: it soon began to sink in that she was missing. It is just so horrific to think that someone did this to Fiona, when she was seven-and-a-half months pregnant. It's so frightening to think of what she may have gone through. Not knowing what happened to Fiona, or where she is, it's just horrible. It is an empty death: nobody can grieve, there's no grave to visit.

Another aspect of the disappearance of Fiona Pender has intrigued detectives who worked on Operation Trace, set up in

1998 to investigate any links between the missing women in Leinster. It is claimed that a man from the midlands visited the home of a close relative of another missing woman, and suggested that he might have been responsible for Fiona's disappearance. It is claimed that this man, who is known to the Gardaí investigating Fiona's disappearance, said he might have been responsible, but had been on medication at the time and couldn't remember whether or not he had caused harm to Fiona.

While Mary Phelan has been to the forefront of a campaign for the establishment of a National Missing Persons Unit, in Tullamore Emer Condron has also been busy trying to keep the issue of missing people before the public. She co-ordinated a campaign that sought to use the postal system to maintain awareness of the plight that many families suffer. She asked An Post to consider raising awareness of the issue of missing persons by issuing stamps bearing a photograph and details of missing people, but the authority declined. Emer was disappointed, but not deterred.

> I get a little upset when I see what does appear on stamps— musicians and the like. All I wanted was a stamp to honour missing people, or to somehow keep the issue in the eye of the public. I still hope that An Post may take the initiative and be the first to do something like this. In the meantime I printed special appeal envelopes with a photo of Fiona, and a short description, and over 22,000 of those have been circulated.

Josephine Pender and Emer Condron are close. Both women lost their best friend in August 1996, and neither will rest until Fiona's body is found and laid to rest and the killer is brought to justice. Emer told me that they cannot rest, and will not rest.

Fiona was the soundest person I knew. We spent so many happy weekends heading off on our bikes to motorbike rallies around the country. Fiona always made allowances for people's behaviour towards her, even when they hurt her feelings: she didn't want hassle or upset in her life. I miss her friendship— something you cannot replace. It makes me so angry that in relation to all the missing people who are presumed to have been murdered, that for each of these people there is a person or persons responsible for these cowardly acts of murder, and they are walking around freely in our society. And they have a free hand to do it again to another family.

In May 2002, Josephine Pender and her son John attended the unveiling of the Monument to Missing People by President Mary McAleese in the grounds of Kilkenny Castle. Later that day, in a private meeting, Josephine Pender and President McAleese held hands and spoke about Fiona. It was an emotional meeting for both. Josephine introduced John to the President, who remarked that he was a fine young man. 'He's had to grow up too fast,' replied Josephine, as tears streamed down her cheeks.

Gerry Murray retired as superintendent at Tullamore Garda Station in April 1999. He had been a garda for thirty-nine years and had served in all four provinces, including his final service in Tullamore, where he served for twenty-three years. He knew the area, and he knew the people. When he retired he was replaced by Superintendent Peter Wheeler, who had worked on Fiona Pender's case from the beginning as an inspector in Tullamore. A team of detectives led by Superintendent Wheeler continues to search for the clue that will unlock the mystery of Fiona Pender's disappearance. Superintendent Murray says the one regret of his four decades as a garda was that Fiona's disappearance was not solved.

> The people of Tullamore were terrific in their assistance, but that is the one disappointment in my life. We thought we would crack this case; and I still believe that Fiona will be found some day and that the person responsible will be held responsible. Right now we have no scene, no body. But I believe this will be solved.

John Thompson declined to be formally interviewed for this book, but he told me he believes the Gardaí made many mistakes early on in the investigation. He believes certain leads were not followed up or were not followed up quickly enough.

When Josephine Pender and her son John are not together they keep in close contact by mobile phone. John works as a salesman for an underfloor heating company in Cappancur, Tullamore. Just like his father, John is interested in art. He may pursue this in the future, just not right now. Josephine and John have travelled on holidays to Portugal and to Medjugorje in Bosnia. Both trips were gifts from well-wishers, bringing some semblance of normality to a family that has suffered unimaginable pain.

Josephine Pender told me she always wanted a large family. She had two miscarriages before John was born, and two afterwards. She looked at photographs of her dead children, Fiona and Mark, and sighed.

> I should have seven children, now I only have one. Whoever took Fiona damaged so many people. John and myself go out to Seán's and Mark's graves in Durrow to think of Mark, Seán,

Fiona, and the baby. On the twenty-second of October of every year, the date that Fiona was due to give birth, we go to the graves and we light a candle. I bring a little toy for the baby.

4

Ciara Breen

❧❧

Ciara Breen is commonly referred to as one of Ireland's missing women, but technically she was a child, being not yet eighteen when she was murdered in the early hours of 13 February 1997. She was probably murdered by a man she had arranged to meet close to her home in Dundalk, Co. Louth. A local man remains a prime suspect. Two years after her disappearance he was arrested on suspicion of murder, but the Director of Public Prosecutions decided that no charges should be brought. This man is one of a number of men questioned about Ciara's disappearance. Two cousins who live a nomadic life and who were living near Co. Louth at the time of Ciara's disappearance were also investigated, and were also questioned about their movements at the time of the abduction and murder of Jo Jo Dullard fifteen months before. The prime suspect denies he ever had a relationship with Ciara Breen, despite a number of Ciara's friends coming forward with claims to the contrary.

Ciara Breen's disappearance has caused untold anguish for her mother, Bernadette Breen, who has lost her only child. Bernadette is aware of the identity of the prime suspect for her daughter's disappearance. He is a Dundalk man who she once chased away from her front door when he was trying to strike up a conversation with Ciara.

Ciara Breen was abducted and murdered a month before her eighteenth birthday. She would never know that her mother had organised a surprise trip to Disneyland in Florida for her birthday. Ciara and Bernadette had been to Florida the previous October, and Ciara had often said she would love to go back.

Twelve hours after Bernadette Breen's only child vanished from her home in February 1997, a doctor at the Blackrock Clinic in Co. Dublin told Bernadette she had cancer. She had kept her appointment, hoping that by the time she returned home Ciara would be back before her. All Bernadette knew was that Ciara had sneaked out of her bedroom window in the early hours of the morning. She hadn't taken any money from her bedroom, and all the indications were that she had left with the intention of returning before her mother woke.

It was only a few hours after they had said goodnight that Bernadette had discovered that Ciara was missing. In the early hours of the morning Bernadette had woken up and had looked in on Ciara. She wasn't there. The bed was empty, and the bedroom window was ajar. This was the first time Bernadette had discovered Ciara sneaking out of the house during the night. She had once run away for a few days, but that was nearly a year and a half before. Besides, she was more mature now.

For hours Bernadette sat in the darkness waiting to catch her daughter when she came back in the window. But she never came.

At her home in St Mary's Road, Dundalk, Bernadette Breen told me there are many reminders for her of what she has lost.

Ciara was my life. She was my identity: I wasn't Bernadette, I was 'Ciara's Mam'. And I know I always will be. But my baby is lying out there somewhere.

Ciara Breen had many things on her mind the night she disappeared. She was worried about her mother's hospital appointment the next day: Bernadette had already been to hospital to undergo cancer tests and was about to get the results. Earlier that day, at the Ógra Dhún Dealgan FÁS course Ciara was on, she had told her tutor, Rosaleen Bishop, that she was going to go home and make the house tidy and warm for her mother, who had an important hospital appointment the next day. Ciara was also worried about her looks. Like most teenagers, she was very conscious of her appearance. A difficulty with her gums meant she would need the upper row of her teeth re-set. And then there are the other things that were concerning her that we don't know about, and never will. We will never know for certain what made her sneak out of her bedroom that night, though we can speculate. It is most probable that she went to meet a man, perhaps a man much older than her. Was this to be the start of their relationship? Or was she trying to end one? If so, why? Why was she keeping the relationship hidden?

Bernadette Breen recounted with clarity her memories of the night Ciara disappeared. The cancer with which she was diagnosed just after Ciara's disappearance did not get the better of her, though it may return.

I remember the night Ciara disappeared we went out for a meal to the Roma restaurant in Park Street in the town. Ciara and I were like sisters the way we would joke sometimes. And we had fun that night. Ciara really liked the actor Chris O'Donnell, and I remember she recorded him that night in 'Circle of Friends'.

She had marked the tape 'Ciara Breen's tape. Do not touch.' We also watched a film on Sky. 'Bad Boys' was the film, with Will Smith. I was travelling to Dublin the next day for the results of a cancer test. I asked Ciara if she was worried about the results. She replied, 'Not really. Not if you aren't.' We got ready for bed and she came in and threw herself on my bed like normal, and we chatted about a few different things. I joked with her about the cancer results, saying, 'You're not going to get rid of me that easily.' She dropped a hint about her eighteenth birthday. One present that she knew she was getting for her birthday was a bank book with her children's allowance money saved in it. She was very excited, wondering how much was in it. The last thing she said to me was, 'Don't read for too long. I love you.' I said to her, 'I love you too, sweetie.' I always called her 'sweetie' or 'sweet pea'. Ciara went into her own room. A few hours later I discovered she was missing from her bedroom, and her window was open.

Ciara Breen was a good child who at one time fell in with a bad crowd. It started when she was about sixteen-and-a-half. Certain girls her own age began to lead her astray. In October 1995 she ran away with a friend; they travelled across the border and hid in a house in Jonesborough, Co. Armagh, owned by an aunt of Ciara's friend. Bernadette had no idea where Ciara was, and she called the Gardaí immediately. A national appeal for information was issued. Bernadette told me that Ciara looked like a wreck when she decided to come home.

You know the way some kids are kind of hardy—well, Ciara wasn't. She wasn't suited to running away. When she ran away to this house in Co. Armagh she didn't like it. She came home with black rings under her eyes, and she had a cold sore on her mouth. This was during a time that I was having trouble controlling her. She was about sixteen-and-a-half, and I had about six months of trouble. She was hanging around with girls who in turn knew boys that would give any mother nightmares. There were about a dozen times that she was in trouble, and I had to ground her many times. But from about July 1996 up to when she disappeared she was fine. She wasn't mixing with those people any more, and we were getting on so well. She had seemed to settle down and had even told me that she had taken her first drink, a bottle of Ritz. She'd had two bottles, and we had a good chat about drinking responsibly. We were the best of friends.

Bernadette Breen doted on her only child. They shared much; but Bernadette knows Ciara was keeping something from her. Ciara left her bedroom that night in February 1997 to meet someone Bernadette wouldn't have approved of; but all the indications are that she intended to return to her bedroom before her mother woke the next morning. She was never to know that her mother woke up during the night and looked in on her, only to find her missing. Bernadette then sat in the dark waiting for her to return and to give her a stern talking to. Even the next day, when she still hadn't returned, Bernadette thought she might be back; she left a message with Ciara's FÁS tutor, Rosaleen Bishop, to say that if she turned up she was to tell her Bernadette was very angry and they would talk about it later. Bernadette had to go to Dublin for the results of her cancer test.

I was hoping Ciara would be back by the time I got back from Dublin. My daddy brought me down to the Blackrock Clinic, and I didn't tell him Ciara had sneaked out of the house. I went in for the results, and all I could think about was Ciara; I wanted to get back to Dundalk and find her safe and well. I remember I went into the doctor and he said he was sorry to tell me that they had detected cancerous cells. I hardly heard him: I just wanted to get back to Dundalk. A few weeks later that doctor told me he thought that I was the coolest cucumber he ever told such news to, but he now understood why. Going back in the car, I told Daddy Ciara was missing.

Though Bernadette and Ciara lived alone at Bachelor's Walk, they had a large extended family living in the general locality of Dundalk. Bernadette's parents, Brendan and Marie Coburn, lived just around the corner in St Mary's Road, where Bernadette lives now. She also has three brothers living in the area, and a sister in the United States. In the late 1970s Bernadette married a Dundalk man; by the time the short-lived marriage broke up they had a baby girl they named Ciara. Ciara's father left for America and never saw his daughter. Bernadette told me that Ciara was beginning to ask more and more about her father.

We never had any contact with him from the time Ciara was very young. He left Ireland. It was just me and Ciara. But she was beginning to get curious about him. And I always told her that if she wanted to see him, or get in contact, or know more, that she could go to her granddad, my daddy, and he would know what to do. Her granddad would know how to make contact. Around the time Ciara disappeared, her father was to travel to Ireland for a wedding. But she never got to meet him. I've spoken to him on the phone once or twice since she's gone. But that's all. We haven't met again.

Ciara's father arrived back in Dundalk some weeks after Ciara's disappearance to attend a family wedding in Co. Louth. He had never met his daughter, who he knew was now almost eighteen. He held out the hope that his daughter might like to see him just once. As he stepped off the train in late February he was full of expectation and trepidation. The first thing he saw at the station was a poster with a photograph of a girl and beside it the words *Missing—Ciara Breen*.

As detectives began investigating Ciara's disappearance they spoke to the girls with whom she had been mixing during her few unsettled months. Conscious that Ciara had once run away with a friend, the Gardaí investigated all the places she might have visited voluntarily. One detective told me there was a great degree of urgency about the search.

> We knew that Ciara had run away by herself once before. But even if she had done this again, she was still a child. She was only seventeen, and we knew that she might be in danger, even if she had chosen to go somewhere. But we were also faced with a number of clear indications that Ciara had not chosen to run away this time. She didn't take any money with her from her bedroom. There was no note for her mother, and remember, she knew her mother had an important hospital appointment the next day. Every instinct we had told us Ciara was not hiding out somewhere. Not this time.

With the assistance of the RUC, searches were undertaken in a number of places in Cos. Armagh and Down, including Newry and Warrenpoint. The girl with whom Ciara had previously run away knew nothing about her fresh disappearance. She did suggest that Ciara might have had contact with a woman in Dungannon. The Gardaí investigated this possibility, but it led nowhere. As detectives questioned Ciara's friends they discovered that she had recently met a young man from Kilkeel, Co. Down, at a disco in Carrickdale. Eventually this man was tracked down. He had not seen Ciara.

As detectives continued to try to trace her movements after she left her house, they developed a good relationship with the young friends Ciara had been hanging around with during the time she had run away from home in 1995. They knew that from late 1995 to the middle of 1996, by which time she had turned seventeen, Ciara went through a 'wild' period. The girls she befriended knew a particular group of boys and young men that the Gardaí regard as part of the 'rough element' of Dundalk. For Ciara Breen, her new friends were a radical departure from the quiet life she had lived up to then. And even though her mother managed to get her out of this life, Ciara still maintained contact with the girls. It was inevitable that she would bump into them on the street, or at a disco. Later on, after she was murdered, it was one of the girls from this group who told the Gardaí she believed Ciara sneaked out of her house to meet a particular man. These girls were able to give the Gardaí information that was to be of assistance in understanding why Ciara might have sneaked out of the house.

In the house in St Mary's Road in which Bernadette Breen grew up, she fought back tears as she told me that she stayed alone at Bachelor's Walk for three years after Ciara's disappearance.

Ciara disappeared a month and a half before her eighteenth birthday. The home we lived in at Bachelor's Walk was a lovely comfortable home, close to my parents' home here. For months and months after Ciara vanished I couldn't go into her bedroom. I stayed in the house though. I wanted to keep the house going for Ciara. It was our home. But as I began to realise Ciara wasn't coming home I began to think about leaving. But I stayed in the house until what would have been Ciara's twenty-first birthday. It's just something I felt compelled to do. She was my baby. I even kept her on my VHI until she was twenty-one. I left the house on Ciara's twenty-first, on the thirty-first of March 2000. I came home here to care for my Mam.

As the Gardaí began to look at possible suspects for the abduction and murder of Ciara Breen, the name of one man began to crop up. A number of people had described seeing Ciara in this man's company. A derelict house in the village of Louth, six miles south-west of Dundalk, was searched. This house was owned by a relative of the suspect, who denied he had any contact with Ciara. Nothing was found in the house.

In a strange coincidence, one man who emerged as a suspect was found to have previously had links with a convicted double murderer, John Duffy. Duffy, a native of Dundalk, left Ireland for England at an early age. He is now serving two life sentences in England after being convicted in 1988 of murdering nineteen-year-old Alison Day in 1985 and fifteen-year-old Maartje Tamboezer in 1986. He also later admitted murdering 29-year-old Anne Lock. Under the gentle but persistent coaxing of a prison psychologist he later broke an 'oath of silence' and gave evidence against his accomplice, David Mulcahy, who will also be kept in prison in England for the rest of his life. During their investigations into the disappearance of Ciara Breen, detectives discovered that a man who had been seen speaking to Ciara would have been known to John Duffy. However, they are satisfied that this is just a coincidence. John Duffy was jailed in 1988, having left Dundalk many years before. The man who was investigated for Ciara Breen's disappearance would have been in his late teens when he last had contact with Duffy.

Detectives also travelled to a town in south Co. Meath to question two cousins. They had received information suggesting that the two men had been in the greater Dundalk area at about the time Ciara disappeared. These two men were members of the travelling community, and detectives from Operation Trace would also later question them about their movements at the time Jo Jo Dullard was abducted and murdered in November 1995. The two men were able to provide alibi witnesses relating to their movements.

More than two years after Ciara Breen's disappearance, a young man contacted the Gardaí with a story that continues to intrigue detectives. He said he wanted to tell them about an incident that occurred some days or weeks after Ciara Breen's disappearance, related to a comment a particular man had made about it. What immediately grabbed the attention of the detectives was the identity of this other man, as he had already been considered as a suspect.

The young man who came forward said that about two years previously, in 1997, he had been in a pub in Dundalk when there was a report on the television news about Ciara Breen's disappearance. A man sitting beside him in the pub said something to the effect that Ciara would not be coming back. The Gardaí wondered if the comment might imply that the man had particular knowledge of Ciara's whereabouts, or whether he was merely expressing an opinion. Because he was already a suspect, the Gardaí decided to interview him again. Under lengthy questioning, he denied any knowledge of Ciara's whereabouts, but he continues to be a suspect.

Bernadette Breen is aware of the identity of the prime suspect for the murder of her child. The man has denied to the Gardaí that he ever had a relationship with Ciara; but this denial is a flat contradiction of the claim of one witness who confronted this man in the presence of gardaí. The man's denial is also in conflict with the firm suspicion of Ciara's mother, who says that more than a year before Ciara disappeared she had to chase this man away from her house.

> I remember one evening when Ciara was sixteen I heard Ciara at the front door talking to someone. I heard this man's voice. He was saying to Ciara, 'Are you going with somebody?' I went to the door; I knew from the voice it wasn't a boy she was talking to. And sure enough it was this man. I chased him away from the door, telling him he was almost old enough for me, and to leave Ciara alone. I was thirty-eight years old at the time, and this man was in his thirties too; and there he was trying to chat Ciara up. And for him then to later claim that he never knew her, never met her! I saw him talking to her. I chased him from my own doorstep. I never liked the look of him. Three days after Ciara's disappearance he passed by my house at Bachelor's Walk and he looked at me. My blood turned to ice. Every hair on my body stood to attention.

In early September 1999 detectives from Operation Trace had a meeting with detectives in Dundalk. After a number of issues relating to the disappearance of Ciara Breen were discussed, a decision was taken to arrest a man and to question him about Ciara's whereabouts. He is a man in his mid-thirties from the Dundalk area. At eight o'clock on the morning of Monday 12 September 1999 the man was taken to Dundalk Garda Station, where he was held for questioning for twelve hours. Word of the arrest quickly spread; two-and-a-half years after Ciara's disappearance, it took many people by surprise. The man was released without charge later that night. A file was sent to the Director of Public Prosecutions, who decided that no charges should be brought. Bernadette Breen was later told about the arrest.

> I was told about his arrest just twenty minutes before it appeared on the news. A local detective and a woman from Operation Trace came to the house. When they told me, my heart hit my knees. That whole day was just so difficult. And then he was released without charge.

The arrest of this man is significant with regard to an assessment of the progress of all the investigations into missing women in the Leinster area. Of the six cases that formed the object of Operation Trace, the disappearance of Ciara Breen is the only one that resulted in a file being sent to the Director of Public Prosecutions during the lifetime of the special operation. One detective told me:

> Bear in mind that we arrested this fellow over two-and-a-half years after Ciara disappeared. We believed we had enough information to warrant his arrest at that stage. So it took us that long to get adequate information to lead to that arrest. We also believed we possibly had enough information to warrant a prosecution. The Director of Public Prosecutions said no. But the very fact [that] we got the case that far at that time, without a body, is significant. This case is still very much active.

As the Gardaí continued to investigate the disappearance of Ciara Breen, a number of searches were conducted after confidential information was received. A piggery on the Dublin road just outside Dundalk was searched. The Gardaí knew that young people used to gather in the area after dark. That premises is now gone, with a block of apartments on its site. Nothing was found during an extensive search of the area. A section of land near Crossan's Garage just outside Dundalk was also searched after the Gardaí received reports about the movements of a particular person. Again, nothing was found. The Gardaí were also conscious of the vast mountainside and forested areas in the north-eastern corner of Co. Louth that lie just past Dundalk and out towards Carlingford. But without an indication of where to begin, a search of such a vast area would not yield results.

North Co. Louth has an unenviable distinction in relation to the disappearance of a number of people who were murdered and whose bodies have not been found. Two of the best-known cases are those of two people killed by the IRA in the 1970s, both of whom are buried in Co. Louth. In March 1972 Jean McConville, a mother of ten, was abducted from her home in Belfast and killed by the IRA. They say her body is buried at Templeton beach in north Co. Louth; but despite a large-scale excavation of the beach, it has not been found. Five years later Captain Robert Nairac of the SAS was abducted from a bar in Drumintee, Co. Armagh, and taken to Ravensdale, just north of Dundalk, where he was shot dead. His body has not been found, and it is now widely believed that it was disposed of using some type of cutting machinery. The killing of Nairac is significant in that a man was convicted of the murder even though a body was never found. Liam Townson, a native of Meigh, Co. Armagh, who was living in Dundalk, was given a life sentence by the Special Criminal Court in Dublin in November 1977, convicted on the strength of a confession made to the Gardaí and also the discovery of the crime scene under a bridge at Ravensdale, where blood stains and trampled grass were discovered.

The cases of Jean McConville and Robert Nairac are examples of how difficult it is to find a body, even when a general area has been identified within which it most probably lies.

At her home in Dundalk, Bernadette Breen told me how upset she became when she discovered that Ciara's disappearance was being linked with the possibility of a serial killer.

I was never told about the setting up of Operation Trace. I remember clearly it was October 1998, and I was watching the RTÉ news at six o'clock. That's where I learnt about it—from the media. I was distraught. They were talking about all these poor girls and whether their disappearances were connected. I smashed so many cups and plates that night—anything I could find—I was so angry. To hear Ciara's name being linked with a serial killer; and for me to hear about it on television! I'm still angry about it. Even the local gardaí didn't know. One local detective arrived twenty minutes after the news report. He was too late. He didn't know about this Operation Trace either. I was given no warning about that news report. Is that right?

A couple of months after Ciara's disappearance her grandfather, Brendan Coburn—Bernadette's father—became ill. A well-known and popular salesman in the shoe industry, he died two years later, in November 1999, two months after the arrest of the Dundalk man suspected of murdering Ciara. Since Ciara's disappearance her grandmother, Marie Coburn, has suffered a stroke. Bernadette Breen returned to St Mary's Road to care for her mother; and it is here that she still keeps some of Ciara's clothes, the special outfits she wore. She gave other items of Ciara's clothing away, but only on condition that they be sold in charity shops outside Dundalk. She couldn't bear seeing another girl wearing Ciara's clothes.

Ciara Breen was three weeks into an early school-leavers' course with Ógra Dhún Dealgan when she disappeared. She had put her name down many months before, and a place became available with the small group of ten or so in January 1997. She was learning how to sew and also to use computers, and she was doing life and social skills. It was a one-year course, certified by FÁS. Ciara had liked history and English in school but wasn't academically minded, and she left St Vincent's Secondary School in Dundalk at the end of fifth year. She loved working with make-up, especially eye make-up, and wondered about the possibility of working as a beautician. She had only to walk a short distance every day to the Ógra centre in Chapel Street, the old Boys' Technical School. Rosaleen Bishop was Ciara's tutor on the Ógra course; and though she knew Ciara only for a short time, she had a few good chats with her.

I remember Ciara was a quiet young girl. She was shy, and she was conscious of her teeth and that they needed some work done on them. She would put her hand up to her mouth when she'd be talking to you. She was very fond of her mother. I remember the day before she disappeared Ciara came into my office and told me her mother wasn't very well. She said she had to get some results from hospital. Ciara told me that she was going to go home and put on a nice fire for her Mam and tidy up the house for her, to make her feel a little better. Ciara never mentioned her Dad. I wouldn't say Ciara was a 'street-wise' kid. She wouldn't be gullible either but maybe would have a trusting nature. She was a lovely wee girl. She was very good

116

at crafts and flower arranging, and she did T-shirt prints as well. I remember when the gardaí came in to question me and the other staff they were so thorough, they wanted to know everything—like the tone of a voice and facial expressions.

As part of her search for her child, Bernadette Breen hired a private detective, but he failed to find any real leads. She even turned to psychics for help, going as far as the United States to speak to a 'medium'.

When Ciara Breen sneaked out of the house that night she was wearing a three-quarter-length leather jacket and jeans. She was also wearing a limited-edition watch, which also has never been found. The watch was one of 2,500 sold in Florida to mark the holding of the World Cup competition in the United States in 1994. It has a square face with a green background featuring Mickey Mouse on the left-hand side, and has a black leather strap. Ciara got the watch when she and her mother were in Florida four months before she disappeared. As well as the distinctive watch she was wearing a white T-shirt from Sea World in Florida, showing a group of men surrounding a woman and with Ciara's face superimposed on the model.

Detective-Sergeant Con Nolan has been stationed in the Louth area for thirty-seven years and has worked on many murder investigations and other serious crimes. He was part of the team that arrested the man in September 1999 for questioning in connection with Ciara Breen's disappearance. He told me that Ciara's disappearance is unlike any other missing person case he has dealt with.

There have, of course, been other missing people. But Ciara's case is distinctive. I was brought in to work full-time on Ciara's case because I had been working on a separate case involving young people. During my other investigation I had made contact with young girls who were friendly with Ciara. They were able to tell us certain things which were of assistance to us in our investigations. We were trying to learn who Ciara might have left her bedroom to meet that night. We looked at, and continue to look at, a number of possibilities. This case is very much still open and active.

On 17 October 2001 the partially clothed body of a 28-year-old German journalist, Bettina Poeschel, was found in dense undergrowth in Donore, Co. Meath, a few miles from Drogheda. She had last been seen alive three weeks before, on 25 September, as she made her way from Drogheda railway station in the direction of the passage tomb at Newgrange in the Boyne Valley. The place where the body was discovered is very close to where she was last seen. This area had been searched in the initial investigation into her whereabouts; it was during a second search that her remains were found by a garda. This case, which occurred in the Louth-Meath Garda division, serves as a stark reminder that even though searches are carried out for missing people, the searches are not always as thorough as they might be. The fact that this body lay undiscovered for twenty-three days means that it was a number of weeks before it could be formally identified. Bettina Poeschel was identified by the use of DNA. It would be a number of months before a full scientific examination of the body was complete, after which her remains were returned to her parents for burial in Munich.

Bernadette Breen both cries and smiles as she remembers some of the wonderful times she had with Ciara. The mother and daughter were much like sisters: they laughed together, joked together, and cried together. Bernadette told me that Ciara was an open, loving and trusting person.

Ciara couldn't see anything wrong in anyone. She was the type of girl who fed stray dogs. She loved animals, from dogs and cats to sharks. She loved make-up, but she wouldn't wear anything that had been tested on animals. She kept a few dogs. Ciara was her own person, but she was my daughter. She was my baby.

Some of the girls Ciara hung around with during her wild period are now dead. Three of them died in a horrific car crash just north of Dundalk while travelling in a car being driven by a teenage boy who had no driving licence. One detective told me that many young people in Dundalk hurt themselves by falling in with the wrong crowd.

What gets to you is that these were fundamentally good kids. But that's just it: they were kids. And they found themselves doing things that even right-thinking adults would not be doing. So many of them have been hurt or killed in accidents. I met many of them during our investigation into Ciara's disappearance. They wouldn't have always seen eye to eye with the Gardaí, but when it came to the search for Ciara, they really tried to help us. We knew that Ciara probably left her house to meet someone her mother wouldn't have approved of, and we thought her former pals would be ones who might know something. I'll never forget the bravery of some of those girls in giving us information about the people they hung around with, and who Ciara might have hung around with. Information they gave us may yet be crucial in catching the person responsible. It's just sad that so many of them have the lives they have.

Bernadette Breen keeps a journal, a record of her innermost thoughts about her daughter's disappearance. Sometimes there are days on which she cannot write at all. The journal is there to be read by her family after her death.

Every child that goes missing reminds Bernadette of Ciara; every missing child is Ciara. Bernadette has also kept a snip of Ciara's hair, which she keeps in a locket. It may well be of significance in identifying Ciara if she is found. Bernadette believes the local gardaí involved in the search for Ciara have been wonderful, but she has reservations about the wider investigations into the cases of missing people.

> I really think the Government come out with things every now and then to keep the families of missing people quiet. I think there should be detectives working for maybe eighteen months or two years at a time in a dedicated unit, and then bring in fresh people. It's little things that really upset you: the fact that families learn things from the media rather than the Gardaí. It just hurts sometimes. But then there are gardaí who are great. You know they really care. There is one detective who I know keeps a photograph of Ciara with him, just to remind him that it's a teenage child who is missing.

Bernadette showed me a large black-and-white photograph hanging on a wall, of Ciara on her First Communion day, smiling proudly in her white dress. Another favourite photograph is one of Ciara wearing a Mexican hat. In another room hangs a large photograph of Bernadette's grandfather, James Coburn—Ciara's great-grandfather, who was a Fine Gael TD for Louth for twenty-seven years. He died in office; his son George—Bernadette's uncle—succeeded him in the by-election.

Bernadette told me she cries mostly at night.

Every day I think that's another day gone without Ciara. I always think I might get some news tomorrow. Maybe 'tomorrow' is what keeps me going. I just can't bear to think of her lying out there somewhere. Two things I definitely know are that Ciara wasn't on drugs, and she was not pregnant. But I know she sneaked out of the house to meet someone I wouldn't have approved of. I'd like younger people reading this to remember that parents don't warn about evil people just for the sake of it. Ciara was stupid once and paid the highest price possible. When I'm at my lowest I can smell her. Ciara wore 'White Musk', and I can still smell her. I would give anything in the world just to hear just two words again: 'Hi, Mam.'

5

Fiona Sinnott

Of all the missing women who it is feared were the victims of a violent death, Fiona Sinnott is the only one who has left behind a child. Emma was eleven months old when her nineteen-year-old mother vanished in February 1998. Fiona Sinnott was last seen in the isolated home she was renting at Ballyhitt, four miles south-west of Rosslare, Co. Wexford. Apart from complaining of a still unexplained pain in her arm, she had been in good form, socialising with friends in a pub in the nearby village of Broadway.

A number of men have been questioned about the disappearance of Fiona Sinnott, who previously suffered a number of brutal assaults at the hands of one former boy-friend. There are various credible explanations for what might have happened. On different occasions she was hospitalised for injuries, including a damaged jaw and twisted ankle, but she discharged herself. The Gardaí are aware of the violence she was subjected to; but without Fiona to testify, charges will never be brought.

Despite the litany of abuse she had endured, Fiona Sinnott had much to look forward to. She doted on her baby daughter, and she was planning to get solid work as a chef. Though she and Emma's father, Seán Carroll, had ended their relationship when Emma was eight months old, they remained on relatively good terms, and Emma spent her time between the Carroll and the Sinnott families. All the indications are that Fiona Sinnott did not choose to disappear. She was looking forward to Emma's first birthday, and her sister Diane was having her twenty-first birthday later the same month. Her disappearance has devastated her parents and her two brothers and two sisters.

The Gardaí have two main hypotheses. Fiona may have been murdered, possibly by one or more local people; or she may have suffered an accidental death, and the person or persons who were with her panicked and concealed her body. Detectives remain convinced that there are people in Co. Wexford who know what happened to Fiona Sinnott, and who know who is responsible.

Fiona Sinnott's former partner, the father of her baby daughter, is the last person that the Gardaí know of to see her. The account he gave is that Fiona was not feeling very well and was planning to head towards a doctor in a town about eight miles from her home. It was about 9:15 on the morning of Monday 9 February 1998, and Seán Carroll was standing in Fiona's bedroom. He had spent the night on a sofa downstairs and went up to wake Fiona before he left the house. He had stayed the night because Fiona had been complaining of a pain in her chest and arm the night before, and he had agreed to escort her home from a local pub. By Monday morning she said she was still not feeling well. 'I think I'll go to the doctor in Bridgetown,' she said. 'I'll thumb over.' 'Have you any money?' Seán asked her. She replied that she hadn't. He gave her about £5 and headed out the door, to where his mother was waiting in her car to collect him. And that is the last reported sighting of Fiona Sinnott.

The night before she disappeared Fiona was out socialising in Butler's pub, up the road from the house she was renting. On a number of occasions that night she complained of a pain in her arm; but because of her disappearance, and the fact that she never made it to the Bridgetown Medical Centre, we will never know exactly why her arm was causing her pain, or whether this pain had anything to do with her disappearance.

Despite the pain, she was enjoying herself that Sunday night. She was going about her normal routine of having a drink and a chat with some of her friends. Her movements in the last few hours before she vanished were those of a nineteen-year-old woman enjoying herself. On closer inspection, however, her life was far from perfect.

Fiona Sinnott had suffered much during her nineteen years. She had her first boy-friend when she was fifteen; over the next four years she had a number of relationships with other men. Fiona came from a loving and closely knit family, but there seemed little they could do to help her when one boy-friend became violent. On a number of occasions she suffered violent physical attacks. The first time she was treated at Wexford General Hospital it was for bruising to her face and jaw; other hospital visits followed when the same man bit her legs and beat her about the head and back. But each time she attended the casualty department she would discharge herself, or decline to say what exactly had happened.

While she never made a formal complaint against the person brutalising her, the Gardaí were becoming aware that Fiona Sinnott was being physically assaulted by a man from the south Co. Wexford area.

In late 1996 two gardaí sped to a house a mile outside Rosslare Harbour. Garda Michelle Power had just received a 999 call to say that a man had reportedly threatened a woman with a knife. The two male gardaí who arrived at the scene found Fiona Sinnott on the street being comforted by another woman. Fiona and the two gardaí went into a house, where the man who had allegedly threatened her was lying asleep on a sofa. He had been drinking. He awoke and held a conversation with the two gardaí while Fiona collected her belongings. Fiona left the house. The two gardaí noted the night's events in the Garda log. No charges were made.

One detective believes that a pattern of abuse was unfolding but it was never proved.

> Here we had a young woman attending Wexford General Hospital on a number of occasions for bruising to her face, a twisted ankle, a damaged jaw. She never once told the Gardaí that these injuries were caused by another person. Of course we might all suspect the injuries were the result of a violent relationship, but suspicion is not enough. Fiona never pressed charges. Were it not for that incident where a man reportedly threatened to kill Fiona, we might not have looked in that direction. But even then the feeling we got from Fiona was that this fellow was going to sleep it off. No charges were pressed. I believe Fiona was physically abused by a man she was having a relationship with. But I can't prove it. And this man has no convictions for anything. He's clean as a whistle.

The feeling of many people close to the case about who might be responsible for Fiona Sinnott's disappearance is influenced heavily by a particular attack she may have suffered a year before her disappearance. Detectives only became aware of the attack after Fiona vanished; but the circumstances of this reported assault disturbed the gardaí investigating her disappearance.

Fiona confided in a number of people about a particular assault she suffered at the hands of this same man, who we believe might have been responsible for her earlier treatment in hospital. We have more than one report about the nature of this assault, which is a very serious attack on a young woman. If we charged the alleged attacker he would be facing up to life imprisonment. But we can't charge him. We need Fiona.

Before Fiona Sinnott's disappearance very few people knew of the attacks she was believed to have suffered. She had ended her relationship with the man who was believed to be assaulting her. Fiona was a quiet girl, who enjoyed the company of her friends and family. She was also now the mother of a baby girl. Her future looked much brighter.

She spent the whole evening of Sunday 8 February 1998 at Butler's pub in Broadway, in the south-eastern corner of Co. Wexford. The pub is a popular spot for young people. A few local men played pool in the corner, while Fiona sat chatting with her friends Nora Sinnott, Joan Furlong, and Martina Scallan. Martina Scallan would later tell the Gardaí that Fiona was in good spirits, but she had complained a number of times about a pain in her arm. Behind the bar, Brian Breslin served the women. Seán Carroll sat up at the bar, smoking and having a pint. He and Fiona had ended their relationship the previous October, when their baby daughter was eight months old. They would still meet quite often, part of a group that went around together, and they shared access to their baby. That night Emma was staying with Seán's parents, Seán and Kitty Carroll.

At one point during the evening Fiona phoned home to her brother Séamus, asking him to come down to the pub. Séamus Sinnott, a fisherman, had just come in and was drained after a hard day's work. He declined the invitation. Later he would wonder whether Fiona was asking him to the pub because something was wrong. Had she something to tell him? Was she looking for help?

This phone call is the last contact Fiona Sinnott had with any of her family. All the indications are that she was going about her normal routine that Sunday night.

As the evening wore on, Fiona's arm was still paining her. She decided she would head home to her house, about a quarter of a mile away, close to Ballyhitt Racecourse. Martina Scallan asked Seán Carroll if he would walk Fiona home. He said he would. He phoned his mother to tell her Fiona was not feeling very well and that he was going to walk her home and to stay the night in her house. He asked his mother to collect him the next morning at about half past nine. Fiona said goodnight to her friends and took two packets of peanuts with her for the journey home.

Seán Carroll and Fiona Sinnott started going out when Fiona was in her mid-teens. Seán was ten years older than Fiona. He was a 'biker' who had bought his first motorbike when he was seventeen. He had spent time in Australia and in London but had returned to his native Co. Wexford and worked for a time in a local factory. He had married a woman he met while working in London, but that relationship was long over. Fiona was attracted to Seán's exciting life-style, and eventually they began dating. Their relationship was to continue on and off for more than three years. During that time Fiona was also involved with other men. On 28 February 1997 Seán and Fiona celebrated the birth of their daughter. Seán arranged for the three of them to move into a flat in George's Street, Wexford. However, by October 1997 they had decided that the relationship was not working, and they split up. They would still meet often, to share custody of Emma, and would also meet on social outings with other people from the locality. When Seán was asked to escort Fiona home that Sunday night, he didn't hesitate.

Fiona Sinnott was the youngest of five children. Caroline, the eldest, is nine years older; in between are Séamus, Norman, and Diane. When I met Caroline and Diane they told me of the pain their family continues to suffer. Caroline told me she believes something awful happened to her youngest sister.

I fear Fiona is dead, but I don't *accept* she is dead. You can never give up. I know she's dead, or hurt in some way. Fiona was such a curious, nosy person. If she was away by herself she would have to be in contact. She wouldn't be able to stay away. She couldn't bear it. I know something awful happened to her and she was put somewhere. You don't just disappear. Fiona didn't have a penny on her. But there is no clue—nothing.

Fiona Sinnott's two older sisters are passionate about her. Both women want answers. Diane told me about her memories of Fiona.

I last spoke to Fiona that Sunday night when she rang from the pub in Broadway. She was looking for my brother Séamus to go down to her. It was a quick conversation.

Our nickname for Fiona was 'Fifi'. Fiona and I were very close. She wanted to be a chef; she could make the most delicious pastries. She loved all types of music: she went to the Cranberries; Dolores O'Riordan was her favourite singer. She loved partying: she was a real party-bopper. It's the not knowing what happened to Fiona that is the worst thing.

After saying goodnight to friends, Seán Carroll and Fiona Sinnott left Butler's pub late on the Sunday night. The walk to Fiona's home was a short distance along a quiet road. The journey was slow, with Fiona taking her time because of the pain in her chest and arm. Along the way they smoked and chatted and ate the peanuts Fiona had bought. As soon as they got to the house Seán asked Fiona if she wanted a cup of coffee. She said she didn't and that she was going to bed. Seán set the alarm on his watch for nine o'clock, having arranged with his mother to collect him. He went to sleep in a spare bed.

He woke at nine the next morning. He went into Fiona's room and woke her; they spoke briefly, and Fiona said she was going to the doctor in Bridgetown. Seán gave her some money and left; his mother had just arrived to collect him and drove him home to Coddstown, two miles west of Broadway. He later told Garda Jim Sullivan that Fiona was awake and in bed when he last saw her. This is the last known sighting of Fiona.

It was nine days after the last reported sighting of Fiona Sinnott that the Gardaí became aware that she was missing. It was not uncommon for Fiona—like many teenagers—to head off somewhere with friends and perhaps stay with them. On a previous occasion she had travelled to Cork to try to sort out differences in a relationship she was in. Though she hadn't contacted her family or friends by mid-February, alarm bells did not ring immediately. Some of her family thought she might have travelled as far as Wales to see someone; but steadily it began to dawn on everyone that something was wrong. Fiona didn't phone home to her family in Bridgetown; she didn't phone either of her sisters, not even Diane, whose twenty-first birthday was fast approaching; and she didn't make contact with the Carroll family to collect Emma to get her a new outfit for her first birthday. It took nine days for everyone to feel that something very bad had happened—nine days during which the person or persons responsible for Fiona's disappearance were able to cover their tracks.

Pat Sinnott reported his daughter missing on 18 February 1998. He walked into the Garda station in Kilmore Quay, where he met Garda Jim Sullivan and told him he was concerned about his daughter Fiona. He told him that the last time any of the family had spoken to Fiona was on the eighth. On hearing that she hadn't been seen in over a week, Garda Sullivan phoned the Gardaí at Rosslare Pier to alert them also. Word quickly spread that Fiona Sinnott had vanished.

Detectives in Rosslare and Wexford began to examine what was known about Fiona Sinnott's last movements. All her friends and family were interviewed, and people from around Broadway were also questioned. One detective told me that the condition of Fiona's house was unusual.

> The house was spotlessly clean. This was unusual for Fiona. Her family told us that she was not the most house-proud of people; but the house was very clean. And considering that Fiona was complaining of a pain in her chest and arm before she disappeared, we doubted whether she might have cleaned the house. But we searched the house for clues, for any sign of anything that might tell us what happened to her. We found nothing.

The area from which Fiona Sinnott vanished is a quiet townland just west of Ballyhitt Racecourse. Four miles to the north is Rosslare Harbour, with daily ferries to Wales and France. Four miles south is Carnsore Point, the south-eastern tip of Ireland. An extensive land and water search was organised, and the normally quiet area around Broadway became the focus of intense Garda scrutiny as every possible witness was tracked down and questioned. When it was learnt from Seán Carroll that Fiona had intended hitching a lift from Broadway to Bridgetown, all possible witnesses were found and questioned. No-one had seen Fiona Sinnott either standing on the road hitching a lift or in a car travelling to Bridgetown. She never attended the doctor that Monday.

Over the following months the Gardaí carried out extensive searches of land in Co. Wexford, but no trace of Fiona Sinnott was found. One of the areas looked at immediately was Lady's Island Lake, a large lake a quarter of a mile south of where Fiona was last seen; it is almost two miles long and a mile wide at its southern base. Only for a thin stretch of land, known as Grogan Burrow, the lake would be part of the sea. The Burrow stretches from near Kilmore Quay eastwards to Carnsore Point. In the process the Burrow helps to form two large lakes: Tacumshin Lake, which lies two miles from where Fiona disappeared, and Lady's Island Lake, which is just a short walk from the house. Extensive searches were carried out at each lake, with Garda divers searching both stretches of water as well as the small islands in the middle of each. One detective recalled that the search of Lady's Island Lake took almost a month.

We actually drained the lake. Not totally dry, but enough to be able to search in just a few feet of water. It was a massive operation. We had already searched the lake and found nothing, but we were conscious that here was a large stretch of water just a short distance from where Fiona disappeared. So, we decided we wanted to be as sure as sure could be. What we did was we cut a hole in the sand of the burrow, using a JCB, and drained much of the lake water into the sea. We were able to comb the lake. If anything was there we would have found it. We found nothing.

From the time of the first report of Fiona Sinnott's disappearance the ferry terminal at Rosslare Harbour was alerted and issued with a description. Through Interpol, the police at Fishguard, Pembroke, Cherbourg and Le Havre were also alerted about the ominous disappearance of a nineteen-year-old mother. Through interviews with Fiona's friends the Gardaí were able to establish that Fiona had met a Welsh lorry-driver in Rosslare Harbour two nights before she disappeared.

On Friday 6 February 1998 Fiona Sinnott and a number of her friends travelled by minibus from Broadway to the Tuskar House Hotel in Rosslare to attend a pool tournament. During the evening Fiona met a Welsh lorry-driver, Gary James. At the end of the night, when the bus was heading back to Broadway, he called out to Fiona and invited her into his lorry. She agreed and got in. Some time later someone started banging on the lorry, shouting, 'Come out of there, Fiona.' They peeped out of the lorry and saw a man that Fiona identified. She stayed in the lorry, and the man who was shouting outside eventually walked off.

In March 1998 Gary James made a statement to the Gardaí about his recollections of that night. He told them that the next morning he had driven Fiona to Kilrane, a village a mile outside Rosslare Harbour in the direction of Broadway. He had not seen her again.

As the search for Fiona Sinnott continued, her daughter, Emma, had her first birthday. Though she was missing her mother, Emma had many loving relatives to help her enjoy her birthday. On her father's side she had her grandparents, Seán and Kitty Carroll, and her aunts Yvonne and Sharon. On her mother's side there were her other proud grandparents, Pat and Mary Sinnott, and her aunts Caroline and Diane and uncles Séamus and Norman.

As time wore on, the Sinnott and Carroll families would see less and less of each other. Emma would be cared for by her father's family. Later it would be arranged that Pat and Mary Sinnott would see their granddaughter in a hotel for about an hour every fortnight.

Everyone is proud of Emma. One treasured photograph of her at an art competition, which was published in the *Wexford People*, shows a little girl having fun with her classmates at primary school—a little girl doing ordinary things; a little girl whose mother never got the chance to see her daughter grow up.

In June 1998 senior detectives held a conference with members of the National Bureau of Criminal Investigation in Dublin. The investigation into the disappearance of Fiona Sinnott had yielded nothing in the way of solid information on her whereabouts. However, as happens when a trawl for any information is undertaken, facts about other alleged criminal acts had come to the attention of the Gardaí. After a detailed discussion it was decided that six men in south Co. Wexford should be arrested and questioned about alleged drug-dealing.

This is the kind of stuff that might go on in any rural area. There are local fellows who know where to source drugs. It's usually small-time stuff, but the fact that this was happening close to where Fiona disappeared could not be ignored. So we decided to lift them. We were legitimately questioning them about drugs in Co. Wexford, but you never know who might be keeping another secret.

A team of experienced detectives from the NBCI travelled to Co. Wexford to question the six men, who were arrested at different places and taken to Wexford Garda Station. Among them was a man who was a suspect in Fiona Sinnott's disappearance. He had no previous convictions, but aspects of his character, and certain allegations made against him, had made him a suspect. He was questioned at length over two days by two sets of detectives. The gardaí who took part in the questioning were involved in many of the most important criminal investigations of recent times; two of them were among those who would later question John Crerar, who was subsequently convicted of the murder of Phyllis Murphy in 1979.

These senior gardaí were questioning men believed to be involved in relatively small-scale drug-dealing. One local garda noted:

> The irony would have been lost on the boys we were question-
> ing. But we weren't leaving this to chance. One of them might
> have known something about Fiona, but it was for them to tell
> us. We couldn't come out and just ask them. They were not
> being held in connection with Fiona's disappearance. We
> hoped one of them might know something and come clean.
> We still wonder if one of them might know something. These
> fellows would have been aware of covert means of travelling
> around the countryside, without drawing attention to yourself.
> If anyone had seen anything that Monday, or any other day, we
> thought those fellows would have seen it. But we brought in
> the best interviewers we had, and we got nothing.

One of the men questioned later died of a drug-related illness. He had known Fiona Sinnott, as they were from the same general area; he would occasionally give her a lift if he was heading her way. One person who knew both believes this man may have known something about Fiona's disappearance.

He seemed to be edgy whenever anybody would mention Fiona. He seemed to take her disappearance quite hard. But it's only afterwards that you start to analyse like this. The poor man was into drugs in a bad way, and that's what cost him his life. Maybe it was the drugs that were causing him to act edgy—perhaps that's a more likely answer. But we just don't know, and now will never know.

Fiona Sinnott's parents, Pat and Mary Sinnott, met in Co. Donegal. Pat was a fisherman from Co. Wexford; Mary lived in the fishing village of Killybegs. Caroline Sinnott smiled as she told me how her father sailed into Killybegs a single man and left with his wife-to-be.

Dad met Mam when he was working in Donegal. His brother met one of Mam's sisters, and they're married now as well—two Wexford brothers married to two Donegal sisters. Mam and Dad went on their honeymoon to Dublin, and they settled here in Wexford. They're both retired now. They've a number of grandchildren, but they're missing one of their children, and it really hurts them. When the monument for missing people was unveiled in Kilkenny, we all went up.

A year after the disappearance of Fiona Sinnott, a suspected serial killer was found to be living in Co. Wexford. Detectives have investigated this man's movements and have tried to trace where he was when a number of women disappeared in Leinster in the

1990s. But it appears to be pure coincidence that he was living close to where Fiona Sinnott had lived the year before. The Gardaí have established that he was living in England at the time of Fiona's disappearance, and there is no evidence that he travelled to Co. Wexford before he was identified by the Gardaí in Wexford in 1999. This man is a native of Co. Laois but had been living abroad for a number of years. He is suspected of having murdered two teenage girls in other jurisdictions. He already has convictions for assaults on teenage girls in Northern Ireland; he also served a ten-year prison sentence for a vicious attack on an elderly woman in Co. Cork in the early 1970s.

In 1999 this dangerous man arrived in Barntown, Co. Wexford, ten miles north of where Fiona Sinnott was last seen, having travelled to Rosslare by ferry from Britain with his partner and other family members. It is alleged that at this time he had already killed one young girl in another jurisdiction; he would later be charged with murdering another girl in England.

After the Gardaí in Co. Wexford became aware that this suspected serial killer was in the area, they paid him a visit. They informed him that they knew who he was and that they would be monitoring his movements. The man left Ireland a short time afterwards, returning to England, where it is now feared that he abducted and murdered a fourteen-year-old girl in April 2001; her body was found at a cement works in Kent in March 2002.

Though the extent of this man's alleged crimes is still being examined by the Gardaí, the PSNI, and police in Britain, it appears that he was not in Co. Wexford at the time of Fiona Sinnott's disappearance.

In June 1998, four months after Fiona Sinnott's disappearance, the man who is alleged to have assaulted her on a number of occasions met the Gardaí. During their discussion this man, who is from south Co. Wexford, was asked directly whether he knew anything about Fiona's disappearance. He replied that he 'couldn't talk about it.' One detective asked him, 'Why can't you talk to us about Fiona?'

'I've nothing to say,' he replied. More questions met with a similar reply.

'Have you anything to do with Fiona's disappearance?'

'I've nothing to say.'

'It would be better to come clean about this …'

'Lads, I can't talk about it.'

'Why can't you talk about it?'

'I have nothing to say … I have nothing to say.'

'Are you concerned about her disappearance?'

'I have nothing to say.'

One line of inquiry the Gardaí believe may still be a valid one is that the person responsible for Fiona Sinnott's disappearance may have had assistance from one or more other people. It has long been wondered whether the person responsible might have summoned assistance after the crime had been committed, and perhaps there is someone who got caught up in something they didn't realise was a crime until it was too late. Perhaps someone was asked to help move Fiona from one place to another, or was asked to hide certain evidence, or was asked to provide an alibi.

As part of this line of inquiry the Gardaí identified a number of people living in Co. Wexford who it was felt might have something to hide. These people denied any involvement when they were questioned. Detectives dug up a septic tank on private land during this part of the investigation, and part of the foundations of a house were also searched, but nothing was found.

Caroline Sinnott told me that she and the rest of the family think that more than one person may know the secret of what happened to Fiona.

> We believe we know the person who might be responsible for the disappearance of Fiona. We've often wondered if this person might have had assistance from another person in south Co. Wexford. This other person might have been brought into it even after Fiona had been abducted or hurt. Someone knows something; someone has a guilty conscience. There are people in the county of Wexford who know what happened to our sister.

In the weeks before Fiona Sinnott went missing she confided in one person that she wanted to change aspects of her life and essentially to take more responsibility for herself and her baby. However, there was nothing to suggest that she was under any threat from anyone. Her only recent trip to the doctor was for a bout of tonsillitis the month before she disappeared. A farmer in the area later came forward to say that he saw Fiona holding her arm and looking distressed on the weekend she disappeared. Whatever was causing the pain in her arm as described by this witness, and by Fiona's friends in the pub that fateful night, has never been established. Had she been assaulted? Was it some kind of accidental injury she had suffered? Has it anything to do with her disappearance?

The disappearance of Fiona Sinnott is only one of a number of upsetting incidents to occur in the general area of south Co. Wexford. In June 2001, 35-year-old Alan Wright from Tomhaggard, four miles from where Fiona Sinnott disappeared, died after taking a heroin overdose. He had travelled with two friends to Crumlin in Dublin, where they bought heroin; he died as they were driving back to Co. Wexford. The death traumatised his family and shocked the local community, unused to such distressing events. Coupled with the sinister disappearance of Fiona Sinnott, this area has suffered greatly in recent years.

At Wexford Garda Station one filing cabinet is filled to the brim with witness statements, questionnaires and 'job-sheets' that the investigation into Fiona Sinnott's disappearance has generated. A job-sheet is what is used when a piece of information has to be followed up to establish whether it might be true or not. Such investigations in the Fiona Sinnott case have involved liaison with police in Wales, England, and France. The possibility that Fiona's abductor might have taken her by car or lorry on the ferry from Rosslare has not been ignored, and Interpol was issued with Fiona's description almost as soon as she was reported missing. But, frustratingly, because she was not reported missing until nine days after she was last seen, detectives fear that the trail had grown too cold.

The Gardaí also spoke to a married man from Co. Wexford who was rumoured to be linked romantically with Fiona. This man, a self-employed businessman, denies the rumour emphatically. The interest of the Gardaí was sparked when it was learnt that he had travelled by ferry to Britain at about the time of Fiona's disappearance; but this line of inquiry has led nowhere.

The loss of Fiona Sinnott is not the first misfortune to be visited on the Sinnott family. Fiona's father, Paddy Sinnott, is one of fourteen children. One of his brothers, Fintan, then aged twenty-one, drowned in 1977 while responding to an emergency call. In a terrible irony, it turned out to be a false alarm; but Fintan, who had rushed to give whatever assistance he could, drowned in the first few moments. Such disasters are unfortunately common in fishing communities, and the loss of Fintan was something the Sinnott family could understand in a certain way and eventually come to terms with; but the loss of nineteen-year-old Fiona is an agonising mystery that has devastated the family. There are no answers, no body, no clearly identified culprit, and no explanation.

Paddy Sinnott doesn't talk much about Fiona's disappearance. Neither does her brother Norman. Fiona's other brother, Séamus, often wonders what might have been if he had gone down to Butler's pub that night. Might things have been different? Did Fiona need help? Was there something he might have been able to do?

Fiona Sinnott left Bridgetown Vocational School before doing her Inter Cert. Finding that she had a talent for baking, she sought work in restaurants and was thinking of pursuing a full-time career as a chef. Just before she disappeared she was planning to take positive steps to better herself and improve not only her own prospects but those of her young daughter.

Fiona Sinnott was the second-last woman to disappear in Leinster before the Garda authorities decided to set up a special investigation to see if the cases might be linked. Hers is the only such disappearance in the Co. Wexford area; the closest other missing woman case is twenty miles away in Waterford, where Imelda Keenan disappeared from her home in January 1994. Despite the best efforts of the Gardaí, no trace of Imelda Keenan has been found. She was last seen at her home in William Street, Waterford, when she was wearing leopard-skin trousers and a denim jacket. Though her details were also privately analysed by detectives from Operation Trace, there was no evidence that she might have been the victim of a crime. While her disappearance is no less painful for her family, from an investigative point of view the Gardaí do not believe that Imelda Keenan's disappearance is linked to Fiona Sinnott's. In Fiona's case there was a clear history of violence against her by one person who was known to her, and this is where a degree of suspicion still lies.

Operation Trace was unable to establish any links between Fiona Sinnott and any of the other missing women, or with any known convicted offenders who might have attacked women. Caroline Sinnott believes the answer lies closer to home, but that the whole issue of missing women must be tackled.

> We don't think that there's a link between Fiona and any of the other missing women. We don't think that a serial killer was hanging around Bridgetown. But you don't just disappear … We're fed up with bits and pieces. We'd like to see Fiona found and rested.

Caroline recounted in clear detail an evening some years before Fiona disappeared that she says should make everybody think.

> I remember looking at the news about when Jo Jo Dullard disappeared, and we were all talking about it and saying just how terrible that must be for her family. But sure you don't think much about it afterwards. Then it hit our doorstep.

6

Operation Trace

Five months after the disappearance of Fiona Sinnott, another young woman disappeared from her home in Leinster. The circumstances of her disappearance are deeply disturbing. This young woman, who was eighteen years old, vanished in broad daylight from the gate of her home at Roseberry in Droichead Nua, Co. Kildare, on Tuesday 28 July 1998.

This time the response of the Gardaí was immediate. Within hours a massive search was under way; but no sign of the missing woman was ever found. Her parents have campaigned vigorously for any information in relation to her disappearance, and still hold out the hope that she will be found safe and well. Privately, many gardaí fear the worst, knowing that the disappearance was so out of character for the woman, and that no trace of her has been found. The possibility that some person or persons may have abducted her in broad daylight from the roadside beside her home is one that the Gardaí must examine, and have been examining since that summer's day. By the autumn of 1998 senior gardaí were privately voicing extreme concern about the number of young women who had apparently been abducted and murdered. From the disappearance of Annie McCarrick in March 1993 to that of Fiona Sinnott in February 1998 at least five women had been abducted either from the roadside or from their homes at various places in Leinster.

The disappearance of this sixth young woman in July 1998 was just too much; something had to be done. By the end of 1998 a specialist six-member Garda team had been hand-picked in an attempt to establish whether any of the cases were linked. For the first time, a special computer system was developed to cross-reference information on thousands of convicted sex offenders. The investigation would bring the Gardaí into contact with some of the most violent men ever to live in Ireland. And at the back of everyone's mind was one question: was there evidence to suggest that a serial killer was operating?

It was a warm summer's afternoon on Tuesday 28 July 1998 in the bustling Co. Kildare town of Droichead Nua. Families walked along the footpaths, looking in shop windows, eating ice cream. Children hung around the town centre, enjoying the long school holidays. A general feeling of well-being from the continuing good fortune of Kildare footballers in the Leinster championship was evident in the conversations that could be heard around the town. But in total contrast to this almost perfect summer scene, something awful was about to happen to an eighteen-year-old woman that would ensure that this day would be remembered for ever, by people from Droichead Nua and beyond, with shock and sadness. In deference to a request from her family, the young woman is not referred to by name in this book.

The eighteen-year-old woman was in good form earlier that day, and there was nothing to suggest that anything was troubling her or that she intended to disappear voluntarily. She was home from England to spend the summer with her parents and younger sister. She was studying to be a teacher at Strawberry Hill College in London and had just finished her first year. Her boy-friend was going to come over from London and visit her later that summer; in fact a letter she sent to him that arrived only after her disappearance showed that she was in the best of spirits and was looking forward to the future.

The young woman was enjoying her summer holidays at home in Droichead Nua, where she would often walk the short distance from her home at Roseberry into the town centre to help her grandmother in the shop she ran. On the weekend before she vanished she stayed with two girl-friends in Kingscourt, Co. Cavan. She returned home on the Monday evening and was in the best of spirits. Less than twenty-four hours later she vanished from the gate of her house.

Her family point out that any speculation about whether someone is responsible for her disappearance is purely speculation. Nevertheless, many gardaí privately fear that the woman was the victim of one or more killers.

The hours and minutes before this woman disappeared did not betray anything out of the ordinary. Indeed some of her actions that day prove she was making plans for her future. At 2:20 p.m. she went to the AIB in Main Street, Droichead Nua, where she got a bank draft to pay for the second year of her training course in London. She then walked the short distance to the post office to send it off to the college. Along the way she said hello to a number of people.

After coming out of the post office she spoke briefly to a friend as they crossed the road, and they then parted company; nothing she said or did gave any indication that she intended to vanish within minutes. She then began the walk to her home at Roseberry, on the Barretstown Road, just north of Droichead Nua. This is a winding but busy road, close to the River Liffey, where the bustling town gives way to the quiet countryside. It was a road she had walked hundreds of times before.

The last definite sighting of the woman was when she was three hundred yards from her home. There was no scream, no screeching of brakes, no sound of the slamming of a car door—nothing to suggest that a would-be killer snatched this young woman from the roadside. The only definite pieces of information the Gardaí have had to work on are that her bank account was never touched, she has never contacted any of her family or friends, and no trace of her or her clothing has ever been found. When last seen she was wearing white Nike runners, jeans, and a Nike top, and she was carrying a black bag with a Caterpillar logo on the flap. In an inch-by-inch search of the roadside outside her home nothing was found to suggest there had been a struggle as she was pulled into a car or van.

Despite the fact that no crime scene was ever found, many local gardaí remembered the case of 23-year-old Phyllis Murphy, who had disappeared from Droichead Nua twenty years before. In that case also there was no crime scene, and for four weeks Phyllis Murphy was classified as a missing person. But in January 1980 her body was found in the Wicklow Mountains. She had been abducted in Droichead Nua as she walked for a bus, and she had been murdered. By July 1998 the killer of Phyllis Murphy had not been caught. It would be another year before John Crerar from Kildare would be charged. Mindful of that abduction and murder two decades before, detectives investigating the disappearance of the eighteen-year-old woman already feared the worst.

The search began within hours of the young woman's disappearance. Her mother arrived home in the early evening and sensed immediately that something was wrong. Her daughter was the kind of girl who would always let her family know where she was. Her father arrived home, and within minutes they had decided to contact the Gardaí.

The search was exhaustive, with roads, lanes, hedges, fields, bogs, rivers and ponds subjected to a thorough search. Detectives were conscious that the first twenty-four hours were crucial in catching a possible abductor before he could cover his tracks. The Gardaí began to trace the movements of a number of men who were known to show extreme violence towards women. The whereabouts of a number of vehicles owned by known criminals were also sought. One person reported seeing a woman in apparent distress sitting in a white Hiace van spotted near Droichead Nua that afternoon. The witness described seeing two men in the van with the woman, and the driver of the van appeared to have red hair. However, no leads emerged from this sighting.

Another line of inquiry would later emerge in relation to an extremely violent man from Co. Wicklow who had not yet come to the attention of the Gardaí. This would-be killer was in Droichead Nua at about the time the teenager disappeared, working as a carpenter on contract work at a pub in the town. In February 2000 this man's reputation as a quiet family man was shattered when he abducted a woman in Carlow and drove her to a number of places in the boot of his car before subjecting her to a number of vicious assaults. He then tried to murder her. This man remains a suspect for the disappearance of the teenager in Droichead Nua in July 1998, and investigations into his activities are continuing while he serves a fifteen-year sentence in Arbour Hill Prison, Dublin. Yet despite a massive investigation, no trace has been found of the eighteen-year-old, the sixth woman to vanish in Leinster within a five-year period in the most chilling of circumstances.

Within days of the disappearance of the eighteen-year-old woman from outside her home in Droichead Nua, a number of senior gardaí had an informal but detailed discussion. They were worried that this latest disappearance, if it was what they feared, was too much. The other case mainly discussed was that of Jo Jo Dullard, the 21-year-old woman who was abducted and murdered in November 1995 and who was last seen in Moone, Co. Kildare—fifteen miles from Droichead Nua. The close proximity of the disappearances of two young women, both last seen on a roadside in Co. Kildare, was something that could not be ignored. Though the two women disappeared at different times of day—Jo Jo Dullard was abducted as she hitched a lift at around midnight, while the latest missing woman disappeared in broad daylight—detectives were privately wondering whether the same person might be responsible. Had the unknown abductor and murderer of Jo Jo Dullard changed his modus operandi? Was the disappearance of the Droichead Nua teenager the work of an opportunistic violent person or persons? Was there some evil killer roaming the roads of Co. Kildare and beyond?

Certainly, the Gardaí had always feared that whoever took the life of Jo Jo Dullard would strike again. It is almost a certainty that she would not have known her killer before she sat into the mystery car on the night she disappeared. Indeed some gardaí wondered whether Jo Jo Dullard had been the first victim of this unknown killer. Certainly the person responsible for the abduction and murder of Annie McCarrick on the Dublin-Wicklow border in March 1993 would fit the profile of a random attacker; and in both cases the bodies of the victims had not been found. Could the person who killed Annie McCarrick have killed Jo Jo Dullard? And were they responsible also for the disappearance of the Droichead Nua teenager?

Also on the minds of detectives were the three unsolved cases involving women whose bodies were found some months after their murder. Antoinette Smith disappeared in Rathfarnham, Co. Dublin, in July 1987; her body was found buried in the Dublin Mountains in April 1988. Patricia Doherty disappeared from Tallaght, also in south Co. Dublin, in December 1990; her body was found in June 1991, also buried in the Dublin Mountains. And Marie Kilmartin disappeared from Port Laoise in December 1993; her body was found buried in a bog in north Co. Laois in June 1994.

Then there were the cases of three missing women in each of which individual suspects had been identified; but the question had to be asked, What if those suspects were not the people respon-sible? Though is was thought unlikely, what if a serial attacker was responsible for murdering Fiona Pender from Tullamore in August 1996, or Ciara Breen from Dundalk in February 1997, or Fiona Sinnott from Co. Wexford in February 1998? And what about the missing Dublin woman Eva Brennan, who disappeared from her home in July 1993, four months after Annie McCarrick was murdered? Was she a forgotten victim of a random attacker? One Garda superintendent, who was approaching retirement, took another officer aside and said to him,

> I'm not the type to be alarmist, but we have to consider [that] there might be a person or persons actively targeting women. If there is a serial killer out there, we have to find him, and we have to let him know we're here. Remember Shaw and Evans.

This was a reference to two Englishmen who in 1976 abducted and murdered two women at random. The senior garda said he would bring the concerns to the attention of the Garda Commissioner as a matter of urgency. And so it was that, twenty years after the last serial killers to terrorise Ireland were put behind bars for the rest of their lives, the Gardaí were once again faced with the distinct possibility that a serial killer or killers might be at large in Ireland.

Detectives privately knew that the disappearances of Annie McCarrick and Jo Jo Dullard would fit the profile of random attackers. But what about the other missing women? A top-level conference was held at which it was decided that six specific cases of missing women, all feared to have been the victims of violent abduction, should be cross-referenced to see if there were any similarities.

In September 1998, two months after the disappearance of the Droichead Nua teenager, Commissioner Pat Byrne announced the establishment of a special Garda operation to investigate the cases of six missing women. Called Operation Trace, it was to be under the command of Assistant Commissioner Tony Hickey from the Garda Eastern Region, from where the missing women had vanished. He had previously directed the team that investigated the murder of the journalist Veronica Guerin and was still working on that case when he hand-picked a team of detectives. The task of the operation was to trace, review and collate the evidence about Annie McCarrick, Jo Jo Dullard, Fiona Pender, Ciara Breen, Fiona Sinnott, and the missing Droichead Nua teenager.

Of paramount importance to the operation was the setting up of a computer system by means of which every scrap of information, every suggestion and innuendo about each case could be cross-referenced. Detectives were hoping to find a common name of a suspect in at least two of the cases, someone who was in the area at the time of two disappearances but had seemed to be in the clear; or perhaps a vehicle was spotted in the area of two or more of the disappearances. As the establishment of Operation Trace

was announced, there was a degree of optimism among the Gardaí
that something positive was about to emerge.

Assistant Commissioner Hickey selected an experienced
superintendent to oversee the day-to-day running of the Operation
Trace team, which would be based in Naas, Co. Kildare. Superintendent Jerry O'Connell had worked with Hickey on the
Veronica Guerin murder investigation and on a number of other
murder cases in the 1980s and 90s. The other members were
Inspector Mark Kerrigan, Detective-Sergeant Maura Walsh,
Sergeant Pat Treacy, Detective-Garda Marianne Cusack, and
Detective-Garda Alan Bailey. Between them the six gardaí had
decades of experience in investigating serious crime, including
murder cases and missing persons cases. Mark Kerrigan was a
former murder squad officer, who was based in Carlow. Maura
Walsh was working with the National Bureau of Criminal
Investigation at Harcourt Square, Dublin. Pat Treacy worked with
the murder squad and had investigated the disappearance of Philip
Cairns and the murder of Patricia Doherty. Marianne Cusack was
a member of the National Drugs Unit and had been involved in a
number of serious cases, including the prosecution of the prominent Dublin criminal 'Dutchy' Holland. Alan Bailey was attached
to the Bridewell Garda Station in Dublin, where he had been
involved in preparing the book of evidence in nearly every recent
murder case in the north Dublin area.

Jerry O'Connell, now retired, told me that every member of
the Operation Trace team brought some individual expertise or
knowledge to the operation.

Among the six of us we had detectives who were experienced
interviewers, and we had men and women who had experienced previous major criminal investigations. We also had a

Annie McCarrick, who was abducted and murdered in the Wicklow Mountains in March 1993

Annie McCarrick at Long Island

Jo Jo Dullard, who was abducted and murdered while hitching a lift in November 1995

Jo Jo Dullard in her bedroom in Callan

Annie McCarrick enjoying a stroll in a park

Jo Jo Dullard (centre) with her sisters Mary (extreme left), Nora (second from right) and Kathleen (extreme right) and three nieces

Jo Jo Dullard's sister Mary Phelan with her husband, Martin, at the unveiling of the National Monument for Missing People in Kilkenny (Edward Cody)

Fiona Pender, who was seven months pregnant when she was abducted and murdered in August 1996

Fiona Pender with her nephew Dean, whose father, Mark—Fiona's brother—was killed in a motorbike accident in June 1995

Josephine Pender (second from left), her remaining child, John, and two family friends meet President Mary McAleese (Edward Cody)

Fiona Pender worked as a model for a company in Tullamore

Ciara Breen, who was abducted and murdered in Co. Louth in February 1997 (Tom Conachy)

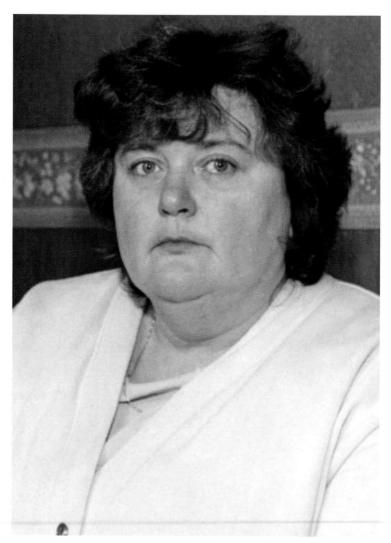

Ciara Breen's mother, Bernadette, who has lost her only child
(Tom Conachy)

Fiona Sinnott, who disappeared from her home in Co. Wexford in February 1998

Fiona Sinnott at her home shortly before her disappearance
(Wexford People)

Mary Boyle (on left) with her brother Patrick and twin sister, Ann, pictured shortly before her disappearance in March 1977

Mary Boyle's parents, Charlie and Ann, her twin sister, Ann, and older brother, Patrick, at the memorial to Mary's memory in Cionn Caslach, Co. Donegal (Eoin McGarvey)

A computer-generated image of what Mary Boyle might have looked like in 1994, seventeen years after her disappearance

Philip Cairns, who was abducted near his home in Dublin in October 1986

Phillip Cairns's mother, Alice, with a treasured memento of her missing son (Maxwells)

A computer-generated image of what Philip Cairns might have looked like in 1994, eight years after his disappearance

mixture of ages, and we had gardaí who had worked in both towns and cities. In Pat Treacy, for example, we had someone who had worked on previous missing persons cases, such as Philip Cairns. I myself had worked on the investigation into the murder of Antoinette Smith, whose body was found in the Dublin Mountains in April 1988, nine months after she had disappeared. We had detectives experienced in tackling organised criminal gangs. Although we were looking at six specific cases of missing women, we were all bringing our collective experience of other major cases with us.

The compilation by computer of information about specific crimes for cross-referencing purposes had never been done before in Ireland. The Gardaí wanted to choose a program that was 'non-judgmental', whereby the information on each disappearance would be treated in the same way and in turn might throw up connections that otherwise might not be found. In each of the six missing women cases there were no witnesses and no crime scene. The task of trying to establish any possible links between them would be painstaking. In choosing a suitable computer program, the Gardaí looked at countries where such cross-referencing of cases was already in existence. Jerry O'Connell and Alan Bailey travelled to meet the English police at the National Crime Facility at Bramshill, outside London, and learn about the Home Office Large Major Enquiry System (HOLMES). They also looked at a system used by the Canadian police, the Violent Crime Linkage Analysis System (VICLAS). This was introduced in the mid-1980s to identify and track the movements of serial violent criminals, including rapists and suspected murderers. Among other systems used for finding common features among unsolved crimes is the FBI's Violent Criminal Apprehension Program (VICAP).

Crucially, certain aspects of the Canadian system deal specifically with solved and unsolved sexual assaults, and with missing persons where there was a strong possibility of foul play. After studying the different programs available, the Gardaí decided to adapt aspects of the Canadian model to form their own Offenders, Victims and Incidents Data-base (OVID).

The OVID system allowed detectives on Operation Trace to collate information about three distinct and crucial areas of their investigation: all known sexual and violent offenders, all known victims of attacks by such people, and information on all reported violent incidents, including attempted abductions. Every scrap of information on each of the six missing women was also compiled and assimilated in the search for any kind of link.

Within weeks of the setting up of Operation Trace the detectives who had worked on the original investigations into the disappearances of Annie McCarrick, Jo Jo Dullard, Fiona Pender, Ciara Breen, Fiona Sinnott and the Droichead Nua teenager met the Operation Trace team at Naas Garda Station. Over a full day the team was briefed to bring them up to date on each of the cases, including any recent developments. One detective who helped to brief the Operation Trace team told me there was an optimistic mood at the conference.

> None of us were upset or anything like that at these new detectives coming in to look at our work. It's not like that, anyway: the missing women are what's important, not office politics. We were all happy to co-operate with Trace, and we all actually felt that a fresh pair of eyes would be quite welcome after all this time. Sometimes you might be so close to a case that you can't see the wood for the trees. And we were all thinking that maybe this computer analysis of the cases might do the trick.

The OVID system was used to compile a list of all known sexual and violent offenders dating back to the early 1980s. It included hundreds of convicted rapists and dozens of men jailed for murdering women; it also extended to men convicted of exposing themselves in public and men who stole underwear from clotheslines. The list covered everything that might label a person as a sexual deviant. The names of many men who had no previous convictions were also nominated for inclusion. In the weeks after Operation Trace was set up the Gardaí received hundreds of phone calls from members of the public naming people they thought might be serial killers. All these names were examined, and if there was any suspicion at all the name was put in the data-base. Within a short time OVID contained the names and details of more than 7,500 people.

The publicity generated by the establishment of Operation Trace led also to a number of women contacting the team directly. These were women who had never made a complaint but had been the victim of sexual assaults, or attempted assaults, or attempted abduction. Some had been beaten or sexually assaulted by former boy-friends; some had been attacked by other people known to them; others had been attacked by strangers. Detectives found themselves meeting women who had never come forward before with their chilling stories of sexual attacks. Each victim said she was coming forward not necessarily to bring criminal complaints herself but to try to help find any of the missing women.

While many phone calls received were anonymous, a number of people with a professional involvement also contacted the Gardaí with their concerns about certain individuals. They included other gardaí who said they had little to base their suspicions on other than a hunch, as well as social workers and teachers, all of whom gave information in confidence.

In addition, the Operation Trace team did an extensive trawl through the cases of the six missing women. When the operation was established, in September 1998, there had been no arrests in connection with the disappearance of Annie McCarrick, Jo Jo Dullard, Ciara Breen, or the Droichead Nua teenager. Three women and two men had been arrested in April 1997 in connection with the disappearance of Fiona Pender, but no charges had been brought. And while no-one had been arrested directly in connection with the disappearance of Fiona Sinnott, a number of people who the Gardaí hoped might have information were held in June 1998 and questioned about other crimes, including drug-dealing in south Co. Wexford. All had been released without charge.

At the back of the minds of the detectives working on Operation Trace was the hope that the computer might throw up a link that would lead to an arrest and in turn to the discovery of one or more of the missing women.

While the Operation Trace team were beginning their work at Naas Garda Station a Co. Fermanagh man was anonymously contacting newspapers and radio stations claiming that in late July 1998 he had given a young woman a lift from Droichead Nua to Carrickmacross, Co. Monaghan. The description he gave of the woman fitted the description of the missing teenager, and the timing of the sighting coincided with the time of the disappearance. The fact that Carrickmacross was only ten miles from Kingscourt, Co. Cavan, where the teenager had stayed with friends the weekend before her disappearance, also made the Gardaí hopeful that the caller was genuine. One detective ruefully remembered that everyone got their hopes up.

The information this man gave us put the missing woman in

the north of the country, and it suggested she left Newbridge [Droichead Nua] of her own free will. We were all naturally excited and hoped that this might all have a happy ending; but the man was lying right from the start: he had concocted the whole story. In his communications with the media the so-called witness said he didn't want to identify himself and didn't want to get involved. But before we had established that the man's story was false, the young woman's parents had travelled to Ulster to appeal on local radio for the man to come forward and help them find their daughter. We released a tape of the anonymous man in the hope that the public could help us find this man.

Following the release of the tape, a 44-year-old man was arrested in January 1999 and held on suspicion of wasting Garda time. However, no charges were brought. This man had suffered the loss of his young daughter in a horrific road accident, and detectives did not believe that malice was the reason the story was concocted.

This hoax caller is only one example of dozens of hoaxers who contacted the Gardaí in the weeks following the launch of Operation Trace. Each phone call and each tip-off had to be investigated fully, but it was a source of frustration to detectives that, for whatever disturbed reasons, some people were simply making up stories to get attention. In the process they were wasting valuable Garda time.

The closest the Gardaí have ever come to bringing a prosecution in relation to any of the missing women is in the case of Ciara Breen, the seventeen-year-old who disappeared from her home in Dundalk in February 1997. On 12 September 1999, a year after Operation Trace began its work, a Dundalk man in his thirties was arrested and questioned about the abduction and probable murder of Ciara Breen. The Gardaí had this man earmarked as a suspect from early on in the investigation, but new information came to the attention of detectives from Operation Trace that lent more weight to the suspicion. After being held and questioned for twelve hours, the man was released without charge. A file on the case was sent to the Director of Public Prosecutions, who directed that no charges be brought at that time. The investigation into the abduction and murder of Ciara Breen is the only one that got this far. However, detectives from Operation Trace did carry out a number of other arrests as OVID threw up new lines of inquiry.

One woman from the travelling community contacted the Gardaí soon after Operation Trace was set up to say she had information that might be of assistance in the search for missing women. This woman was serving a prison sentence at the time for robbery. She sent word from the prison that she had particular information in relation to the disappearance of one missing woman. Detectives met this woman and listened carefully as she outlined the information she had. They were conscious that they were dealing with a person who was serving a prison sentence, and that any such person might be looking for something in return, such as temporary or early release. One detective told the woman that if she had any information at all that could ease the suffering of one family she had a duty to help. The woman said she did want to help and that she was trying to better her own circumstances and do the right thing. She took the Gardaí to a place in Co. Kerry where she said she thought there might be evidence that would assist them. Unfortunately she was unable to pinpoint an exact site that could be searched. The Gardaí are still pursuing this line of inquiry, but without a more exact site detectives say that any search would be futile.

Nine people, including a number of women, were questioned by detectives from Operation Trace in connection with the disappearance of Jo Jo Dullard. Detectives were also hopeful that one or more of these people might have information about the more recent disappearance of the Droichead Nua teenager. On foot of certain information a number of people in the Waterford area were arrested and questioned about a number of crimes, including the abduction and murder of Jo Jo Dullard. Other people were also arrested throughout the country and taken to Naas Garda Station to be questioned. One of those questioned had a previous conviction for a violent sexual assault on a woman. However, all those arrested were released without charge.

While detectives analysed information relating to the six missing women they were specifically assigned to investigate, those cases could not be looked at in isolation. There were other missing women who were not receiving as much attention, and there were four unsolved murders where bodies had been found weeks or months after those women had gone missing in Leinster. So while Operation Trace was officially looking only at six missing women, privately detectives were also looking at five other unsolved cases. Those were the cases of the missing Eva Brennan and the murdered Phyllis Murphy, Antoinette Smith, Patricia Doherty, and Marie Kilmartin.

Before Operation Trace was a year old there had been a breakthrough in relation to one of the unsolved murders that gave all the other investigations renewed vigour and enthusiasm. On an evening in July 1999 Chief Superintendent Seán Feely emerged from Naas Garda Station and addressed the large group of journalists waiting outside. He confirmed that a man was due in court the next morning charged with the murder of Phyllis

Murphy twenty years before. The next day the man was named as John Crerar, a 51-year-old former army sergeant from Woodside Park, Kildare. 23-year-old Phyllis Murphy had last been seen alive on 22 December 1979 as she walked towards a bus stop to travel from Droichead Nua to Kildare. Her naked body was found four weeks later in the Wicklow Gap. For two decades the Gardaí had feared that her killer might strike again. In October 2002 John Crerar was convicted of murdering Phyllis Murphy after the jury accepted the evidence of forensic scientists that semen taken from the body of Phyllis Murphy was John Crerar's. An alibi witness who had lied for twenty years also changed his story.

Though Crerar had no previous convictions, his name was known to the Gardaí in Kildare since 1980, after many gardaí had privately had their suspicions raised about the security guard who volunteered a blood sample. It was to be another nineteen years before that blood sample could be matched with the specimen recovered from Phyllis Murphy's body. It was detectives from Operation Trace who co-ordinated the questioning of Crerar, and they also prepared the book of evidence and kept the valuable exhibits safe.

Crerar's movements have also been examined in relation to the disappearance of the other missing women in Leinster. This is a difficult task, and one that is continuing. One detective told me the Gardaí do believe that the solving of this murder will at least lead indirectly to progress being made in other cases.

You should see the amount of calls we get when some break-through happens in a case. The conviction of John Crerar has shown not only detectives but the general public that hard work does pay off, and that the guilty people will never be allowed forget their evil deeds, whether it's a year or ten years or twenty years or more before gardaí come knocking on their door. Solving the murder of Phyllis Murphy has added much impetus to the investigations into the missing women in Leinster. And that was a clear case of showing that someone giving a false alibi will be found out. There are other people out there of course who have given alibis for friends, or sons, or husbands, and they know it is wrong.

The three murder cases that remain unsolved are much more recent than those of Phyllis Murphy. While her body was hidden under ferns in a densely wooded area, the bodies of the three other victims who were originally classified as missing were buried on bogland.

On 11 July 1987, 27-year-old Antoinette Smith travelled to Slane, Co. Meath, with a friend to a David Bowie concert. It was a lovely summer's day and she danced the afternoon and evening away at the concert. Afterwards she and her friend travelled to the La Mirage night club near Parnell Square, Dublin. They met two men while they were there, one of whom was a barman whom Antoinette knew. The four left the night club at about 2 a.m. and headed down O'Connell Street. There was a minor dispute about where they might go next, and Antoinette and her friend parted company. Antoinette and the barman walked on, but they too parted company a short time afterwards. Antoinette walked over to Westmorland Street close to the Abrakebabra restaurant, where she met two unidentified men. The three of them got a taxi to Rathfarnham, close to the Yellow House pub. The taxi driver seeing Antoinette Smith getting out of the taxi with these two men in Rathfarnham was the last time she was seen alive.

For nine months the disappearance of Antoinette Smith was treated as a missing person case. Antoinette was separated from her husband, who had quickly reported her missing, as she had not arrived to visit her two young children in Clondalkin. For nine months there were no leads; then, on 13 April 1988, her body was found in a shallow grave at the Feather Bed in the Dublin Mountains. She had been strangled, and a plastic bag had been put over her head. Her body had been left in a drain at the side of a turf bank but had become exposed when rain washed away part of the soil. The body had been preserved to a certain extent because of the soil in which it lay. From evidence gathered in what soon became a murder investigation, the Gardaí are satisfied that two men were involved in the attack and murder of Antoinette Smith.

Detectives with Operation Trace looked at the Antoinette Smith file to see if any similar names were cropping up in relation to any of the other missing women. The abduction and murder of Antoinette Smith would fit the profile of two random attackers, but what detectives were trying to establish was whether these violent men were opportunistic killers who had killed once or were serial killers who had struck again.

Operation Trace detectives were fully aware that whoever murdered Patricia Doherty in December 1991 buried her body less than a mile from where Antoinette Smith's body had been left four years before. The Gardaí still wonder whether the two women were murdered by separate killers and the burial sites were close purely by coincidence or whether the murders were the work of the same two men.

Patricia Doherty, a native of Anascaul, Co. Kerry, was last seen alive on 23 December 1991. She had travelled to the Square in Tallaght to buy Santa hats for her two children. She and her husband, Paddy Doherty, were living at Allenton Lawns, Tallaght, close to a road that heads south into the Dublin Mountains.

Patricia Doherty had been working as a prison officer in Mountjoy Prison for about six months before her disappearance, having trained in Port Laoise Prison. Her disappearance was out of character for her, but the alarm was not raised until Christmas Day, because her husband thought she had gone to work on Christmas Eve. He first realised something was wrong when he arrived to meet her at her mother's house in Rathfarnham, as they had arranged, only to find she wasn't there. Weeks became months, and still there was no sign of the missing woman. Then, in June, everyone's worst fears were realised.

Patricia Doherty's body was found by a man out cutting turf close to the Lemass Cross at Killakee in the Dublin Mountains. A full-scale murder investigation immediately began, headed by detectives in Tallaght. Patricia Doherty had been strangled, and her body had been left in a bog drain. She was identified by dental records and by rings she was wearing. The key of her front door was found close to the body. Detectives are satisfied that the body had lain in the Dublin Mountains from about the time she went missing the previous Christmas.

Whoever abducted and murdered Patricia Doherty chose to bury her body less than three miles from her home. The place is also less than a mile from where the body of Antoinette Smith was left by her killers four years earlier. No-one was ever arrested in connection with the murder of Patricia Doherty.

The third missing woman case that is now officially an unsolved murder case is that of the abduction and murder of Marie Kilmartin in Port Laoise on 16 December 1993. The 34-year-old single woman, a native of Ballinasloe, Co. Galway, was lured out of her house at Beladd on the Stradbally road by some man who phoned her from a public phone box in the town. When it came to investigating the disappearance of Marie Kilmartin the Gardaí had more precise information to go on than in the Antoinette Smith and Patricia Doherty cases. They knew that Marie Kilmartin had earlier attended a Christmas party at the day centre where she worked in Port Laoise. She got a lift home with two women, who she invited in for a cup of tea, but they declined. She was due to meet a friend later that night, at about six o'clock; but when the friend called around, Marie's shopping was still on a chair in the kitchen, and Marie was nowhere to be seen.

Detectives would later establish that a phone call was made to her home at about 4:30 p.m. that afternoon. The call, from the public phone box on the Dublin Road in Port Laoise, lasted about two-and-a-half minutes. Whoever made that call has crucial information relating to her murder; but that person has never been clearly identified. Detectives have established that no other phone calls were made from that call box between 4:11 and 4:42 p.m. This information could yet prove crucial, as a witness has told the Gardaí that she saw a man in the phone box at about half past four as she was hitching a lift on the road. She described him as about five feet eight inches tall and about thirty years old. While the description may be vague, it establishes that there was one person who made the phone call to Marie Kilmartin, and that it was a male caller. This would suggest that whoever managed to lure her out of her house was a man who was known to her in some way.

For six months Marie Kilmartin was classified as missing. Then, on 10 June 1994, Thomas Deegan from Mountmellick, Co. Laois, made a shocking discovery. He was visiting his son, who was cutting turf at Pim's Lane, Barnanaghs, off the Portarlington–Mountmellick road. He had given his son a flask of tea and was looking around. He spotted the wheel of what looked like a pram in a nearby drain; then he saw what looked like a black boot also in the drain. He looked a little closer, and he saw the body of a woman.

For six months the body of Marie Kilmartin had lain in a bog drain near Mountmellick. It was only when the bog water in the drain had subsided in hot and dry weather that the body became visible. The area where she was found was covered with gorse, ferns, and bracken. The gardaí who arrived on the scene saw that there was a six-inch-wide concrete block over the woman's chest and shoulder. It was a distressing scene, which left many detectives speechless. Before they could reach the body they had to remove a pram and a gas cylinder, which had also been put in the drain. Marie Kilmartin was still in the clothes she was last seen wearing at the Christmas party she had attended the previous December, with a three-quarter-length tweed coat, the buttons still fastened. Uncannily, the watch she was wearing began to work again when her body was removed from the drain. The state pathologist, Dr John Harbison, found that the cause of death was manual strangulation.

Within weeks of the discovery of Marie Kilmartin's body, two Co. Laois men were arrested and detained for questioning. Both were held for twelve hours but were released without charge. A file was not sent to the Director of Public Prosecutions, and the case remains unsolved. One man identified as a suspect—a former soldier living in Port Laoise—had previously given Marie a lift. He was unemployed at the time of the murder, and he had previously cut turf in the area where the body was discovered. His van was thoroughly searched during the investigation, but no evidence was found of any crime having been committed. A mobile home was also searched as part of the investigation, but nothing was found. Soon after being questioned by detectives, this suspect was admitted to hospital with chest pains. The murder file remains open, and this man remains a suspect.

Detectives working at the Operation Trace headquarters in Naas entered all the information relating to the murders of Antoinette Smith, Patricia Doherty and Marie Kilmartin in the OVID system, as well as the information on the murder of Phyllis Murphy—which would later be solved. There were no common features between the cases that would suggest that the cases were linked. The private feeling of many gardaí is that the murder of Marie Kilmartin is not linked to other unsolved cases, but that the murders of Antoinette Smith and Patricia Doherty may be linked.

Even if the same killers were not responsible for each murder, the proximity of the places where the bodies were left is suspicious. Detectives have also wondered whether one killer might have told another killer of an isolated spot where a body could be concealed. There are definitely two men responsible for the murder of Antoinette Smith, but it is not known how many people have information about Patricia Doherty's murder. The Gardaí are satisfied that Antoinette Smith did not know the men who murdered her. Detectives have long feared that the same pair might have struck again, perhaps abducting Annie McCarrick or Jo Jo Dullard, or that one or both of these killers may be responsible for unsolved sexual assaults in the greater Dublin area. But Operation Trace did not turn up any concrete evidence linking the three unsolved murders with any of the missing women.

The murder of a young woman in the foothills of the Dublin Mountains in July 1982 was also considered by members of Operation Trace. Nineteen-year-old Patricia Furlong was strangled near Glencullen, Co. Dublin, after she travelled there with friends to attend a festival. Nine years after this brutal murder a Dublin disc-jockey, Vincent Connell, was convicted of the murder. He later appealed against his conviction, challenging the admissions he was alleged to have made while in custody. His conviction was quashed in April 1995; but he was later convicted of assaulting four former girl-friends, all of whom made complaints to the Gardaí about his violent tendencies. Connell was given a suspended sentence, and he emigrated to England, where he died of a heart attack in 1998, while continuing to protest his innocence of the murder of Patricia Furlong.

Though the murder of Patricia Furlong occurred sixteen years before the establishment of Operation Trace, detectives were still conscious that officially the case remains unsolved, and that there was a distinct possibility that Patricia Furlong's murderer was still free. It was also on the minds of many detectives that this victim was strangled close to where the missing American woman Annie McCarrick was seen at Johnnie Fox's pub in Glencullen in March 1993. Could Patricia Furlong's killer have struck again in the same general area eleven years afterwards? If so, why did he go to the extreme lengths of hiding her body?

As well as examining the unsolved murders that might fit the profile of a serial killer, detectives from Operation Trace considered whether there were any other missing women who might have fallen prey to a random attacker. It was later felt that one case not included in the original six of Operation Trace should be analysed thoroughly. Though the age profile did not fit that of the other missing women, the timing and place of the disappearance of Eva Brennan in July 1993 was too significant to be ignored.

Eva Brennan, who looked younger than her thirty-nine years, was last seen alive on 25 July 1993, when she angrily left her parents' house at Rathdown Park, Terenure, Dublin, after a minor argument. She had looked in the oven and said something like, 'Oh, no, not lamb again,' and one of her brothers had responded, 'If you don't want it you don't have to stay.' It was a trivial dispute, the kind that happens every day; but Eva Brennan left the house and walked down Templeogue Road towards her own apartment at Madison Avenue in Rathgar. The Gardaí are satisfied she arrived safely, as a raincoat she had been wearing was in the apartment when it was later checked; but her handbag, keys and bus pass were missing. It was almost a week after she went missing that her family reported her disappearance. In an effort to do everything they could to assist the Gardaí, they told them she had suffered on and off from depression since she was a teenager. Detectives at first feared she had gone off by herself and might have done herself harm. Eva's sister, Collette McCann, believes the answer may be more sinister.

I know that Eva left my parents' house in a huff, and she had had depression before, but you don't just disappear; you don't just vanish. And if you do something to harm yourself, how do you hide your own body? You have to look at other things going on at the time to really think about what might have happened. Eva disappeared just twelve weeks after Annie McCarrick was abducted and murdered. Eva could very well have gone for a walk that Sunday afternoon to cool off or clear her head, and before she knew anything a car had stopped and she'd been attacked. Her attacker wouldn't have known about Eva's previous bouts of depression: he wasn't being selective. We simply don't know; but when I initially asked a senior officer why Eva's case wasn't part of Operation Trace he said something like 'It's not my jurisdiction.'

Eva's a missing woman, last seen on a Sunday afternoon in a well-populated suburb of south Dublin. Surely that's a matter of concern for any right-thinking person. Eva's remains are most probably in the Dublin Mountains. I know Eva is quite happy now, giving God a sore ear with all her yapping. I just wish the Gardaí could do more to find her and the other missing people.

The OVID computer system, which compared Eva Brennan's disappearance with those of the other missing women, did so in a non-judgmental way. It wasn't concerned with whether she suffered from depression or not: it was merely trying to establish whether any of Eva's habits or acquaintances might have cropped up in any other investigations. No such links were established.

There was no suspect in connection with Eva Brennan's disappearance. A man from Co. Donegal who had met her at a prayer group was tracked down, but he had no information for the Gardaí. A former boy-friend was found in Liverpool, but he also had no information. Detectives who worked on the case looked at the convicted double killer Michael Bambrick as a possible suspect. He was not caught until May 1994, when his daughter told detectives about her father's violent behaviour. Bambrick later admitted killing two missing women—his wife, Patricia McGauley, in September 1991 and Mary Cummins in July 1992. Both victims were killed at Bambrick's home in Ronanstown, Dublin. The fact that he had not known his second victim until hours before he killed her made the Gardaí wonder whether he might be able to assist them in finding Eva Brennan. But this line of inquiry led nowhere.

As detectives continued to assimilate thousands of pieces of information and to enter it in the OVID system, a number of violent convicted criminals contacted the Gardaí claiming to have information about some of the missing women. Over the following months detectives would find themselves in communication with criminals in Ireland, England and Canada who claimed to know something about one or more of the cases. Frustratingly, just like the hoax calls that came from members of the public, each of the criminals had concocted an elaborate story of lies, a figment of their disturbed imagination. Yet the Gardaí are acutely aware that some of those people who made up stories about abducting and murdering women are capable of acting out such violent deeds. One of them was a young man from Athlone who would later be jailed for twelve years for one of the most shocking crimes to be committed in Ireland in recent times.

At the time this teenage criminal contacted detectives from Operation Trace he was serving a prison sentence and was also being treated at the Central Mental Hospital in Dundrum, Dublin. He claimed that a man he knew was responsible for at least one of the disappearances of women in Leinster. Detectives met the man, and he eventually named two sites at which they might find some evidence. He was taken to Athlone to pinpoint the places where the evidence might lie. Looking back now, one detective told me that at first this man had a lot of people convinced he had solid information.

This young man was having psychiatric difficulties, but he had concocted an elaborate tale, and it was one that initially swayed a lot of people, from prison officers to gardaí. This man named another man who he said had harmed at least one of the missing women. On foot of this information we searched an area of land near Clara in Co. Offaly and at Creggan bog, just outside Athlone. Sure when we brought this fellow down to Athlone to help us pinpoint where we should be looking, all he wanted to do was see his donkeys that he had down there. He led us on a merry dance; but based on what he did later on he is not only a fantasist but a very dangerous man.

It was in June 2001 that this young criminal proved he was capable not only of fantasising about evil deeds but of carrying them out. Though the victim in this case was a young man, the circumstances of the assault prove that fantasists can become killers.

In June 2001 the young Athlone criminal had recently been released from prison. Detectives from Operation Trace were satisfied by this time that he had no credible information that would help them in their search for missing women. In the early hours of the morning of 30 June 2001 he abducted at knife-point a seventeen-year-old youth who had travelled into Athlone to buy chips. He sat behind the terrified teenager on his parked scooter and forced him to drive first to Moate, then to Clara, and eventually to Creggan bog, off the Athlone–Dublin road. The teenager was forced to push his bike out of view of the roadside and was then frogmarched further into a remote part of the bog. The criminal forced his petrified victim to take off his runners and his football jersey, which was used to gag him. His hands were chained behind his back with the chain from the scooter, and his feet were tied together with the laces from his runners. The criminal then pushed his victim into a bog-hole, and pushed the scooter in on top of him. As the teenager fought to keep his head above the water his attacker said to him: 'Goodbye, and good luck.'

Sergeant Seán Leydon and Garda Brian Lee were on patrol around Athlone that night when they noticed the criminal loitering on the street. The young man was well known to both gardaí, and they were aware that he was back on the streets after serving a prison sentence in Dublin. As they approached him to assess what he was doing out so late at night he said to them, 'I've done it this time. Now you'll believe me.' Within seconds the young man was confessing that he had left a teenager bound and gagged in a bog-hole.

The story shocked the two gardaí, who asked the criminal to show them where he had committed this crime. When they arrived at the scene, only the victim's face was above the water, but they managed to pull him to safety. One of this criminal's first questions for the gardaí when he was arrested was 'How long will I get for this?' In July 2002 the now 22-year-old criminal was jailed for twelve years for false imprisonment, reckless endangerment, and assault. His young victim was too upset to give evidence in court.

This episode graphically reminded the Gardaí that while some people who contacted Operation Trace might have concocted stories because they were attention-seekers, there was still the possibility that some of them might one day try to act out their sick fantasies.

Another extremely violent man who contacted the Operation Trace team with false information was a convicted child serial killer in Canada. The first time detectives came across the name Clifford Robert Olson was when a sergeant at Baltinglass Garda Station in Co. Wicklow answered the phone one day to find himself speaking directly to one of the most dangerous men alive. From his prison cell in Québec, Olson had managed to obtain access to information on the internet about the Garda operation to find Ireland's missing women. He concocted an elaborate tale, saying that a now deceased friend of his, Colin Miller, had murdered five women in Ireland.

Detectives at first kept an open mind about Olson's claims, but eventually they ruled out his 'information' as nothing more than twisted fantasy. The fact that Olson is serving a life sentence for murdering eleven children in Canada in the late 1970s and early 80s had at first made the Gardaí sit up and listen. Here was a self-confessed serial killer claiming to be in a position to solve the mystery of certain missing women in Ireland. His own crimes had caused waves of panic in the Vancouver area before he was caught and jailed in January 1982. In a deal that later caused widespread debate, Olson was paid by the Canadian authorities to identify the unmarked graves of the children he had murdered. The money was not paid directly to Olson but was put in trust for members of his family. The arrangement sparked intense debate about whether killers should be rewarded for giving such information. The Canadian police were satisfied in the knowledge that the recovery of the children's bodies brought some form of relief for the devastated families, while Olson would never again set foot out of jail. However, the deals negotiated by Olson allowed him to obtain access to the outside world by way of the telephone and the internet; and so years later, when he saw an opportunity to cause mischief, he was able to make contact with the Gardaí without any difficulty.

Clifford Olson claimed he knew where the bodies of five missing women were. He claimed that the five women—whom he named—were buried in Co. Kildare. But he wanted to be brought over to Ireland to find the bodies, something the Gardaí were not prepared to contemplate. One detective told me that Olson wasted a lot of their time.

This Olson fellow is a serious killer, an evil man, but he also lives in a fantasy world. He learnt about our operation through the internet and newspapers, and then he tried to get in the middle of it. He's tried it before with other countries as well.

He claimed he could get us photographs of the locations where bodies were buried, but he would have to be brought over. Can you imagine us flying this serial killer over from Canada on a whim? He tried it on with police in Seattle and Hawaii, and in England too, claiming he knew information about murders and other crimes. He led us a merry dance for a little while, but because he had killed at least eleven children we were taking great notice of him; but he was lying all the way.

Detectives with Operation Trace travelled to meet a prisoner in Britain who also contacted them with information about missing women in Ireland. As with the conversations with the young Athlone criminal and with Clifford Olson, the 'information' this person had amounted to nothing.

As the Gardaí examined the files of all known sex offenders who might be capable of killing their victims, the name of one man came strongly to the fore. Already a suspect in the murder of a teenage girl who disappeared in Northern Ireland, he would later be charged with murdering another teenage girl in London in April 2001. This man is a recidivist criminal who previously served a ten-year sentence for raping an elderly woman in Co. Cork in 1974. He had broken into the woman's house and subjected her to a prolonged attack before robbing her. He was later convicted of raping a young girl and given a three-year sentence in 1995. This criminal also has a number of convictions for robbery, and in between his many spells in prison he has lived in Ireland, Scotland, and England. He was earmarked as a suspect for the murder of a teenage girl in Northern Ireland early on in the investigation but was not charged, and he later travelled to Scotland and then to London. That girl's body has never been recovered.

During the 1990s he returned to Ireland and spent time in a number of places in the midlands and the south-east. He was known to the Gardaí as a convicted rapist, but he was not identified with any crimes in the Republic during the 1990s. However, it is now believed that in April 2001, after returning to England, he murdered another teenage girl, this time a fourteen-year-old. Her body was found at a cement factory in March 2002, and shortly afterwards the man was charged with her murder. The Gardaí, RUC and English police met in Dublin for a day-long conference, at which they discussed their information relating to this extremely violent man.

The man's first conviction, for housebreaking, was in 1957, when he was thirteen years old, and he was sent to St Joseph's School for Boys in Clonmel. He later spent time in other detention centres for young offenders, at Daingean, Co. Offaly, and St Patrick's Institution, Dublin. He was thirty in 1974 when he raped the elderly woman in Co. Cork. It is now believed that twenty years later the man killed his first murder victim, a teenage girl. The fact that in the mid to late 1990s this violent man later travelled by ferry between Ireland and Britain a number of times has not been lost on detectives investigating the cases of missing women in Ireland. However, trying to establish where exactly he was at the time of each disappearance has been a massive task. He remains a suspect in relation to a number of the disappearances, most notably those of Annie McCarrick and Jo Jo Dullard. He is a suspect, however, not because he was seen in the vicinity of those abductions but because he is now believed to have killed two teenage girls in different countries.

While this man was already known to the Gardaí by the time Operation Trace was set up, other violent men had not yet come to their attention. The crimes for which they were later jailed were attacks on women that shocked the detectives who investigated them. While the name of Larry Murphy from Baltinglass, Co. Wicklow, is the most prominent of those who have been convicted of abducting and raping women in recent times, there are other men who have been put behind bars for similar crimes, and one thing they all have in common is that they have no previous convictions. But for the courage of the rape victims in coming forward with their harrowing tales, coupled with the dogged determination of detectives in pursuing them, these criminals would still be as 'clean as a whistle.'

In September 2000, nineteen-year-old Daniel Moynihan from Raheen East, Rathmore, Co. Kerry, set out in his car posing as a hackney driver. He headed for Killarney, where he began driving around. In the early hours of the morning two young women got into the car, thinking it was a hackney cab. Moynihan drove one woman to her intended destination and then set off towards where the other young woman wanted to go. However, instead of driving to the woman's home he drove to an isolated spot, where he raped her. He later brought her to another place, where he attacked her again. When he was arrested he told the Gardaí he was glad he was caught and had 'wished to be found out.' He was later jailed for twelve years after admitting two charges of raping the woman, with the final two years of the sentence being suspended because he pleaded guilty.

Another violent young man who is now serving a lengthy prison sentence for abducting and sexually assaulting a woman is Thomas Callan from Shanmullagh, Carrickmacross, Co. Monaghan. He was twenty-one when he abducted a seventeen-year-old girl, who he put in the boot of his car in Carrickmacross in June 1999. After abducting the terrified teenager he drove her to a secluded area outside the town, where he sexually assaulted her and tried to rape her. It would later emerge that this was not the first time Callan had tried to abduct a girl. In February 1999 he approached a fourteen-year-old girl in Carrickmacross and tried to force her to go to an isolated spot, but she managed to flee. In May 2001 Callan was sentenced to ten years' imprisonment for his attack on the seventeen-year-old and to four years for falsely imprisoning the fourteen-year-old. As he passed sentence, Mr Justice Paul Carney remarked that this was the second case in a month in which he had to sentence a violent man who had abducted a woman and put her in the boot of his car. The other man was Larry Murphy.

There has been a great deal of speculation about what information Larry Murphy might have about a number of unsolved crimes. The now separated father of two is serving a fifteen-year sentence for abducting, repeatedly raping and attempting to murder a 28-year-old Carlow woman in February 2000. Murphy disarmed her by punching her full in the face, fracturing her nose. He was trying to kill his victim in a remote woodland area in Co. Wicklow when two men came upon the scene, and Murphy fled. Detectives investigating the disappearance of women in Leinster have studied Murphy's case in an effort to find new leads. Like Daniel Moynihan in Co. Kerry and Thomas Callan in Co. Monaghan, Larry Murphy had no previous convictions and therefore did not feature in the OVID data-base when it was set up by Operation Trace. The difference between Murphy and the other two men is that he was seemingly a happily married man, while the other two were single. Murphy was thirty-five when he carried out the heinous crime for which he was convicted. He was twenty-eight when Annie McCarrick disappeared in March 1993; he was thirty when Jo Jo Dullard disappeared in November 1995; he was thirty-three when the Droichead Nua teenager disappeared in July 1998, and he had been working in the area at the time.

After he was arrested and charged with raping and attempting to murder the Carlow woman in February 2000, Murphy's car was scientifically examined to see if any information relating to any other crimes might be found, but nothing came of this. When two senior gardaí visited Murphy in Arbour Hill Prison he told them he had no information about missing women. When he was given his fifteen-year prison sentence the last year was suspended because he pleaded guilty. Murphy will be in his late forties when he walks out of prison a free man.

Another name that did not feature on Garda files when Operation Trace was set up in September 1998 was that of Thomas O'Connor, who at the time was working as a curator at Dublin Civic Museum. By the time Operation Trace was set up, O'Connor, a married man with two children from Rock Road, Booterstown, Co. Dublin, was already subjecting a number of women to a reign of terror by threatening them over the phone and sending them obscene packages through the post. O'Connor picked on at least nine single women and widows and threatened them that they would meet the same fate as Annie McCarrick and Jo Jo Dullard. He terrorised the women by phoning them anonymously, grunting and groaning into the phone, and ordering them to hang their underwear out their windows. One woman reported receiving a letter with faeces on it. O'Connor sent one of his victims a news-paper headline, 'Theory of serial killer rejected.'

The Gardaí in south Co. Dublin had been pursuing the unidentified stalker for five years before Thomas O'Connor was caught in February 2001 as he stalked the house of one of his victims. In July 2002 he was jailed for three years. He told the

Gardaí he had stalked his victims because he loved the control he had over the women and the fear he could put them under. Detectives, conscious of O'Connor's references to missing women during his reign of terror, conducted a thorough examination of his previous life. No information could be found to suggest that he had ever met any of the missing women.

Detectives investigating the disappearance of women in Leinster were always conscious that a killer might have travelled from Britain or elsewhere to commit crimes in Ireland. A recent example of the transient nature of some violent offenders is the fifty-year-old Englishman who was charged in January 2002 with raping a woman in Bantry, Co. Cork. This man, who was living under an alias, is wanted by the English police for questioning about the murder of a 23-year-old woman in Norwich in October 2001. The body of Hayley Curtis was found buried in a shallow grave along a lay-by in Hampshire in January 2002 by a couple out walking their dog. She had been reported missing by her family only two months after she disappeared, as she had been known to go missing by herself before. The English police believe that the man who was arrested in Ireland in January 2002 after the alleged rape in Cork might be the last person to see Hayley Curtis alive. An examination of this man's history has not revealed any links with any of Ireland's missing women.

This case is just one example of murders committed in other jurisdictions being considered by the gardaí investigating Ireland's 'missing, presumed murdered' cases. As one senior garda put it, 'Criminals do not respect borders.'

The work of Operation Trace involved both a reassessment of the original investigations and the following up of new lines of inquiry.

More than five thousand people were interviewed and four thousand statements taken, leading to more than seven thousand lines of inquiry. The detectives looked at every conceivable motive that might link some or all of the cases; they looked at the different months in which the women disappeared, the days of the week, and the time of day. The phases of the moon were even assessed and logged to see if any link might be established. A number of searches were carried out in Leinster, Connacht and Ulster, some of them at the request of the families of the missing women. Sniffer dogs trained in Britain were used to search fields and bogs. Detectives used metal probes, which they stuck deep into the ground at the various sites; these were then assessed by the sniffer dogs to see if anything suspicious might be buried there. But nothing was found.

A number of graveyards were also looked at, to see whether any efforts might have been made to hide bodies there. In the investigation into the disappearance of two of the missing women—Fiona Pender and Fiona Sinnott—the idea had already been raised that the bodies of the women might have been hidden in graveyards, but detectives could find no evidence of this. Old graveyards were also looked at as possible places where killers might try to hide their tracks. One detective told me they once thought they had found such a grave.

It happened that a 'psychic' came and told us that she could see some image of an old graveyard in west Dublin, and she named one of the missing women and said she had a feeling she might be there. Officially we can't just act on somebody's feeling, but we looked at the graveyard, and we thought that it would definitely be a location that could conceivably hold some evidence. We did a cursory look around the graveyard. It was an old graveyard, and we found evidence of soil disturbance. We found finger bones, and we immediately sealed off the area. However, a forensic examination of the area revealed that the bones were old bones, the remains of someone who had been buried there centuries before.

But it made us think, and we still look at that possibility. It's a terrible thing to contemplate, that someone would do such a thing, but that's what we're dealing with: killers who will go to extraordinary lengths to hide the evidence of their crimes.

By December 2001 Operation Trace had not established any clear links between any of the cases of missing women. With all conceivable lines of inquiry examined, the six gardaí on the Operation Trace team had begun to be reassigned to their original duties. The OVID data-base was closed and is now locked in a room at the Carlow-Kildare Divisional Headquarters in Naas, together with all the files on the missing women. But the investigations into the missing women are still continuing at individual Garda stations, and members of the Operation Trace team still reassemble to investigate any leads that suggest that two or more cases might be linked.

Detectives from Operation Trace were in attendance at the Central Criminal Court in October 2002 as a jury unanimously found John Crerar guilty of the murder of Phyllis Murphy in December 1979. Unlike the cases that Operation Trace was assigned to examine, the discovery of Phyllis Murphy's body had given the Gardaí a crime scene, from which the necessary evidence was gathered that would eventually lead to the case being solved twenty-three years later. Members of the Operation Trace team played a prominent role in the prosecution of Crerar, conducting a number of interviews, preparing the book of evidence, and keeping safe the clothing and other scientific evidence that other gardaí had held for more than twenty years. John Crerar had no previous convictions and was apparently a dedicated family man. Like Larry Murphy, he continues to be of considerable interest to the gardaí investigating a number of unsolved crimes, including the cases of missing women.

From the time Operation Trace was set up in September 1998 to the time it was decided to reassign members of the team to their original duties, no other women disappeared in sinister circumstances in Leinster. One detective believes there could be a number of reasons for this.

> To put it at its most simple, if there is a serial killer, or if there was a serial killer, he may just be lying low; he could be in prison serving a sentence for other crimes, as we suspect might be the case; he could have travelled abroad and is now living elsewhere; or he may be dead and has taken his evil secrets with him. The same analogy can apply to any of the cases, whether it's a serial killer or a once-off 'crime of passion' killer.

One detective who worked on Operation Trace pointed out that drawing assumptions about any of the cases is hazardous.

> If we could say for definite that such-and-such killed so-and-so, that would be the case solved. As it stands, we have three individual prime suspects in relation to the suspected abductions and murders of Fiona Pender, Ciara Breen, and Fiona Sinnott. And we have a number of hot suspects in relation to Jo Jo Dullard and the Newbridge teenager; and the same men would be in the frame for Annie McCarrick. But suspicion is one

thing, proof is something entirely different. They say, for example, that all serial killers are men who are loners and who start off stealing underwear from clothes-lines, and killing animals to see how they suffer. That analogy would be partly true of a man from Co. Laois, for example, who's facing murder charges in two other jurisdictions. But there's another man we are looking at who could be a serial killer who was the most courteous and friendly of men, a real family man, a 'boy next door'. Now he was having affairs with a number of women, so he wasn't totally clean, but he never ever showed a violent tendency towards any woman we could find who knew him. And then next thing he snaps and abducts, rapes and tries to kill a woman who was a total stranger to him. Serial killers— or killers in general—do not fit one profile.

Detectives who have investigated the cases of missing women believed to have been murdered are acutely conscious that having a prime suspect does not mean the case is solved. There is always the possibility that the prime suspect, while capable of killing, might not in fact have committed the crime. The Gardaí are mindful of one case from the 1970s in which a young woman had a row with her boy-friend and stormed off. A short time later she was abducted and murdered by a complete stranger. At first detectives looked at the boy-friend as a suspect, based on the ill-feeling between the two of them on the night the woman disappeared. From a prosecution point of view the boy-friend had a motive and opportunity. It was more than two months before the killer was caught, and the utterly distraught boy-friend was cleared of any suspicion.

There was also a case in the early 1980s in which a young woman was murdered by a married man she had met only that day.

By sheer coincidence she had earlier been in the company—unknown to her—of another sexual deviant. At first the Gardaí thought this man was the killer, but after a number of months they established that he wasn't and that it was the other, the 'upstanding' man, she had met later that day.

When the door was locked on the Operation Trace investigation room in December 2001 many gardaí privately felt that the detectives should have been left to continue their work full-time. There was always the possibility that the computer system was about to throw up a link between two or more of the disappearances. Perhaps the next piece of seemingly innocuous information to be given to a garda might unlock the mystery of where the bodies of the women lay. Other gardaí argue that all possible leads had been exhausted, and it was pointless to leave the detectives in a room in Naas with no more leads to work on.

The commitment of the gardaí who worked on Operation Trace could never be called into question. All of them worked long hours, often in their own time, in an effort to bring closure for the families of the missing women. Members of the Operation Trace team had many other successes in their careers, solving many murders and other serious crimes; but Operation Trace did not achieve what the public wanted it to achieve.

Was Operation Trace a failure? Certainly it failed to establish any links between any of the cases of missing women in Leinster; but there always remains the possibility that none of the cases are linked. The feeling of the Gardaí is that the abduction and murder of Annie McCarrick and Jo Jo Dullard may be linked, and the disappearance of the Droichead Nua teenager may be linked also; but the tens of thousands of pieces of information gathered by OVID failed to show any firm links. Many detectives feel that

Operation Trace was established too late, believing that something similar should have been operational soon after Jo Jo Dullard's disappearance and therefore before Fiona Pender, Ciara Breen, Fiona Sinnott or the Droichead Nua teenager had disappeared.

While Operation Trace failed to find the women's bodies, it did throw the spotlight on new suspects in a number of the cases. Nine people, including a number of women, were questioned during the operation, and investigations into the activities of these people continues. The Gardaí were always conscious that they were collating information relating to sexual deviants and violent men who were either already convicted or strongly suspected of carrying out attacks. There was always the possibility that those responsible for murdering the missing women had never come to the attention of the Gardaí. One detective, however, believes that most if not all of the names of the murder suspects are contained in OVID.

The list is still updated whenever another violent man is convicted in the courts. His details are fed into the data-base, and there are a number of such cases where seemingly upstanding members of the community, with no previous convictions, either admit or are convicted of some of the most heinous crimes this country has witnessed. We examine each of these individuals, and we are monitoring Northern Ireland and Britain as well. I think we have most of the names of the killers at this stage, but we just need that little bit extra: we need a wife or girl-friend to break the false alibi they have given to the killer, or we need a neighbour who saw what they thought was a body in someone's car or garage. We need something like that, something tangible to match with the names we have circled as suspected killers who are either at large or behind bars for other attacks.

Members of the team are still in regular contact to discuss certain suspects whose names cropped up repeatedly in their original investigation. They still get calls from fellow-gardaí around the country about men who may be responsible for the disappearance of women in Leinster. The number of phone calls and tip-offs from members of the public increases whenever any murder cases are reported. Whenever any fresh and credible leads are found, members of the Operation Trace team reassemble to investigate the information. OVID remains on stand-by in Naas Garda Station, but it needs to be fed.

It was the disappearance of the Droichead Nua teenager in July 1998 that sparked the intense concern by the public and the Gardaí that led to the establishment of Operation Trace. As well as a massive search by local gardaí of bogland, rivers, fields and roads around Co. Kildare and beyond, it was hoped that the Operation Trace team might be able to throw up a computer-generated lead that would bring the teenager home. Her disappearance is one of the most eerie occurrences this country has known, the eighteen-year-old apparently disappearing from the gate of her home in broad daylight. If, as is feared, she was abducted, it was one of the most audacious and most cruel crimes Ireland has known. But there is no proof that a crime was even committed, and that is what scares those closest to the case. Unlike other cases of people who have vanished without a trace, the response time of the Gardaí to this disappearance could not be faulted: the young woman was reported missing within hours of her disappearance, and extensive searches began the same night. This was far faster than any of the other missing women cases; and yet not a shred of evidence was found on the roadside, not one witness could be found who could throw light on what continues to be an agonising mystery for her parents.

In the years since then a number of possible suspects have been identified. Most of these violent men are in prison for other offences. Indeed, for whatever reason, this was to be the last such unexplained disappearance of a young woman in the 1990s.

7

Mary Boyle

❖

M ary Boyle is Ireland's youngest missing person; but her case is one of the oldest. Long before the disappearance of thirteen-year-old Philip Cairns in 1986, or the disappearance of women in the Leinster area in the 1990s, something terrible and so far unexplained happened to little Mary Boyle. Six years old, going on seven, she vanished in March 1977 at Cashelard, near Ballyshannon, on the southern tip of Co. Donegal.

What happened to the little girl who was last seen eating a packet of sweets? It's a heartbreaking question that her parents, Ann and Charlie Boyle, her twin sister, Ann, and older brother, Patrick, still ask every day. It's a case that has touched the hearts of the gardaí who worked on the original investigation, all of them now retired.

There are only two possible explanations for Mary Boyle's disappearance. Did a desolate patch of marshy ground swallow up the little girl? Or is there a more sinister answer? Was she abducted from the quiet Donegal countryside that Friday afternoon? Is there a person in Co. Donegal or beyond who is responsible for Mary's disappearance? Whatever the reason for her disappearance, why has no trace of her been found a quarter of a century later?

Mary Boyle disappeared seven years after the murder of ten-year-old Bernadette Connolly, who was abducted thirty miles away in Collooney, Co. Sligo. Bernadette's body was found four months after her disappearance in a bog drain in Co. Roscommon. Mary Boyle and Philip Cairns remain Ireland's only long-term missing children who are still the subject of intense Garda investigations.

Everyone who knows anything of the story of the missing girl has a hypothesis; but no-one has an answer. The gardaí who worked on the case believe the key to this mystery lies somewhere in south Co. Donegal.

Mary Boyle's uncle and godfather Gerry Gallagher is the last known person to see Mary. It was about 3:30 on the afternoon of Friday 18 March 1977, and he was carrying a ladder back to the house of his neighbour, Patrick McCawley, in the quiet countryside of Cashelard, three miles north-east of Ballyshannon. His little niece followed at a distance, her black wellington boots occasionally getting stuck in the mud along the isolated laneway between the Gallagher and McCawley houses. The walk was only about 450 yards but was over marshy ground. No cars could travel along this laneway. Its main use was as a short-cut between the Gallaghers and their nearest neighbours.

Gerry Gallagher chatted with his niece as they walked, but the conversation was stilted, because he was carrying a heavy ladder and Mary couldn't keep up with her uncle's big strides. About seventy yards from the end of the journey, Gerry, with the ladder over his shoulder, made his way through mud up to six inches deep. Mary, who was only 3 feet 11 inches tall, hesitated. She pointed over her uncle's shoulder and asked him if he was going up to that house in front of them. He said he was, and he saw her turn back in the direction of his own house, from where they had begun their short walk. He turned to continue his journey. Mary Boyle would not be seen again.

Mary Boyle was three months short of her seventh birthday when she disappeared. She was a bubbly character, a chatterbox, always smiling for photographs. She was wearing her favourite lilac-coloured hand-knitted cardigan, and her brown jeans were tucked into her black wellington boots when she disappeared. She was born on 14 June 1970 at the Sorrento Maternity Hospital in Birmingham to Ann and Charlie Boyle, both natives of Co. Donegal. Shortly after Mary's arrival her twin sister, Ann Theresa, was born. Twins run in both Ann's and Charlie's families, but the arrival of beautiful twin girls bowled the proud parents over.

A quarter of a century later I met Ann and Charlie Boyle in their home in Burtonport on the west coast of Co. Donegal. This is the home they were in the process of building in 1977 when they lost their little daughter. But in one way Mary is in the house: she smiles down on visitors from a large photograph above Charlie's seat. It's a photograph of the three Boyle children: the twin sisters and their brother, Patrick, taken just before March 1977.

Though Ann and Charlie Boyle are both natives of Co. Donegal, they met and married in Birmingham. Ann grew up on a farm at Cashelard, near Ballyshannon, where Mary was to disappear years later. Charlie Boyle was an island man, from Owey Island, one of the many small islands that dot the western coast of Co. Donegal. He left school at fourteen, and in the late 1950s, hearing tales of money to be made on building sites in England, he left Owey Island and his beloved Co. Donegal to make his living as one of the large Irish community in Birmingham. One of his five brothers was already in Birmingham, and within a short time Charlie was working as one of Birmingham's youngest builders. At a dance in Birmingham he met Ann Gallagher from Cashelard, and in 1967 they were married. Two years later Ann gave birth to their first child, Patrick, in Birmingham, and on 14 June 1970 Mary and Ann were born.

Looking back on their time in Birmingham, Ann and Charlie Boyle find it sad and ironic that a conscious choice they made about their family's future was to lead inadvertently to a terrible event in their home country. Charlie told me it was his choice that the family should return to Co. Donegal.

> There was this drugs problem developing in Britain in the early 1970s. Birmingham had been good to us, but we wanted our children to be safe, and to have a good future. Ann actually wanted the family to go to America, but I wanted to go home. I love the sea, the water; I missed it so much when we were in England. I'd been away from Ireland many, many years before I met Ann. And so we brought the family home to Donegal.

In 1972 they said goodbye to their friends in Birmingham and brought three-year-old Patrick and the two-year-old twins home to Co. Donegal. Five years later, Mary Boyle would disappear.

On 17 March 1966, while Ann Gallagher was living in Birmingham, one of her older brothers, Patrick, aged thirty-two, was killed in a tractor accident at the family farm at Cashelard Lower, three miles north-east of Ballyshannon. It was the second calamity to hit the Gallagher family: Ann's eldest brother, John, had died when he was three months old. Patrick's death left seven siblings: Lily, Michael, Alice, Anthony, Gerry, Ann, and Bríd.

After returning from Birmingham, the Boyle family first settled on Owey Island, from where Charlie had left for England two decades before. He began working as a fisherman, and the Boyles fitted in perfectly in the closely knit island community. There were fifteen or twenty people on the island at this time, with the mainland towns of Anagaire, Cionn Caslach and Burtonport just a short distance away. Owey Island gave the Boyle children a wonderful open playground of streams, fields, old walls, hidden nooks, and crannies, all within a short distance of their home. Ann Boyle told me that while living on Owey Island, Mary was the most cautious of the three.

> There was a small river on Owey Island where Patrick and Ann would run across a small pathway to get to the other side of the river. The pathway was a couple of feet wide, but Mary was so cautious that she lay on the pathway and crawled from one side to the other. She was very careful when out playing, but she never wanted to be left out either.

The family later moved a few miles to the mainland, first living in Burtonport, then Belcruit, near Cionn Caslach, while they began building a house in Burtonport. In March 1977 the future was bright, and Patrick, Mary and Ann Boyle were all in primary school and full of wonder and adventure. The three children naturally became excited when they were told they were going to visit their Granny and Granddad Gallagher, Uncle Gerry and Auntie Eva and cousins Gregory and Gerard in Cashelard. They were to leave Cionn Caslach on 17 March and travel the forty miles down to Cashelard to a memorial Mass for Patrick Gallagher junior, who had died eleven years before. They were to stay over and travel home the next day. Though the reason for the visit was a sad occasion, it was also an opportunity to visit loved ones.

Early on St Patrick's Day 1977 the five set off in the family car from Belcruit down the coast, through Dunglow, the Glenties, Donegal, on to Ballyshannon, and up to Cashelard.

Ballyshannon lies at the southern tip of Co. Donegal. The seaside resort of Bundoran is a couple of miles south-west; Finner Camp, along the coast just west of Ballyshannon, is another prominent feature. Cashelard is three miles north-east of Ballyshannon, close to the border town of Belleek, Co. Fermanagh.

The Gallagher house in Cashelard is on a hill, with access by a narrow laneway. Today it is in ruins. The gateway, about eight hundred yards down to the right, is tied up. The house can be reached only on foot, over a rusty gate and up an overgrown incline. The nearest neighbours are still the McCawleys. Their house is not visible from the Gallagher house but is up to the right, over a wall and up the isolated laneway that holds the secret of what happened to Mary Boyle. Beyond the McCawleys' house, also out of view, is a narrow roadway that can lead to the right and to the border and Belleek or to the left and a turn back to Ballyshannon.

On the afternoon of 18 March 1977 Ann Boyle, her sister-in-law Eva Gallagher and her mother, Lizzie Gallagher, were in the kitchen. Charlie Boyle was chatting with his father-in-law, Patrick Gallagher. Mary's twin sister and her brother were playing outside with their cousins Gregory and Gerard to the left of the house, towards the forested area about thirty yards away. Gerry Gallagher was working at the front of the house, doing odd jobs at a wall.

A quarter of a century after Mary Boyle's disappearance her mother broke down when she told me of her memories of that terrible day.

We had travelled down to Cashelard on the seventeenth of March 1977 for the memorial Mass for my brother Patrick. We stayed over in the house in Cashelard where I grew up. My mother and father were living there, and my brother Gerry, and his wife, Eva, and their two sons, Gregory and Gerard. In the early afternoon of Friday the eighteenth of March 1977 we had our dinner in the house. I remember clearly we arranged it that the adults sat at one table and the kiddies sat at another table beside us. So we had our dinner; and the children went outside and we were clearing up after dinner. The kids were playing out to the left of the house as you go outside the door. We could hear their voices. I remember my father saying something like 'Is those kids all right?' I was sweeping the floor and I remember he said it again. I said, 'I'll check. I'll look out.' I looked out and could see Paddy and Ann and Gregory and Gerard in a field. I asked them if they'd seen Mary, and one of them said, 'We haven't seen her since dinner time.' Immediately I had this terrible feeling.

What happened over the next couple of moments was a scene of utter panic. Ann Boyle knew immediately that something was wrong. Even before a search was under way, she knew something was wrong.

Once the kids said they hadn't seen Mary, I went back into the house in a terrible state. Charlie said to me that he was sure she would be found in a minute. But I just had this feeling. I said to my mother that if she had a blessed candle in the house she should light it. I got some holy water and shook it out around the house as well. Then I thought of the well close to the house. I ran out there to make sure Mary hadn't fallen in there. There was no sign of her there. I started shouting, screaming her name. I remember telling my brother Gerry and his wife, Eva, that Mary was nowhere to be seen. Gerry immediately ran off in the direction of our nearest neighbours, the McCawleys. I was in a total panic. I remember Daddy saying to me, 'Stop that shouting, Ann. The neighbours will hear you.' But I just knew something was terribly wrong. I just had this feeling. The others thought that perhaps Mary was around somewhere and would be back shortly. Then Gerry arrived back at the house from the McCawleys' and said Mary had followed him when he was leaving the ladder back to the McCawleys. Gerry had retraced those steps to the McCawleys' house, but Mary was nowhere to be seen.

Gerry Gallagher is the last person known to have seen Mary Boyle. In the panic that engulfed him and the rest of the family after it became apparent that Mary was missing he had run back immediately towards the McCawleys' house. When he couldn't find her he ran back to the house and told Ann and Charlie that Mary had followed him earlier that day when he was bringing the ladder back to Patrick McCawley. It was a story he was to relive again and again.

After finishing his dinner, Gerry Gallagher had gone outside the house and picked up a ladder from the front yard to bring back to his neighbour, who had lent it to him earlier. He set off over a wall and over a rough, hilly pass of marshy ground, along a broken track that acted as a short-cut to his neighbours' house. Mary saw her uncle head off with the ladder and decided to follow him. Her brother, sister and two cousins were playing nearby, but Mary wanted to go on a walk, following her uncle. The walk takes only a couple of minutes.

Mary and her uncle spoke to each other as they walked, but it was difficult to have a proper talk, because he was carrying a large ladder over rough terrain and was some distance ahead of his niece. Eating her sweets, Mary followed him at a distance, her black wellington boots getting ever more muddy as she continued on her latest adventure. It was about 3:30 p.m.

About seventy yards from the McCawleys' house Gerry Gallagher came upon a muddy patch in a laneway where the depth of mud would cover an adult's wellingtons up to six inches. Mary saw the muddy patch and hesitated. She could see the McCawleys' house and asked her uncle if that was where he was going. It was at this point that he saw her turn back in the direction of her grandparents' home. He continued on the last leg of his journey with the ladder, and stayed about twenty minutes chatting with Patrick McCawley. It was now about 4 p.m.

Ann Gallagher had grown up in the same house, and so she knew the surrounding area, the nooks and crannies, like the back of her hand. Once she realised that one of her daughters was missing, and despite her panic, she was able to think of the likely danger areas if Mary had wandered off.

> I immediately thought of Lough Colm Cille, which is some dis-
> tance from the back of the house. I ran down there in a total
> panic. I remember there were three men out on a boat on the
> lake and I called out to them to see if they had seen a wee girl.
> They said they hadn't, and that a man had just asked them the
> same thing. I saw Gerry: he had thought of the same thing and
> had gone down to the water too. I asked the men if they could
> contact the Gardaí for us. We had no phone in the house. The
> men said they would call the Gardaí in Ballyshannon.

The men Ann Boyle spoke to that afternoon did not hesitate in contacting the Gardaí. This was the era before mobile phones; the nearest phone was about half a mile away. On of the men, 'Happy Harry' Coughlin, knew a lot of local people. He made his way to a phone and contacted the Gardaí in Ballyshannon. Garda records show the call being made at about 6:30 p.m., some two-and-a-half hours after Mary was last seen by her uncle Gerry.

The three men in the boat on Lough Colm Cille that day were to become important witnesses in the Garda investigation. Harry Coughlin would later tell one detective that he and his two friends had had their eyes peeled for gardaí while they were poaching on the lake and so would have spotted any vehicles or people, or indeed would have heard any sounds out of the ordinary. The Gardaí knew that the three men watching and listening intently for any sudden or unexpected movements would have been the best witnesses to spot anything out of the ordinary. They heard nothing.

Inspector P. J. Daly at Ballyshannon Garda Station immediately took charge of the investigation. When the alarm was raised there were still some hours of daylight left. Conscious that the Boyle and Gallagher families had checked the main likely areas that Mary might have wandered off to, the gardaí took a decision immediately to call in an army helicopter from the nearby Finner Camp to help in the search. With the helicopter hovering over the mountainside, dozens of gardaí and local people combed the countryside around the Gallagher house. A drama festival under way in nearby Ballyshannon, and those involved, hearing that a little girl was lost or missing, came up to Cashelard to give a hand. As the hours went by, Ann and Charlie Boyle had terrible thoughts of their daughter lying injured somewhere close by.

As dusk turned to night, the search had to be called off until morning. It was just too dangerous to walk on the marshy, hilly ground in the dark.

In Ballyshannon Garda Station a discussion took place between a number of gardaí. Piecing together the information from Gerry Gallagher and Patrick McCawley, they saw there was a slight chance that instead of heading back towards her grandparents' home, Mary might have walked on past the McCawleys' house. This would have brought her to a quiet roadway that to the right would lead to Lough Colm Cille and to the left to another quiet country road. But it is likely that if she had walked this way, either Gerry Gallagher or Patrick McCawley, or both, would have seen her. Neither saw or heard anything during their conversation, which had lasted about twenty minutes. On the other hand, the 450 yards between the Gallagher and McCawley houses was searched by dozens of people that evening. There was no sign of Mary—not even a wrapper from the sweets she was eating when she set off to follow her uncle.

On hearing the first details of Mary Boyle's disappearance, and knowing the layout of the countryside, the Gardaí feared the worst. If she couldn't be found after a few hours' search over what was a relatively small area, perhaps she wasn't lying injured: perhaps she had been taken against her will. It was just a possibility, and twenty-five years later it is still just a possibility, though a realistic one. It was against this background that at 6 a.m. on 19 March 1977 the search was extended for miles around Cashelard.

The landscape around Cashelard is dotted with lakes, rivers, streams, ponds, bog-holes, and drains. All were searched in March and April 1977, and indeed many have been searched again since then. Nothing was ever found. As well as Garda divers, other divers came to lend a hand in the search. The Sligo Aqua Club, Ballyshannon Canoe Club and Bundoran Inshore Rescue Team searched the lakes and rivers. As well as Lough Colm Cille there were nearby Lough Uinsinn, Lough Aghvog, Lough Nagolagh, Lough Meenasallagh and Lough Atierna. It was exhausting work, but the divers were spurred on by the thoughts of a little girl lying alone somewhere, and her inconsolable parents hoping against hope.

Local alsatians were used as sniffer dogs in the search from the second day. It would have taken too long to get sniffer dogs up to Co. Donegal from the Garda Dog Unit in Dublin. The RUC across the border in Co. Fermanagh were also contacted. The Gardaí say that every river and lake was searched in the immediate locality. Every search that could be done was done.

In the days immediately after Mary Boyle's disappearance, Ann and Charlie Boyle were hoping that perhaps Mary might have wandered off the beaten track on her way back to her grandparents' house. Perhaps someone had picked her up wandering on the road and was just minding her. Ann Boyle told me she has many vivid memories of the following few weeks, but in other ways the memories are all jumbled together.

We stayed in Cashelard, and the house was packed tight with people. Charlie would be out helping in the search, and another brother of mine, Michael, was heavily involved in the search. I just felt so sad. Mary wouldn't have known the area. Cashelard was my home. Mary wouldn't have known where she was. Patrick and Ann were so upset. It was to affect Ann for a long time afterwards—her twin sister gone …

It was such a sad time for us, but we had such support from people. People came from as far as Co. Mayo and Co. Down to help search for Mary.

Within days, as the search of the Cashelard countryside was yielding nothing, the Gardaí decided to take a somewhat unorthodox approach. Conscious that Mary and her twin sister, Ann, were close, and with all other avenues yielding nothing, Detective-Garda Martin Collins and Detective-Garda Aidan Murray arranged a reconstruction, after informing the Boyle family. Aidan Murray recounted the tale as if it was yesterday, the strain of the unsolved mystery evident in his voice.

The last known sighting of Mary Boyle was by her uncle Gerry, about seventy yards from the McCawley house, in a quiet, muddy laneway, which would be about 370 or 380 yards from her own grandparents' house. And these are the only two houses in the immediate area. What we decided to do was to bring Mary's twin sister, Ann, on the same journey under the pretext of doing an errand or something like that. We thought that because they were twin sisters, and because we knew they were very close, that perhaps Ann might do whatever Mary had done, and might lead us to Mary. Maybe something would catch her eye and she would walk this way or that way. We had gardaí dotted around the laneway, so she was never in any danger. What we did was, Martin Collins walked with Ann towards the McCawleys' house, and at about the same location that Mary disappeared he said something like, 'Oh, Ann, I've forgotten such-and-such; could you run back to your Nana's and get it for me?' So Ann turned back to walk the same walk that Mary had walked—over marshy, bumpy land.

Now we were keeping a very close eye on Ann, but we were lying low, out of sight, trying to see if, being a twin, Ann might do the same as Mary had done, whatever that was. As she started to walk back towards her grandparents' house she couldn't see the house. There are some hills and trees in this area, you see. At one stage she stopped and seemed to sway, not knowing where the house was. Was it over this little hill or that one? But she got her bearings—and got back to the house. It was worth a shot, but nothing came of it.

The effect of Mary's disappearance on her twin sister and her brother was immediate and deeply saddening. Ann, especially, became much quieter. Her twin sister had been the more chatty one; often Mary would speak for Ann. Mary, Ann and Patrick had been on endless journeys and adventures in the fields and laneways around their homes on Owey Island and in Cionn Caslach and Burtonport. Now one of the three members of the gang was gone. Despite her own anguish, their mother noticed the effect on her two remaining children.

Both of them were badly affected. It got to the stage that you couldn't read Ann's writing any more. She didn't seem focused. She wouldn't talk. Mary wasn't talked about for a long time. We just couldn't. It was—it still is—heartbreaking. But we can talk now.

During the next few weeks the land around Cashelard and Ballyshannon was combed for clues. Hundreds of questionnaires were circulated in the Ballyshannon area. Five hundred people helped gardaí climb Behy Mountain and surrounding mountainous terrain around the Gallagher home.

The Gardaí also investigated whether any strangers had been in the area of Cashelard that Friday afternoon. There were no reports of any outsiders driving or walking in the area. The people who were attending the drama festival in Ballyshannon that weekend were also questioned, and their movements were traced, but nothing came of this either. While there had of course been visitors to the general Ballyshannon area that afternoon, no-one was seen up in Cashelard near the Gallagher home.

To put it at its simplest, there are only two possible explanations for the disappearance of a little girl on a quiet afternoon in Co. Donegal. Either she was abducted or she wandered into a part of the countryside where she accidentally met her death.

The landscape around Cashelard is dominated by marshy bogland. One of the first fears of gardaí and other searchers was that Mary might have become stuck in a marshy area and have fallen into a 'swallyhole'—a bog-hole that can become covered over with vegetation to give the illusion that it is firm ground. Such bog-holes can be up to twenty feet deep. However, over the weeks and months after Mary's disappearance gardaí searched every such bog-hole they could find around the Gallagher house. Nothing was found.

The missing child may have fallen into one of the rivers or lakes in the area; but each one was searched, and searched again. The Gardaí say they searched every inch of the surrounding countryside. One detective, in explaining the extent of the search, recounted a distressing tale of how the body of a boy had been found in the north-west many years before.

We had been searching the bogland for Mary, and we searched the water. We covered every inch of this bloody mountain. And then a senior officer remembered how a body of a young boy had been found in a tree. Yes, in a tree. This young fellow had disappeared maybe forty years before. It turned out he had been climbing a tree and had fallen into a hole in the tree. The

poor lad was identified by a medallion he wore. But it made us
think: feck, we're looking down all the time. What about
looking up? Even though Mary was only seven years old, and
wouldn't have been capable of climbing a tree in her wellies,
we hadn't been looking above our heads. We checked every
tree. Nothing was found. But it just shows you. Sometimes you
need to take a step back and think: are there any areas we're
not covering? I think we searched every inch of the area
around Cashelard. But it's over twenty-five years later, and still
nothing. If Mary was close to her home, I really believe we
should have, and would have, brought her home.

If Mary Boyle did not accidentally meet her death, somebody
abducted her. This possibility has caused much discussion within
the Gardaí, and a quarter of a century later there are questions still
to be fully answered about the movements of certain people that
day. No-one has ever been arrested in connection with Mary
Boyle's disappearance, but certain people have been questioned
intensively. And there is one man—a convicted killer of three
girls in Scotland and England—who the Gardaí would still like to
question.

One detective who served in the region for ten years before
Mary Boyle's disappearance told me the Gardaí first investigated
the movements of local men who would have been known as
potential suspects. All were ruled out.

There were at least six what you'd call perverts in the area,
around the Donegal-Sligo area. These were fellows who'd be
known to be unstable, and would have had convictions or
been accused of sexual attacks, mostly against women. None
had ever gone as far as abduction, but we of course checked

them out. We ruled them out early on. But I suppose these were only the fellows we knew about. At the back of our minds was the case of that poor girl Bernadette Connolly in Sligo in 1970. They never got to charge anyone for that abduction and murder, and we wondered if the same fellow was at work in Mary's case. We still don't know. But if Mary was taken against her will I think it's like that saying: 'Those who talk don't know, and those who know don't talk.'

If a local suspect could not be found, the other possibility, and one that remains to this day, is that a person from outside the locality, possibly a foreigner, abducted Mary Boyle. It is such speculation that has led to the name of one of Britain's most evil killers being linked with that of Mary Boyle. After an extensive investigation the Gardaí believe that on the day Mary Boyle disappeared a Scottish child-killer, Robert Black, then thirty years old, may have been travelling in Northern Ireland. An analysis of the employment records of the poster delivery company he worked for shows that he travelled from England to make deliveries at some time in the early part of 1977. He travelled by ferry to Northern Ireland and drove around the eastern part of the North delivering posters. Unfortunately the paper trail does not extend to showing whether or not he travelled as far west as the Co. Donegal border; but the fact that such a violent man—who would later abduct and murder three girls in Scotland and England—was travelling in Ireland in 1977 is something that the Gardaí have always had in their minds.

Robert Black, a native of a suburb of Edinburgh, is serving eleven life sentences in Britain for sexually assaulting and murdering three girls and kidnapping two others. By the time he had been given his first life sentence—for kidnapping and sexually assaulting a six-year-old girl in Scotland in July 1990—he had already kidnapped and killed at least three girls. It would be another four years before the full extent of these crimes would be revealed and his name would be linked with a number of unsolved cases of murdered and missing children, including that of Mary Boyle.

On 20 May 1994 Robert Black stood in the dock at Newcastle Crown Court as a jury found him guilty of murdering three girls. They had been abducted and murdered over a five-year period in the 1980s and their bodies hidden within an area 26 miles wide dubbed the 'Midlands Triangle', encompassing parts of the English counties of Nottinghamshire, Staffordshire, and Leicestershire. Black, a balding man with a thick beard, stood impassively as he was found guilty of the murder of eleven-year-old Susan Maxwell from Northumberland in 1982, five-year-old Caroline Hogg from Edinburgh in 1983, and ten-year-old Sarah Harper from Leeds in 1986. He was also convicted of kidnapping fifteen-year-old Teresa Thornhill in Nottingham in 1988.

Black was convicted after the jury was told of his previous conviction for sexually assaulting the six-year-old girl in 1990 and of circumstantial evidence that put him and his van at the scene of each of the abductions. He was given ten life sentences for the abduction, sexual assaults, and murders, to add to the life sentence he was already serving. As he was being led from the dock he turned to the police who had solved the three murders and said, 'Well done, boys.'

Robert Black was thirty-five when he killed eleven-year-old Susan Maxwell in 1982. The police in Newcastle, conscious that Susan might well not have been his first victim, began to make contact with police forces in a number of other countries, including the Gardaí in Co. Donegal.

At the time of Mary Boyle's disappearance Robert Black was thirty years old and was working as a long-distance delivery driver for a poster company. His work took him all over England, Scotland, and Northern Ireland. It is now believed that on the day of Mary Boyle's disappearance he was probably in Northern Ireland. There is no evidence that he was in the Republic on the day Mary disappeared, but a petrol receipt discovered by British police in 1994 shows that he bought petrol somewhere in the North in March 1977. Unfortunately the receipt does not give the exact date in March, but this fact, coupled with other information gathered by detectives, leads them to believe that Black was in Northern Ireland on 18 March. It would be another five years before he would abduct, sexually assault and murder eleven-year-old Susan Maxwell; but police in England now believe that by 1977 Black may already have killed two other girls in England—one in Norfolk in 1969 and another in Scunthorpe, Lincolnshire, in 1973. But in March 1977 nobody knew what Robert Black had done, or the terrible deeds he would later do. He was in a position to travel freely around Britain and Ireland and as far as France, which he is also known to have visited during the 1970s and 80s.

There are people in Co. Donegal who claim to have met Robert Black in the years before and after Mary Boyle's disappearance. He is reported to have travelled across the border to Anagaire and Dunglow, close to where Mary's family live today in Burtonport. Those who say they met him describe a strange but smiling and friendly man with a Scottish accent who drove a white van. After the meticulous piecing together by police in Britain of the movements of Robert Black since the early 1970s—using petrol receipts, delivery logs, shop receipts, and eye-witness accounts—it is the informed opinion of the Gardaí and police in the North that Robert Black was in Ireland in early 1977 and was most probably in the North the day Mary Boyle disappeared four or five miles from the border.

In July 1994 the Gardaí were invited to meet police in Newcastle to discuss the possibility that Robert Black might have been involved in the disappearance of Mary Boyle or in the murder of Bernadette Connolly in 1970. Inspector (later Superintendent) Michael Duffy and Detective-Sergeant Aidan Murray travelled from Ballyshannon to Newcastle to liaise with police from England and Scotland. On further investigation it was thought that Black was not a likely suspect for the abduction and murder of Bernadette Connolly. However, he was certainly a likely suspect in relation to Mary Boyle. A number of years later the Gardaí learnt of the reported sightings of Robert Black in the Dunglow area of Co. Donegal in 1976 and 78. Inspector Duffy decided that Black should be questioned about the disappearance of Mary Boyle.

> I retired from the force in 1998, but shortly before I did we received information from a number of people suggesting that Robert Black might have been around Anagaire and Dunglow in the 1970s. We always knew that we could put him over the border at around the time Mary disappeared, but now we had reports that he had been in this jurisdiction. I decided that we were in a position now to seek to question Robert Black about Mary's disappearance. I wrote to Garda Headquarters requesting that we be allowed travel to Britain and interview Black. I hadn't received a reply before I retired. I don't know where the request lies now. But I should say that, while I think Black should be interviewed about Mary, we never closed our minds to every other possibility.

Neither English nor Irish law allows the questioning of a prisoner about a crime without their consent, unless they are formally arrested. Many in the English police, seeking to solve other unsolved murders, believe that a 'carrot and stick' approach should be used in relation to Robert Black. As things stand, he will be eligible to apply for parole in 2029, when he will be eighty-two years old. Having exhausted every other line of inquiry, many think that a trade-off with Black, however unpalatable—granting parole when he is no longer physically capable of killing—might be the only way to find out whether he has any knowledge of other missing and murdered children.

Ann and Charlie Boyle are well aware of the name of Robert Black. They have heard the stories and read the newspaper articles, many of which have drawn conclusions, but without proof. For Ann and Charlie Boyle, if Black, or someone of his sort, was responsible for their daughter's disappearance, it is the not knowing that is the worst thing.

In 1978, a year after Mary Boyle disappeared, her grandfather Patrick Gallagher—Ann's father—died. Ann told me that within a short time the home she had grown up in became derelict.

> Daddy died in 1978. He was so upset at Mary's disappearance, and then we lost him. Mammy later came to live with us here in Burtonport. She was supposed to stay two weeks, and she ended up staying nine years. She had Alzheimer's when she died. My brother Gerry owned the house in Cashelard, but he closed it up in 1981. He and Eva and the kiddies moved a short distance away.

When I met Ann and Charlie Boyle at their home in Burtonport there was a busy feel. They are now proud grandparents, and as we spoke about their lost daughter, their grandson Ultan—Patrick's son—played with jigsaws spread out on the sitting-room floor. Both Mary Boyle's siblings are now married and have children.

In November 1994 a computer-modified photograph was issued by the Gardaí that showed what Mary Boyle might look like at that time, seventeen years after her disappearance, using a process developed by the National Center for Missing and Exploited Children in Alexandria, Virginia. Mary would have been twenty-four at that time. Unlike other cases of missing people, however, the Boyle family already knew exactly what Mary would look like, for the simple reason that Mary has an identical twin sister. The Boyle family have been able to see just what Mary would have looked like at different times in her life: on her Communion day, as a teenager, going out with friends, getting married, having children.

Throughout the late 1970s, 80s and 90s and into the new century the Gardaí examined every line of inquiry open to them. During their initial investigations in the late 1970s they interviewed hundreds of people. Though no-one was ever formally arrested for questioning, the Gardaí did question a number of people closely about their movements on the day Mary Boyle disappeared. One detective ruefully remembered how he and a colleague thought they were about to crack the case.

We had this man we were questioning—you know, in general, about whether he had seen or heard anything that afternoon. He'd been in the Ballyshannon-Cashelard area at the time of Mary's disappearance, and he was one of many men who we wanted to rule in or rule out as suspects. He was a married man and had children. I remember we were chatting with him, and all of a sudden he started to cry. He put his head in his hands, and there he was, sobbing. My experience before that was that lads cry because their conscience is at them. I thought we were about to get somewhere. But then he raised his head and wiped his eyes and said he knew nothing. And he repeated it. 'I know nothing.' Who knows why he cried? Who knows?

In the years since Mary Boyle disappeared a number of extensive searches have been undertaken in the south Donegal area. Some of these searches have been as a result of anonymous information provided to local gardaí. In November 1995 members of the Garda Sub-Aqua Unit spent a week searching a lake near Cashelard, but nothing was found. In September 1996 a patch of bogland in Cashelard was searched after a request from the Boyle family. A mechanical digger was brought in and a quarter of an acre of swampy bogland, about half a mile from the old Gallagher home, was drained. In an intensive two-day search, nothing was found.

The Gardaí also suspect that the body of a fifteen-year-old Co. Tyrone girl lies in the area between Ballyshannon and the Co. Tyrone border. Arlene Arkinson from Castlederg, Co. Tyrone, disappeared in August 1994 after attending a disco in Bundoran. During searches in the late 1990s around the Pettigo area of Co. Donegal for Arlene Arkinson's body the Gardaí were also privately hopeful that some trace of Mary Boyle might turn up. Nothing was found; but the Gardaí know that any effort to excavate any land around south Co. Donegal may inadvertently turn up a lead in either case.

In 2002 Sergeant John Kennedy retired. He was one of the original team to investigate Mary Boyle's disappearance, and the last of that team to retire. At the time of his retirement he and Superintendent John McFadden travelled to meet Ann and Charlie Boyle in Burtonport to assure them that although the original Garda team were all now retired, the investigation into Mary's disappearance was still at the top of the agenda of the

Gardaí in Co. Donegal. File no. C31/32A/77 will remain open until Mary Boyle is found.

A memorial to Mary Boyle was unveiled in Cionn Caslach, Co. Donegal, in June 2000. Ann Boyle told me that the time was right for the memorial.

> We knew about the memorial to missing people that was being planned for Kilkenny. It's a great idea, but it's just a bit too far for us to get to. So I started to wonder about setting up some memorial closer to home. Now we've a lovely little grotto at Cionn Caslach. I didn't want anything too big. This is just right.

The memorial features a small statue of a guardian angel, a plaque bearing a photograph of Mary Boyle, and the inscription *Faoi choimirce an aingil choimeádaí go raibh tú. Mary Boyle, who disappeared from her family on 18 March 1977—aged 7 years.*

Ann and Charlie Boyle say they can't be sure whether someone knows what happened to their daughter. How can they be sure of anything? Ann told me that it's the not knowing that's the worst thing.

> Newspapers report on Mary's disappearance and they mention certain things and draw conclusions. But nobody knows the real answers. Until Mary is found, who knows anything?

8

Philip Cairns

❧⊱∘⊰❧

In October 1986, in a Dublin suburb, something terrible and as yet unexplained happened to a thirteen-year-old boy walking to school. It was just after lunchtime, and Philip Cairns was making his way back to Coláiste Éanna in Rathfarnham, Co. Dublin, where he had recently started first year. He never made it to school. Somewhere on the fifteen-minute walk from his home in Ballyroan Road, Philip Cairns was abducted.

Despite a massive investigation, Philip Cairns has never been found. And there is another dimension to this distressing case—an extraordinary event that continues to both baffle and intrigue everyone involved in the search for Philip Cairns. A week after Philip was snatched from the roadside, the schoolbag he was carrying when he disappeared was left in a laneway a short distance from his home. Was it dumped there by Philip's abductor hurriedly trying to get rid of evidence? Or was it left there by a young person who had found it on the day Philip disappeared, perhaps someone who was too afraid to come forward? Or was it left there by someone related to the abductor, who continues to keep their dark secret?

The violent abduction of Philip Cairns continues to shock a country in which child abductions are extremely rare. Philip Cairns's disappearance happened nine years after the disappearance of seven-year-old Mary Boyle in Co. Donegal; these remain the only unsolved missing children cases in Ireland that are non-parental abductions.

The disappearance of Philip Cairns from a busy road in a populous Dublin suburb still deeply disturbs the gardaí who originally worked on the case, and those who continue to work on it; but their pain is nothing compared with the constant anguish endured by Philip's parents, Alice and Philip Cairns, his four older sisters, Mary, Sandra, Helen, and Suzanne, and his younger brother, Eoin.

Philip Cairns sat at the table in his home in Ballyroan Road and began doing homework. It was after one o'clock on the afternoon of Thursday 23 October 1986. He was doing his maths homework, and he had a few minutes to spare before heading back to school. The lunch break at Coláiste Éanna was from 12:45 to 1:45 p.m., and the walk to school would take him about fifteen minutes. Also in the house were Philip's sister Suzanne and his granny, May, who was living with the Cairns family. Philip's mother, Alice, was also at home but was getting ready for a trip to town: another of Philip's sisters, Helen, had a toothache that needed to be treated.

Philip gathered the books he'd need for his afternoon classes and got ready to head back to school. He had religion, geography and maths in the afternoon; having started in secondary school two months before, he was beginning to learn off by heart what classes he had each day. He went to talk to his granny and then went back to another room to get his schoolbag. From the hallway he called out, 'Cheerio, Gran. I'm off,' and he pulled the front door shut behind him. Within minutes, he would be abducted from the roadside.

Nobody saw Philip Cairns leave his house to go back to school that afternoon. It was an ordinary day in the Cairns house, and Philip was following his normal routine of coming home for lunch. To this day his mother cannot even remember whether she left for town before or after Philip left for school. The fact that little can be recalled about that lunchtime is precisely because it was so ordinary. But some time around 1:30 p.m. that afternoon, somewhere along the curving Ballyroan Road in Rathfarnham, or on a side road close to the school, Philip Cairns was abducted.

All through that Thursday afternoon no-one was aware of the ordeal that Philip Cairns was going through. To this day only Philip and his abductor can know what happened in the hours after he was snatched from the roadside, where he was taken, and what happened to him after that. All that afternoon Philip's family thought he was in school, while at Coláiste Éanna his teachers assumed he was at home because of illness, or a family emergency.

When Philip didn't come home from school that evening, his family began to worry. He was a dependable boy and followed a particular routine. His father was not very worried at first, thinking Philip might be out with new friends from school. Starting in secondary school is a daunting time for any teenager, but Philip was beginning to find his feet. It was only when his mother arrived home from town that the first feelings came that something wasn't right. She was met by her eldest daughter, Mary, who said to her: 'Philip isn't in. He didn't come home from school.' Alice was concerned, and she went around to the house of Enda Cloke, Philip's best friend in school, hoping Philip would be there, but he wasn't. She then checked at the school, where a teacher told her that Philip had never returned that afternoon. It was then that everyone realised that something serious had happened.

At 6:30 p.m. a garda at the desk at Rathfarnham Garda Station received a phone call from Paddy Cloke, Enda's father, who was also a garda. That conversation was to set in train an investigation that continues to this day.

The pain suffered by Alice and Philip Cairns and their five remaining children has not diminished, despite the length of time since Philip was cruelly taken from them. For Alice and Philip, who still live in Ballyroan Road, there are feelings of hope, anger, frustration, and sadness. The fact that a boy could be abducted on a busy Co. Dublin road, and never be found, is a matter of terrible concern for all parents; for the parents of the missing boy, it is an agonising and unrelenting mystery.

Alice and Philip Cairns know their son was abducted by an unknown attacker. But after that there is just speculation. Tears well up in the eyes of both parents when they think of the boy they have lost. With clarity, Alice recounted her memories of the night on which all their lives changed for ever.

Once I arrived home and heard Philip hadn't come home, I went around to his friend Enda Cloke, but Philip wasn't there. I contacted the school, and found out he hadn't been there in the afternoon. Another friend that Philip had was Gareth, who also lived a short distance away; but Philip wasn't there either. We called in the Gardaí immediately. I remember it was getting dark quite early by the end of October, and the weather was quite bad that night. An inspector called down from Rathfarnham Garda Station and said that because of Philip's age, and the weather, they were putting out a full alert, contacting all gardaí immediately. And then the full-scale search began.

The disappearance of Philip Cairns is a mystery that continues to haunt both the Cairns family and the Gardaí, who have often feared that the same violent person might strike again. At whatever point Philip Cairns was snatched on the walk back to Coláiste Éanna, the road would have been quite busy. It was a fluke that the abduction most probably happened just seconds before and seconds after other cars and pedestrians travelled past the same spot. Perhaps the abduction happened just moments before or after someone went in or out their front door, someone who, but for a few seconds, could have been a crucial witness. Perhaps there actually is a witness, someone who did see a neighbour or a motorist acting suspiciously, a person who has kept what they saw secret all these years. Certainly, if you walk from Philip's house, turning to the right towards Coláiste Éanna, the first thing to strike you is the volume of traffic. Rarely a minute goes by without a car travelling along the road that links the residential areas of Templeogue and Ballyboden. The large semi-detached houses on each side of the wide road would also have provided a vantage-point for a potential witness to Philip's abduction. But no-one has come forward to say they saw Philip being dragged into a car, or speaking to anyone on the roadside.

The Cairns family have lived in Ballyroan Road since the late 1970s. Photographs of Philip making his First Holy Communion and his Confirmation have a prominent place in the sitting-room. Alice showed me a St Brigid's Cross that Philip made in school a short time before he disappeared; it now has pride of place in the hallway of the house. Alice told me Philip was a quiet and conscientious pupil.

He enjoyed his time in primary school and was very good at arts and crafts. When it came to essays and written tests, Philip would shine. He played a bit of sports, including hurling, and I remember he joked that he didn't know if he'd play for Dublin or Kilkenny—because I'm from Kilkenny, you see. Philip had settled into secondary school and had good friends. He also had interests outside of school and would play out in the garden with his friends and his brother. Everything was normal when this happened.

Philip Cairns was born on 1 September 1973. For the first five years of his life the family lived at St Columba's Road, Drumcondra, Dublin, after which they moved to Rathfarnham, to the south of the city. When Philip disappeared in October 1986 his four sisters—Mary, Sandra, Helen, and Suzanne—were aged from twenty to fifteen. His only brother, Eoin, was a year and two months younger than Philip, and the two boys were very close.

The loss of their brother has deeply affected all five remaining siblings. Eoin was in primary school when Philip vanished; he later went to the same secondary school that Philip should have been in.

The intensive and exhaustive search for Philip Cairns began on the night he disappeared, 23 October 1986. Never in living memory had a boy been snatched from the roadside in Ireland in such circumstances, and the case remains the only such abduction. Detectives were conscious that, assuming Philip was abducted some time around half past one that afternoon, the person responsible had seven or eight hours in which to cover their tracks. House-to-house searches began in the immediate area, and the Gardaí in nearby Terenure and Tallaght were alerted. In the days immediately following Philip's disappearance, lanes, rivers, ponds, fields and parks were searched throughout south Co. Dublin in an increasingly desperate effort to find the missing boy. The searches took place in terrible weather, as the remnants of Hurricane Charlie brought howling winds and heavy rain. But despite the weather, hundreds of volunteers, gardaí and members of Civil Defence conducted extensive searches in the Dublin Mountains, which begin a couple of miles south of Rathfarnham.

There was of course the possibility that Philip had wandered off somewhere by himself, but that possibility fizzled out within days. With the numerous searches by hundreds of gardaí and volunteers, it quickly became apparent that Philip had not chosen to disappear. Privately detectives knew that they were looking not only for Philip but also for the person or persons responsible for keeping him away from his family.

Philip Cairns was five feet tall, with dark-brown hair. When last seen he was wearing dark-grey trousers, a dark-grey V-neck jumper, his grey school shirt, a grey jacket with black shoulder corners, and black leather shoes with laces. He was carrying his grey schoolbag. None of Philip's clothing has ever been found; however, a week after he was abducted something extraordinary happened, something that has never been explained but may yet shed some light on what happened to Philip Cairns. On Thursday 30 October 1986, at 7:45 p.m., in a laneway a few hundred yards from Philip Cairns's home, Philip's schoolbag was found.

Two teenage girls, Catherine Hassett and Orla O'Carroll, were walking through the dark, curving laneway that serves as a short-cut between Anne Devlin Road and Anne Devlin Drive when they spotted a schoolbag lying on the ground close to a telegraph pole. They picked it up, looked inside, and quickly discovered that it belonged to Philip Cairns. With their hearts in their mouths they ran to Rathfarnham Garda Station, where Detective-Garda John Harrington was that evening working on other leads in the search for Philip Cairns. He took possession of the bag and arranged for it to be searched thoroughly, while still keeping open the hope of gaining some scientific evidence from it.

Looking back on that evening, John Harrington, who is now retired, told me that he believes the schoolbag holds the key to this case.

The discovery of Philip's bag one week after his disappearance is the best clue we've ever had. The bag was only in the laneway for a short time before it was found by the two girls. The laneway had been thoroughly searched before the bag was discovered, and nothing was found. But dozens of people had passed through the laneway even on the day the bag was found and they didn't see anything. Also, it was drizzling quite heavily that night, but the bag was relatively dry. Whoever left it there did so just a short time before the girls walked through— just before eight o'clock that night. So the bag was deliberately left in that laneway one week after Philip disappeared. The questions remain: Who left it there? Why did they leave it there? What more do they know?

Whoever left Philip Cairns's schoolbag there chose to do so when it was dark and at a time when few people would be walking along the laneway, which is only about a hundred yards long. Each side of the laneway is also the side wall of two back gardens, which back onto each other. Whoever left the bag dropped it at a spot where the laneway curves, so they would not have been seen from either entrance as they dropped it. The identity of the person who left the bag has never been established. That person holds information that is crucial to establishing what happened to Philip Cairns.

There are a number of hypotheses that detectives believe may explain why the bag was left as it was. Philip Cairns believes his son first dropped the bag when he was abducted, and that it was then picked up, perhaps by a young person.

I think Philip was dragged into a car, and in the struggle that ensued he dropped his schoolbag. Maybe some teenagers found the bag and took some of the books out to sell them to make a bit of money for cigarettes, or a disco. Could it be more than a coincidence that the bag was left in the laneway just hours after all the children were called back into Philip's school?

On the morning of Thursday 30 October the boys in Coláiste Éanna were supposed to be enjoying their mid-term break, but they had all returned to the school voluntarily, with their teachers, to be addressed by the detectives investigating the case of their missing fellow-pupil. The detectives who spoke to the boys were friendly and approachable; but the arrival of gardaí in a classroom must still have been somewhat disturbing. Hours after the boys were quizzed by the gardaí, Philip's schoolbag was found in the laneway.

The belief of Philip Cairns's father that the schoolbag was found on the roadside by other schoolchildren on the day Philip was abducted is one that also holds currency with a number of detectives involved in the case. One believes that if the bag was left in the laneway by an innocent person, they could still help in finding Philip Cairns.

Say the bag was dropped on the road when Philip was attacked and some young kid or kids picked it up. With all the publicity and all the Garda activity, that kid may have kept the bag hidden at home. They may have then dumped the bag in the laneway, or maybe one of their parents or brothers or sisters dumped the bag for them. If this is the case, that person or persons still hold so much information that they may not even know they have. They were a child when they did this, and the natural instinct of a child is not to get in trouble. That child is now an adult, and needs to act like an adult. If they could tell us exactly where they found the bag, then we have our crime scene and, believe me, we would begin to make progress. Maybe the witness dreams about that day, or under hypnosis they could remember the colour of a car, or a person they saw. It is so wrong for them to stay silent. That person is now definitely an adult; they may even have children of their own. I'm convinced that that person is tormented every single day by this whole case.

This schoolbag is unique in all the investigations into the disappearances of missing people in that this is the only one in which a trace of the missing person has been found after the disappearance. Today the most famous schoolbag in Ireland lies in a plastic evidence bag locked in a safe. When the bag was found, Philip's school journal, a copybook and a maths book were inside. Three books were missing: a geography book, and two books that would have been required that afternoon for religion class. Those three books have never been found.

When a person close to the Cairns family asked whether the bag and the books still in it could be checked for fingerprints against all the people in the school, a garda told them it would be too big a job, and also that all the pupils would have to do so voluntarily. A scientific examination of the bag in November 1986 did not reveal anything of value. However, the bag may yet reveal a clue, as Detective-Sergeant Tom Doyle, the person now in charge of the case, explained to me.

There are many advances that have been made in forensic science in recent years, and there will be even more advances made in the future. Something which we were unable to detect from a search of Philip's bag in 1986 may be revealed in the future. Philip's schoolbag is kept in a secure location, and it may yet become crucial.

Philip Cairns had a happy life as part of a closely knit family. A number of newspaper articles suggested that in the weeks before his abduction he may have been physically attacked, or have been under threat from some unknown person. The informed belief of those closest to this case is that those claims are simply not true. Not one member of Philip's family has a suspicion that anything untoward happened to Philip before the day on which he was abducted. The family are adamant that he was sleeping normally, eating normally, and playing with his friends—all the actions of a boy without a care in the world. His concentration in school was so good that only hours before he disappeared, as his class took turns to read aloud, Philip was able to pick up reading when it wasn't even his turn, after his name was called in error.

Philip spent many happy afternoons fishing with the Dublin City Sea Angling Club and would often travel with his father to the open competitions along the east coast. A few weeks before he disappeared he had taken part in the All-Ireland Juvenile Championships at Garryvoe, Co. Cork. On the day he disappeared he had been looking forward to going away the following weekend fishing with his father. He had also started to learn to swim, and was involved in sports in his new school.

In the days and weeks following the disappearance of Philip Cairns, a sense of fear hung over the country. That fear had been compounded by the eerie dumping of Philip Cairns's schoolbag close to his home a week after the abduction. Parents around the country refused to let their children walk to school alone and insisted on walking with them or driving them to the school gates, or even keeping them at home. Yet no similar abductions followed that of Philip Cairns. One detective told me that this fact has led the Gardaí to examine a number of possibilities.

The fact that no other boys, or indeed girls, were abducted in the greater Dublin area would indicate [that] the abductor was not necessarily a predator with constant uncontrollable urges to attack. The person would more likely be someone who committed an evil act on impulse, and has managed to control that impulse. That doesn't mean they haven't attacked other children in other ways, but they haven't snatched other children from the roadside.

We've also considered the possibility that Philip knew his attacker, and was singled out by the abductor because of this. Another reason that no other abductions occurred might be because the abductor is now dead, or in prison for something else. But we're conscious that there have been a number of reported abduction attempts every year since Philip disappeared. No children have been actually abducted, and no-one has been arrested, but it always crosses our mind that Philip's abductor may still strike again.

Philip Cairns's father told me he fears that the person who abducted his son might have tried to strike again.

Even in June 2002, at a spot out on the roadside very close to where Philip would have been walking, a boy about the same age as Philip was approached by a stranger in a car. A car came down from the Rathfarnham area and made a U-turn and stopped close to the boy. The driver said something to the boy like 'Come on, you're late. Get in.' The boy didn't get into the car, and told his parents about the incident that night. The Gardaí later said they hadn't made the abduction attempt public because 'nothing happened and nobody had seen anything.' I would wonder if it's the same person who picked up Philip sixteen years before.

In November 1986, as the Gardaí continued their search for Philip Cairns, a twelve-year-old boy, Ultan Whelan, was chosen to take part in a reconstruction of Philip's last movements for a television appeal. He was nominated by the principal of Coláiste Éanna after Philip's friend Enda said that Ultan was a good likeness of Philip. A jacket similar to the one Philip was wearing when he disappeared was bought, and Philip's own schoolbag was used. As part of the televised appeal, Philip's mother pleaded with the abductor. 'If Philip has been abducted, please let him go. We just want Philip back.'

More than a hundred leads were suggested in the hours after the televised reconstruction, as people phoned Rathfarnham Garda Station or called in with information. This brought to over six hundred the number of separate leads the Gardaí were following up by November 1986. In the first two weeks of the investigation detectives took more than 1,500 written statements, followed up more than two hundred reported sightings of Philip Cairns, checked every hostel in Ireland, alerted all ports and airports, carried out house-to-house searches in the Rathfarnham area, and combed woodland and wasteland close to Philip's house. Nothing was found.

In the weeks and months after Philip Cairns was abducted, his family were emotionally and physically drained. Alice Cairns spoke to numerous journalists in order to generate publicity, hoping to trigger a break in the case. Philip Cairns senior was out taking part in searches day and night. Two weeks after Philip's disappearance another tragedy struck the family when a young relative of Alice's died in Kilkenny following an illness.

The pressure on the whole family was almost intolerable. Philip's four sisters had always looked out for him, and his little brother, Eoin, missed his best friend terribly. Eventually Eoin, Helen and Suzanne were persuaded to return to school, something they all found extremely difficult. Establishing some degree of normality for Philip's brothers and sisters was something that was very important, but almost impossible.

No-one has ever been arrested for questioning about the abduction of Philip Cairns. There has never been a prime suspect. However, detectives who continue to investigate this disturbing case believe there are a number of issues that may be significant. One detective believes the answer may lie close to where Philip disappeared.

Philip was a sensible boy, and wasn't foolhardy. He would never have willingly got into a car with someone he didn't know. Therefore, he was either dragged into a car in the space of a few seconds or he accepted a lift from a person he knew. We're only guessing now, but it's an educated guess. If he was dragged in by someone he didn't know, there would have been more of a chance of a struggle, or a scream, or Philip might have dropped his bag. Now, that might have happened and would certainly explain the bag being found dumped close by a week later; but it's almost unbelievable that a child could be basically kidnapped on a busy street and no-one to see anything. If I had to guess, I'd say someone he knew stopped and offered him a lift, someone he trusted. If this is true, perhaps it was someone living in the Rathfarnham area, or who worked in the Rathfarnham area.

Some weeks after the disappearance of Philip Cairns a man contacted the Gardaí in Rathfarnham. What he told them was at first to intrigue them but ultimately to frustrate them. He told them he had been driving along Ballyroan Road from Ballyboden Road between 1:20 and 1:30 p.m. on Thursday 23 October 1986—the time Philip is believed to have been abducted. Close to Ballyboden Road he noticed a red car, which he described as being badly parked and obstructing traffic. He said he had seen a boy wearing a grey school jumper and carrying a bag approaching the front passenger door of the parked car. The witness had been angered by the way the car was parked and told the gardaí he had written down the registration number of the car. However, he no longer had the number. He had gone on to the airport, and while he was away his wife had cleaned out his car, and the number was lost. It was only after he learnt of the disappearance of Philip Cairns that he remembered about the badly parked car.

Detectives gritted their teeth, and thanked the man for his help. They knew it wasn't his fault: it wasn't as if he had seen anything that he thought was really suspicious. It was just frustrating that the man had the foresight to write down the registration number of the car, and then should lose it. He was able to describe the driver of the car as possibly about fifty years old, with grey hair sticking up. The red car might have been a Renault or a Mazda.

In October 1989, three years after Philip Cairns's disappearance, the Gardaí in Rathfarnham believed they might be about to unlock the mystery. The optimism developed after detectives received four anonymous phone calls from a man who said he knew 'who had killed Philip Cairns.' The mystery caller, who has never been found, had phoned the confidential number with particular information, which at first convinced the Gardaí that he was genuine. Over the course of four phone calls he told them that Philip had been driven away from Ballyroan Road that day by a man whose identity was known to the caller. For weeks the Gardaí spoke to the anonymous caller, each time getting more information from the man, who seemed worried and nervous. Then the calls stopped. By 23 October 1989 the man had still not been in contact, and Superintendent Bill McMunn of Rathfarnham went on television to reveal that the anonymous calls had been made, and to appeal to the caller to get in contact again.

Looking back on that time, Bill McMunn, now retired, told me he now believes the calls may have been a cruel hoax.

This man told us he knew who was responsible for abducting Philip, and he called four times. Yet he wouldn't give us the crucial information we wanted. And then the calls stopped. The mystery caller may have met with an accident, or couldn't call us again for some reason; or, as many of us subsequently believed, it might all have been a hoax. It's not right that someone would do that, if that's what happened. We were trying to find a young boy: it's a serious business; but we have to check out all leads, we have to check out everything.

I was in the force for forty-three years, and despite all the successes, the unsolved cases do affect you. Gardaí don't like to be beaten.

The abduction of Philip Cairns is only one of a number of distressing crimes to have been committed in the Rathfarnham area in recent decades. During the 1980s a now convicted paedophile, Derry O'Rourke, lived in the area and appeared to be an upstanding member of the community, happily married and raising his five children. He was a prominent national swimming coach, but beneath it all, over a period of thirty-two years, he was sexually abusing girls he was teaching to swim. From July 1970 until December 1992 he abused at least thirteen girls in changing rooms and other places. In 1997 he was caught and jailed for twelve years for his litany of hidden abuse.

Another violent man from Rathfarnham who appeared to be a committed family man is now serving a life sentence for murdering his wife and a baby girl in 1992. Frank McCann—who, like Derry O'Rourke, was a prominent member of the swimming community—was convicted in 1996 of deliberately starting a fire at his home in Butterfield Avenue, Rathfarnham, in September 1992. His wife, Esther, and an eighteen-month-old baby girl whom the McCanns were rearing died in the blaze. Local people who witnessed the fire were traumatised by being powerless to do anything to save the victims from the raging fire that engulfed the house. McCann had used a fire accelerant to start the fire, which he lit while standing in the front doorway and throwing in a match as his wife and the baby girl slept upstairs.

Another violent man from Rathfarnham is a single man who is now serving a life sentence for raping one of his nephews at a place in the west of Ireland in 1993. This man also admitted sexually assaulting three other boys at his home in Rathfarnham and at hotels around the country on dates between 1989 and 2000. He was also convicted of taking pornographic images of children in the bedroom of his home. This violent man was thirty years old when, in 1989, the first of the known sexual assaults occurred. He did not come to the attention of the Gardaí until eleven years later, in June 2000, when one of his victims found the courage to contact the Gardaí.

On 12 November 1994 the Gardaí issued a computer-modified photograph showing what Philip Cairns might look like at the age of twenty-one. The process used photographs of Philip's parents and siblings at a similar age, and tried to interpret Philip's appearance eight years after his disappearance. The technique is similar to the one used as part of a fresh appeal for information on Ireland's only other long-term missing child case that is not a parental abduction, that of seven-year-old Mary Boyle. Despite the 'aged' photographs of Mary Boyle and Philip Cairns, neither appeal ever led to a definite sighting.

Because Mary Boyle has an identical twin sister, her family has been able to see exactly what Mary would look like as an adult. In contrast, the 'aged' photograph of Philip Cairns was the first opportunity Alice and Philip Senior had to see what their eldest son would have looked like as a man.

The part of Co. Dublin where Philip Cairns disappeared is a densely populated suburban area, with Templeogue and Rathfarnham to the north and Firhouse, Knocklyon and Ballyboden to the south. Assuming that Philip stayed on the same side of the road as he walked south from his house towards Coláiste Éanna, he would have been walking on the footpath with oncoming traffic to his immediate left. If an oncoming car stopped on the near side of the road and then travelled on in the same direction, it would have brought Philip back past his house and to a junction that links roads to Tallaght, Templeogue, and Rathfarnham.

Another possibility is that he was abducted by a person in a car that stopped at one of the side roads to Philip's right as he walked; this car might then have driven either north towards Templeogue or south towards Ballyboden. Philip may also have crossed the road, so that he would have had the busy road to his right as he walked; however, this would have been unusual, as he would have had to cross back later to get to the school. If he was on this side of the road and was driven away by a car that came up behind him, the car would have travelled towards the junction with Ballyboden Road, where a turn left leads to Rathfarnham and the turn to the right leads to the Dublin Mountains at Killakee and Tibradden.

Detectives have had to consider many possibilities that can leave even the most focused of minds confused. These possibilities assume that the motorist did not make a U-turn, something that might have stuck in the minds of other motorists. There are no reports of any such U-turns being made. There is also the possibility that whoever abducted Philip did not travel very far but drove towards one of the nearby estates, avoiding the main roads. There is not one report of a boy being seen in a distressed state in a car in south Co. Dublin that day.

It is possible that whoever left Philip Cairns's bag in the laneway a week after his disappearance holds the key to catching the abductor. That person might be able to pinpoint the site of the abduction and so narrow the search, even now.

There is also the possibility that the person who left the bag is the person who abducted Philip. This hypothesis is credible when we consider that Philip's normal practice was to put the bag over his head and wear it across his chest. The bag had not been cut or damaged in any way, so that if he was wearing it over his head it would have taken a number of seconds for the abductor to take it off and throw it on the roadside, an action that would have been unusual for someone trying to cover their tracks.

A more credible possibility is that if Philip knew his abductor, the bag was removed later at an unknown place. The abductor may then have thrown the bag some distance from the scene of the abduction, where it was found by some schoolchildren; or he may have kept the bag and then left it in the laneway himself a week later. If it was left by the abductor, detectives believe this was only to try to throw them off the scent. It is not thought likely that a person who had committed such a violent and callous act would have risked capture close to the scene of the crime, unless it was to throw some type of smokescreen over the investigation.

When all the available evidence is weighed up, the most likely explanation remains that the bag was left by an innocent person, whose conscience probably still troubles them.

The search for Philip Cairns has extended to a number of continents. While the feeling of many detectives is that the answer to Philip's disappearance lies somewhere in south Co. Dublin, every conceivable lead has been followed up. One hypothesis that received some attention was that Philip was abducted by a religious cult. This possibility was privately examined by the Gardaí—indeed premises owned by certain religious groups were searched—but this line of inquiry was ruled out in the early weeks of the investigation. The idea had been fuelled by the fact that two of Philip's religion books were missing from his schoolbag when it was found; but it ignores the fact that a geography book was also missing, and that all these books had been in Philip's bag only because he had those particular classes that afternoon. The Gardaí also point out that the kind of religious groups that might be capable of such an action are quite rare in Ireland, and such people might well have stood out in south Co. Dublin. Whoever abducted Philip Cairns is more likely to be someone who was able to blend into the community and not arouse suspicion.

Another idea put forward was that some other unknown person might have abducted Philip and taken him abroad. In the years since the disappearance of Philip Cairns there have been reported sightings as far away as America and Argentina. All reported sightings are investigated, but none have ever stood up as genuine.

Detectives have also been frustrated by a number of people using Philip Cairns's name when they are stopped by the police in different countries. Either through malice or idiocy, a number of young Irish men arrested for various offences in England and Scotland have been known to give their name as Philip Cairns. The Gardaí have been immediately alerted, and an inspector and a detective-sergeant have been despatched to investigate the reported sightings, only to return empty-handed, having established the true identity of the culprits.

Alice and Philip Cairns have suffered a number of false hopes and hoaxes since their son disappeared. Some mistakes have been genuine and without malice; but a number of people have acted in a callous manner towards a family whose grief has been laid bare for everyone to see. This is a family who know what most probably happened to their thirteen-year-old son and brother but who naturally still hold out hope that something positive may some day develop. A person close to the family told me of the added traumas that the family has had to suffer down the years.

I'll never forget the night that the schoolbag was found in the laneway. One garda in his excitement actually came into the house and said, 'Philip is around; we've found his bag; we'll have him back home in the next half hour.' Can you imagine hearing that and waiting that night, and waiting, and nothing: Philip doesn't come home, Philip doesn't ever come home; can you imagine?

And while that's an example of a false hope that happened through over-enthusiasm or stupidity, there have also been really sick people who've targeted the Cairns family. One man once phoned them up pretending to be a garda at a station in north Dublin, saying that he'd found Philip and that he was bringing him home. Again the family waited, and of course nothing happened. That man phoned from what sounded like a busy Garda station, so he was in some type of office when he made this hoax call. What type of sick person does something like that?

A female garda stayed with the family for weeks after Philip went missing. Some of the phone calls were very upsetting. But you have to answer the phone: the next call could be the one.

A number of newspaper articles have suggested that Philip Cairns was the victim of more than one attacker, and that he might have been murdered because he was about to expose a paedophile ring. These distressing articles quote an unnamed source who has never confided this information to the Gardaí. Such articles have caused untold pain to Philip's family, who are adamant that Philip had nothing troubling him in the weeks before he disappeared. The articles have also angered the gardaí involved in the case.

Just because a journalist writes something doesn't make it true. We've had a number of people come into us with their theory about what happened to Philip. We've had everything suggested to us, from a foreign child-trafficking ring to aliens. It's all wild speculation, and it doesn't help. These journalists need to remember that there is a family left behind here, and there is a memory of a young boy to be honoured and protected. In relation to the 'paedophile ring', there is absolutely no proof. Certain journalists quote unnamed sources, people who have never contacted us with this information. Show me the proof.

Alice and Philip Cairns's five remaining children are by now all adults, making lives for themselves. Philip Cairns senior retired from his job as a purchasing manager at the end of 1994. In 2003 he and Alice celebrated their fortieth wedding anniversary. Their first child, Mary, was born in 1965, and over the next nine years they had three more daughters—Sandra, Helen, and Suzanne—and two sons—Philip and Eoin. In October 1986 the world of this happy and loving family was cruelly turned upside down.

The other boys in Philip Cairns's class in 1986 are now grown men; most are married, most have families of their own. And all the while, the search for Philip continues.

At Rathfarnham Garda Station, Detective-Sergeant Tom Doyle told me that the investigation into Philip Cairns's disappearance is very much active.

I will go anywhere, at any time, to meet with anyone who has information about Philip. They can talk to me in confidence, and there are other gardaí here who also work on this case on a regular basis. This case is alive: we are continuously checking out leads. We undertake searches as new information comes in. We keep in regular touch with the Cairns family. Detective-Garda Mary Fallon is the liaison officer, and she would speak often with Philip's parents and with his sisters and brother.

It all comes down to one thing: someone knows something that can help us solve this mystery. In all probability there is some person who is tormented every day by their secret and would love to speak out in confidence. It could be a seemingly trivial piece of information that someone has that might fit what we're looking for. Despite the passage of time, the search for Philip will never end.

One day a number of years ago the Cairns family came face to face with another family who continue to suffer similar pain. Alice and Philip Cairns met Ann and Charlie Boyle, the parents of Mary Boyle, who was seven years old when she disappeared in Co. Donegal in March 1977. The families met in the RTÉ grounds in Donnybrook, Dublin, where they had taken part in a radio discussion about missing people. It was a deeply emotional meeting, and many tears were shed. Later, at Ballyroan Road, the two families talked late into the evening. It was an extraordinary meeting of two families both living a life of uncertainty and both clinging to a chink of hope that their children will some day be found.

9

Ireland's Missing

⪻≫∘≪⪼

Five people on average are reported missing in Ireland every day. Most of them have left of their own accord, for personal reasons, for space, or time to reflect. It is not a crime for an adult of sound mind to go missing. Most such people return to their home after a few days or weeks, or at least contact their family to let them know they are safe. Many missing people are depressed, some suffering from long-term depression, while others are upset after a family funeral or a dispute with another family member.

The families of these missing people suffer the same unrelenting pain that is felt by the families of missing people who have been murdered. There is no closure, no definite information; families grieve but cannot say their last goodbyes. They do not know if their loved ones are still alive, or if not, where their bodies might lie.

Of the two thousand people reported missing in Ireland every year, between five and fifteen will never be found. Some of these will have gone away by themselves, perhaps not being in full health, while others will have disappeared because they have been murdered. More than a dozen of Ireland's long-term missing people, such as Annie McCarrick, Jo Jo Dullard, Fiona Pender, and Ciara Breen, did not choose to go away but were murdered, their bodies hidden in unmarked graves in unknown places.

In other long-term missing persons cases it is less clear what happened: it is as if these people just vanished off the face of the earth. But that didn't happen: these missing people must be somewhere. They include an elderly couple who disappeared from their home in Co. Cork in 1991, a young man who vanished while walking home from a Christmas party in Dublin, and a number of young men in different parts of the country who disappeared without a trace.

There are many questions and few answers. But the answers lie somewhere. Thanks to the sterling work of the families of missing people, it is certain that their missing loved ones will never be forgotten; but what more can the state, the Gardaí and the public do to find them and bring them home?

In May 2002 a landmark event took place in Kilkenny that formally acknowledged the legacy of Ireland's missing people. Amid emotional scenes, dozens of families who have lost a member through violence, illness or accident came together to share their grief. The event that brought these brave families together was the unveiling of the National Missing Persons Monument in the grounds of Kilkenny Castle. After a memorial Mass for all missing people, the families travelled to a quiet part of the castle grounds that will commemorate for ever those people who have vanished in cruel and unexplained circumstances.

The sun shone on a calm afternoon as President Mary McAleese unveiled the monument, while dozens of families of missing people looked on, some of them quietly sobbing. The steel monument features the handprints of members of the families of missing people, the hands of people who have written countless letters, made thousands of phone calls and conducted numerous searches of their own in a desperate effort to find their loved ones. In her speech, President McAleese acknowledged that every family of a missing person has a different story: each case is different. But uniting all families is the need to know what happened to their loved ones.

The creation of the National Missing Persons Monument was the brainchild of Mary Phelan, whose younger sister Jo Jo Dullard was murdered in November 1995. Mary Phelan is a quiet-spoken woman who has found herself thrown into the spotlight. Though at first she found interviews daunting, she was compelled to speak out by the need to find her sister, and she has transformed herself from a hard-working farmer's wife into a voice for many families who cannot cope with intrusion by the media. As she made a short speech from the podium in the grounds of Kilkenny Castle she thought of Jo Jo, her 21-year-old sister brutally murdered by a person who has not been caught. With tears streaming down her face, Mary Phelan thanked everybody who came to the unveiling of the monument.

Later that afternoon, President McAleese had a private meeting with a number of the families. Among those she was introduced to were Bernadette Breen, whose seventeen-year-old daughter Ciara was abducted and murdered in Dundalk in February 1997, and Alice Cairns, whose thirteen-year-old son Philip was abducted from a roadside in south Co. Dublin in October 1986. Also there was Josephine Pender, whose only daughter, Fiona, was abducted and murdered in Tullamore in August 1996 while seven months pregnant. Josephine's only surviving child, John, now a young man, was there to support his mother.

Another brave woman in Kilkenny that day was Christine O'Sullivan, whose six-year-old daughter Deirdre was shot dead by her father, Christopher Crowley, in August 2001, who seconds later took his own life. From December 1999 to August 2001 Deirdre Crowley was classified as a missing child. All the Gardaí knew was that she had been abducted by her father from her home in Co. Cork, after Christine and Christopher had separated. The Gardaí mounted an extensive search for Deirdre, both in Ireland and abroad. It failed to find her; and when they eventually stumbled on the little girl and her father at a rented house in Clonmel in August 2001 it was too late. Two gardaí called to the house and spoke briefly to Christopher Crowley, who was using an alias. Seconds after they left the house Crowley took a shotgun and fired at his daughter, killing her instantly; he then turned the gun on himself. The failure to find Deirdre Crowley before her father harmed her has been the subject of much debate within the Gardaí and has deeply affected many detectives who were close to finding her before her father killed her.

Christine O'Sullivan had made many friends among the families of other missing people in the time since her daughter was taken from her in December 1999. For almost two years she suffered the same uncertainty that every family of a missing person suffers. For two years she prayed that her little daughter would be brought home to her. The shocking death of Deirdre Crowley has affected the public, who once again were shaken by such unexplained violence against a child.

The unveiling of the National Missing Persons Monument brought together families who might not otherwise have met. While some missing people may have been suffering from depression or may have fled because they were frightened of something, others were taken from their family by murderers. The families of missing people do not differentiate between the circumstances of the disappearances: indeed many families still cannot say for certain why their son or daughter, or brother or sister, vanished without a trace. The monument seeks to honour their memory and offers the opportunity for families to remember their loved ones and all missing people.

The names of many missing people in Ireland are well known to the public—names such as Annie McCarrick, Jo Jo Dullard, and Fiona Pender, women who were murdered by men who have not been found or charged. There is also Philip Cairns, a thirteen-year-old schoolboy snatched from the roadside in October 1986 and not seen since. Mary Boyle, not quite seven years old, who disappeared in the most perplexing of circumstances in Co. Donegal in March 1977, is another missing person whose name is well known for all the wrong reasons. There are many other people who have simply vanished, some names well known because of the publicity generated by their distraught families. An examination of some of the other cases of missing people also makes for worrying reading. Clearly, something more needs to be done.

A recent case that captured the hearts of the public is that of 22-year-old Trevor Deely from Naas, Co. Kildare, who disappeared while walking home from a Christmas party in Dublin in the early hours of 8 December 2000. His movements in the hours before he disappeared have been well documented; they show no indication that he planned to disappear of his own free will. When last seen at 4:15 a.m. he was walking down Haddington Road, close to Baggot Street Bridge. Earlier that night he had been socialising with colleagues from the Asset Management Department of the Bank of Ireland. He had started his night at Copper-Face Jack's pub in Harcourt Street at about 7 p.m., later going to the Hilton Hotel in Charlemont Place at 9 p.m. At 12:28 a.m. he went to the bank machine at the ACC bank in Charlemont Street, then returned to the Hilton. At 2:15 a.m. he left the Hilton and went to Buck Whaley's night club in Leeson Street. He left there at 3:30 a.m. and went back to his office, where he checked his e-mail and picked up a blue ACC golf umbrella. It was a stormy night as he left the office at 4 a.m. An unidentified man was seen on video-tape close to the building as Trevor went in and went out. Trevor Deely was last spotted on closed-circuit television walking down Haddington Road alone at 4:15 a.m. A man and a woman are seen on the tape walking in the same direction a few moments later. Neither of these two people has come forward.

A massive search for Trevor Deely included house-to-house inquiries and an extensive search of the Grand Canal, but nothing was found. Trevor's family, friends and colleagues conducted a huge poster campaign in an effort to find him. Despite the biggest publicity campaign in recent times in relation to the search for a missing person, no trace of Trevor Deely was found.

Trevor Deely is one of a number of young men who have dis-appeared in recent years in unexplained circumstances. Another is 22-year-old Aengus (Gussie) Shanahan, whose disappearance in Limerick in February 2000 later spurred his cousin Father Aquinas Duffy to set up a special web site to help find missing people. The site (at www.missing.ws) has provided a constant source of information on missing people. A special section of the Garda web site (at www.garda.ie) also features the cases of missing people.

Another young man to disappear in Limerick was Patrick O'Donoghue, who was also twenty-two when he vanished one month before Gussie Shanahan. And before that, 27-year-old Desmond Walsh went missing in Limerick in September 1999 after leaving a night club.

Other young men to vanish in recent years include Shane

Curran from Co. Waterford, who was twenty-two when he was last seen in December 1999 in Dunmore East, and Stephen Finnegan from Howth, Co. Dublin, who was twenty when he vanished in February 2000.

A number of cases of missing women have not received the same attention as others because there is no evidence that they were the victims of a crime; but their disappearance is no less painful for their families. Imelda Keenan was last seen at her home in William Street, Waterford, in January 1994. 28-year-old Sandra Collins from Killala, Co. Mayo, disappeared from her home in December 2000.

Ellen Coss from Ballyfermot, Dublin, was last seen in November 1999 as she boarded a train in Manchester for Holyhead, where she was to get the ferry to Dublin. It is now believed that she never arrived in Dublin. In the meantime her family travelled to the unveiling of the National Missing Persons Monument, unaware of the fresh trauma they were soon to endure. In June 2002 Ellen's brothers and sisters were notified of the discovery of a woman's body on a beach at Eastbourne, Sussex, but they were told it would be some time before DNA tests would tell whether the body was that of their missing sister. It was three agonising months before tests proved that the body was not that of Ellen Coss. Ellen remains missing.

There are further cases in which, despite the best efforts of the Gardaí, no trace has been found of people who have disappeared. One that continues to baffle detectives in Co. Cork is that of a married couple, Conor and Sheila Dwyer from Fermoy, who were in their sixties when they were last seen in April 1991. When gardaí searched their home they found all their personal belong-

240

ings, such as clothes, money, and passports, still in the house. The only thing missing was the couple's car—a Toyota Cressida, registration number ZT-5797. Despite the assistance of the police in other countries, no trace of the car, or of the missing couple, has been found.

Another long-term missing person is Michael Farrell from Donaghmede, Dublin, who was thirty when he disappeared from the B&I ferry *Isle of Inishmore* in September 1994 while the ship was en route from Rosslare to Pembroke. He worked as a cinema projectionist on board the ferry, and his disappearance has left his family devastated. Despite a thorough search of the ship and the sea, no trace of Michael Farrell has been found.

In January 1996, 73-year-old Alpho O'Reilly, who suffered from amnesia, disappeared from his home in Strand Road, Sandymount, Dublin. His car, a green Mitsubishi Colt, registration number 95-D-6446, is also unaccounted for. What many people find disturbing about this case, and that of the Dwyers in Co. Cork, is that two cars, whose registration numbers are known, have not been found anywhere. Neither car has turned up abandoned or stolen. How can cars vanish?

While the great majority of people who go missing return home safely of their own free will, or are found by the Gardaí, there are some who will not return alive. Some missing people have taken their own lives; others have died in accidents; others still have been murdered. Whatever the circumstances of the deaths of these missing people, the fact that many of their bodies have not been found is a source of great distress to their families.

Unfortunately, there have been a number of significant instances in which the Gardaí have failed to find the bodies of missing people even when they are within a few hundred yards of the search areas. While detectives stress that they have learnt from their mistakes, it is still unfortunate, to say the least, that murder, accident and suicide victims have lain undiscovered for days or weeks before being found. These failures deny the distraught families the opportunity to grieve properly for their loved ones.

For almost three weeks Paul McQuaid's body lay in a lane a few hundred yards from Grafton Street, Dublin. While thousands of people walked along one of the city's busiest streets during May 2001, a young man who had wandered down the lane and fallen off a railing lay dead a short distance away. Though the body was found on private property belonging to a bank, it seems almost incredible that an isolated lane so close to where the man disappeared was not searched. Paul McQuaid had last been seen outside Judge Roy Bean's bar in Nassau Street. It seems clear that later that night he wandered up Grafton Street and turned to the right down Wicklow Street. For some unexplained reason he then turned right again into a dark lane and tried to climb a high fence at the end but fell and suffered fatal injuries.

One of the most distressing aspects of this case is the fact that it was later discovered that there was closed-circuit television tape of a figure—later confirmed as that of Paul McQuaid—walking towards the lane. Detectives had conducted an intensive search, including the River Liffey and numerous areas between Judge Roy Bean's and Paul McQuaid's home in Clontarf in north Dublin. But one of the gardaí who worked on the case accepts that they failed to fully search the immediate area around Nassau Street.

Basically, we should have tried to put ourselves in Paul's shoes. He had come out of the pub in Nassau Street, and he had had a few drinks. What we failed to do was try and think like Paul.

We were thinking that, logically, he might have tried to make his way home to Clontarf, but for some reason he headed up Grafton Street instead of down towards Trinity College. So we were wrong from the start. The exact place where his body was found was actually private property, a back entrance in the basement of a bank, and it was a security guard from the bank who found Paul's body. Even if we had looked in from the alleyway it would have been almost, if not totally, impossible to see Paul; but that is still not good enough. We are truly sorry for his family. We could have found him sooner.

Another recent case in which the Gardaí sadly failed to find a body very close to their search area was that of the murder of the 28-year-old German journalist Bettina Poeschel in Donore, Co. Meath, in September 2001. For twenty-three days the body lay in dense undergrowth about fifteen yards off the main Drogheda road close to Donore. A massive investigation had been launched soon after her disappearance on 25 September, yet search parties failed to find the murdered woman until a garda made the shocking discovery while searching the almost inaccessible terrain on 17 October. The fact that it took the Gardaí more than three weeks to find the body caused a great deal of discussion among detectives. Unlike the case of Paul McQuaid, Bettina Poeschel's body was found very close to where she was most probably travelling. The Gardaí knew she had taken the train from Dublin to Drogheda, and she had told a friend she was planning to visit the passage tomb at Newgrange, about three miles from Donore. Yet for twenty-three days the body lay hidden in undergrowth in Donore, exposed to the elements. During that time the woman's distraught father and sister travelled from Munich to appeal for help in finding her. The failure to find the body sooner was to lead in turn to a delay of several months before it was released to her family by the coroner for bringing back to Germany. Because the body had lain exposed for so long, it took longer than usual to conduct all the necessary examinations for the purpose of assessing the exact cause of her death, and other elements of the criminal investigation. The family later thanked the Gardaí for their hard work in eventually finding Bettina; a memorial now stands close to where she met her death.

There are two recent examples of young men who have been murdered as part of the activity of criminal gangs in Dublin but whose bodies remained undiscovered for long periods relatively close to where they disappeared. Seventeen-year-old Patrick 'Whacker' Lawlor was murdered in January 1999, and for three years his body lay in a shallow grave close to the Ninth Lock of the Grand Canal at Clondalkin, Dublin. He was murdered after getting involved with a violent heroin dealer who was distributing drugs in west Dublin. It was in January 2002 that the Gardaí found Lawlor's remains after a tip-off. From the time of his disappearance three years before, detectives believed he had been murdered and his body buried somewhere in west Dublin, but all searches for his body were fruitless. It was eventually recovered only because the tip-off was extremely precise in identifying where it was buried. For three years people walked and drove by the spot where this body lay, and for three years the Garda investigation was hampered by the failure to find the body. The investigation into the murder of Patrick Lawlor continues.

The other recent example was the killing of 22-year-old Neil Hanlon from Crumlin, Dublin. For five months his body lay in a shallow grave on open land close to Crumlin Vocational School in the centre of a heavily populated area. He was last seen in

September 2001 close to his home, less than a quarter of a mile from where his body was found. He had been abducted and murdered in a horrific attack after he was involved in a dispute with a Dublin drug-dealer. He suffered a prolonged attack before being murdered, after which his grave was dug under cover of darkness. As with the discovery of the body of Patrick Lawlor, detectives found Neil Hanlon's body in February 2002 only after precise information was received about where they should search. For five months children played close to the unmarked grave, while pedestrians and motorists travelled along the busy Sundrive Road, a few hundred yards away.

The fact that these two young Dublin men could be abducted and murdered and their bodies buried so close to the murder scenes is a source of extreme concern to the Gardaí, who naturally want to find such bodies as soon as possible, not only to aid their investigations but also for the sake of the grieving families. One detective pointed out that neither body would have been found but for very precise information.

When it comes to finding bodies of such missing people, we need to have information indicating, preferably within a few feet, where the bodies might lie. Giving general information, such as a part of a town, or a golf course, or part of a large farm, is not really going to help us. Naturally we will search such areas as best we can, but it's just not practical to get large diggers in to search acres and acres of land. You have to remember that we carry out inch-by-inch searches of possible locations for bodies, but it's just not humanly possible to search massive tracts of land without strong indications that we might find something.

The clearest example of the problems faced by the Gardaí is the difficulties they had in trying to find the remains of people who were abducted and killed by the Provisional IRA in the 1970s and early 80s. In March 1999 the IRA admitted that it was responsible for the deaths of nine missing people who were abducted and murdered between 1972 and 1980. The organisation forwarded information to the Gardaí about a number of places where the remains had been buried in unmarked graves in Cos. Monaghan, Louth, Wicklow, and Meath. By the time detectives had finished extensive searches of each of the sites, only three of the nine bodies had been found.

A mysterious and sinister story remains to be told about the disappearance and suspected murder of a number of men in Cork in the mid-1990s. In April 1994, 23-year-old Cathal O'Brien from Co. Wexford and 42-year-old Kevin Ball both disappeared from a house in Wellington Terrace, Cork. In December the same year 32-year-old Patrick O'Driscoll, who lived in the same house, also vanished. The Gardaí began an intensive investigation, and within months Fred Flannery, who had also been living in Wellington Terrace, was charged with the murder of Patrick O'Driscoll. When his trial began at the Central Criminal Court in June 1996 his seventeen-year-old nephew Michael told the jury he had seen body parts in a cupboard in the house, and he had been shown a coalbag in which, he was told, Patrick O'Driscoll's body was hidden.

However, the trial was halted amid extraordinary scenes after Mr Justice Robert Barr found that certain evidence had been suppressed. Mr Justice Barr directed that Fred Flannery be acquitted of the murder charge, and he walked free from court.

A month later Patrick O'Driscoll's dismembered body was found buried in a sports bag in a shallow grave in the grounds of Lotabeg House in Cork. Cathal O'Brien was a graduate of Waterford RTC and was a socially concerned young man who worked with the Simon Community in Cork. During his work he met and befriended Kevin Ball. The failure to find their remains is a source of great distress to their families and a hindrance to the Garda investigation in bringing charges against their killer. Detectives are also conscious of the disappearance of Frank 'Blackie' McCarthy, who vanished in Cork in February 1993 and is believed to have been murdered also.

The reluctance of the Garda authorities to establish a National Missing Persons Unit, to be involved in continuous searches for missing people, is a source of anger and frustration to many families of missing people. From her home in Co. Kilkenny, Jo Jo Dullard's sister Mary Phelan is leading a campaign for the establishment of such a unit. In relation to her own sister, who was abducted and murdered in November 1995, Mary Phelan believes that detectives have not searched every area they should have in their efforts to find Jo Jo.

> Right from the start we have been calling on the Gardaí or the state to make sure that a full search for Jo Jo is done in a twenty-mile radius around Moone, where she made the phone call that night. Such a search should cover both public and private land. The Gardaí have not searched areas that they really should be looking at, and it's just not right. We need better-trained detectives who know exactly what they are looking for, and who are given the time and the equipment to do their job. What we need in this country is something like the Murder Squad that we used to have, where they would travel around the country and investigate the big cases.

The feeling of Garda headquarters is that investigations into missing people are best left to the Garda division in the area in which the person disappeared. It is argued that local gardaí have a particular knowledge of their areas as well as of local people and can therefore better ascertain why a person might be missing.

Mary Phelan has spent thousands of hours writing, phoning and faxing politicians seeking whatever support she can for her campaign for a Missing Persons Unit. She and her husband, Martin Phelan, spend day after day travelling to meet families of other missing people and fund-raising for various ventures to ensure that the memory of missing people will never diminish. Through the Jo Jo Dullard Memorial Trust the Phelans led the campaign for the National Missing Persons Monument in Kilkenny. They have also campaigned tirelessly for the establishment of a National Missing Persons Day, to commemorate every person who is missing in Ireland.

As part of their campaign for the establishment of a Missing Persons Unit, the Phelans organised a trip to the United States with John McGuinness TD in 2003 to meet members of the FBI and to learn of techniques used by the American police in tracing missing people. They have also established contacts with the families of American missing people, while many American politicians voice concerns about the abduction and murder in the Dublin-Wicklow Mountains of the missing American woman Annie McCarrick. Mary Phelan told me they will continue to fight for more to be done to find Ireland's missing people.

We want to see helicopters out searching for the missing people, and special sniffer dogs, and we want to see continuous searches, in any place where missing people might be. And some of the missing people, like poor Jo Jo, have been murdered. It's just not right that these killers can walk around free like that.

And they will do it again if they are not caught. Ireland is only an island, and there are far too many of these missing persons, and none of them have been solved.

John McGuinness told me that their trip to the United States is part of a continuous effort to fight for missing people.

I never met Jo Jo Dullard, and I only got involved after I really listened to the terrible story that Mary and Martin have to tell of how their lives and the lives of so many others have been affected by losing a loved one in such a way. I've done what I can through questions in the Dáil and the like, but it shouldn't be left to me or any other backbencher to keep this issue alive in the Dáil. The Government has a moral duty to respond in a tangible way to these people. I believe that expertise from abroad in how to find missing people should be brought in or bought in. Ireland is not that big. More can and should be done to find these people.

A number of suggestions about what more can be done have been privately considered by senior gardaí. One of these is enlisting the assistance of the Defence Forces in searching large tracts of land where a body might conceivably be buried. There are thousands of such areas around the country, including hundreds of acres of bog-land and forested land. Soldiers have occasionally been used to conduct certain searches alongside gardaí, at the request of Garda headquarters. One senior garda told me the issue should definitely be looked at more closely.

This should not be about territorial disputes, or who is in charge. The army can only ever be used within Ireland as an aid to the civil power. The Gardaí will always be in charge within our borders; but the Defence Forces could be of immense assistance to us. I'm not only talking about manpower. Of course the more people out searching for missing people the better, but what I mean is that soldiers, like gardaí, are trained to observe the smallest of details. Our soldiers have proven themselves again and again, from East Timor to Eritrea, and such attention, discipline, patience and methodical thought could be of immense assistance in finding what might be the tiniest signs of a body being buried somewhere. Ideally the army could be helping to search for the missing people while gardaí conduct the criminal investigations, trying to establish who might be responsible for these murders, and where the most likely burial areas might be.

The two most likely areas where killers have buried bodies of their victims are on bogland and in mountainous areas. The killer of Marie Kilmartin in Co. Laois in December 1993 hid her body in a bog drain, where it remained for six months. The killers of Antoinette Smith in south Co. Dublin in July 1987 hid her body in a bog in the Dublin Mountains, where it lay undiscovered for nine months. And whoever killed Patricia Doherty in 1991, also in south Co. Dublin, chose to hide her body close to where Antoinette Smith's body was hidden, where it was discovered six months after her disappearance. It is entirely possible that if members of the Defence Forces, or others, were to conduct extensive continuous searches of bogs and mountains they would eventually find bodies or crime scenes, or other evidence.

A good example of how such minute searching can yield results came during the late 1980s in the Dublin Mountains. A team of detectives were carrying out an inch-by-inch search for paintings that had been stolen from the Beit Collection at Russborough House, near Blessington, Co. Wicklow. The Gardaí had established that the paintings had been stolen by a gang led by the Dublin criminal Martin Cahill, who had later hidden them in the mountains. They were combing the woodland and dense undergrowth at a section of the mountains just south of Rathfarnham when one eagle-eyed garda noticed clothing. She looked more closely and saw that it was the partially decomposed body of a man.

The area was immediately sealed off, and the body was examined. It would later emerge that the man had died from a gunshot wound to the back of the head. His killer had hidden his body in the mountains, where it remained undiscovered for several months. The victim was later identified as a Dublin man; but what amazed detectives was that he had never been reported missing by his family or friends. If the Gardaí had known earlier that he was missing, with their knowledge of the man they would have feared the worst and conducted searches in the mountains for his body. As it was, it was only because of the search for the Beit paintings that this murder victim was found.

The Dublin Mountains have long been used by killers as a place in which to hide the bodies of their victims. The extraordinary events this area witnessed in 1971 show that the use of such mountainous terrain for hiding bodies is not new. In a crime that shocked the country, the bodies of two young people from Co. Meath were left at Tibradden, Co. Dublin, in separate but linked killings. The first victim was a young woman, Una Lynskey, who disappeared from her home near Ratoath, Co. Meath, in October 1971. It was not until two months later, on 10 December, that James Williams, out walking in the Pine Forest at Tibradden, found the shallow grave. The Gardaí later established that tarred felt had been used in an attempt to cover the unmarked grave. A watch and a ring taken from the body were identified as being Una Lynskey's, but because the body had lain undiscovered for two months the State Pathologist, Professor Maurice Hickey, could not establish the exact cause of death.

Two young Co. Meath men were later tried for the murder of Una Lynskey. Both were found guilty of manslaughter and jailed for three years. Detectives who investigated Una's death also investigated a second violent death which occurred in December 1971. Nine days after Una Lynskey's body was found in Tibradden, a 22-year-old man was abducted by a group of men in Co. Meath and driven to the same spot in the mountains, where he was beaten and left to die. Three young men, including two brothers, were later convicted of the manslaughter of this man and were jailed for between two and three years.

The murder of Patricia Furlong at nearby Glencullen in 1982, and the murders of Antoinette Smith in 1987 and Patricia Doherty in 1991, also resulted in the Dublin Mountains being used by murderers for concealing the evidence of the killings. It is possible that somewhere close by, the body of Annie McCarrick is hidden, and perhaps also that of Eva Brennan, who disappeared in July 1993. There are other missing persons cases where the Gardaí privately admit they believe the bodies most probably lie in the mountains and forests of Cos. Dublin and Wicklow. Though it is easier said than done, if soldiers were taken out of their barracks to take part in extensive and continuous searches in areas such as the Dublin and Wicklow Mountains, for weeks or months at a time, many more bodies might be found.

Another tool that might aid the Gardaí in their efforts to trace missing people could be new legislation allowing for specific periods of detention for suspects. Detectives often speak of their frustration at being able to hold murder suspects only for twelve hours before having to set them free. Such a short time for questioning is even more frustrating for the gardaí who are investigating possible murders when there is no body, no murder weapon, and no crime scene. One detective who believes he knows the identity of the killer of one of Ireland's missing women says the hands of the Gardaí are tied by some of the laws they work with.

> The Criminal Justice Act allows us to hold a murder suspect for a maximum of twelve hours before they can be charged or released. If we think a firearm has been used in the murder of someone who is missing we can hold the person for up to seventy-two hours. But very often we believe we have a prime suspect who is very much in the frame for some missing person's abduction and murder, and we can only bring them in for questioning for twelve hours, for the simple reason that we don't know how they have killed the missing person.
>
> Compare those laws to the drug legislation, where suspects can be held for up to a week before being charged or released. If we had a week with some of the murder suspects who have just sat across the table and smirked at us when they are under arrest, things might be different. Their consciences might get the better of them, and they might crack.

Another issue that angers detectives is the right to silence that suspects enjoy. If a murder suspect remains silent during questioning, the only sanction they might face is that an inference might be drawn by a jury if the case ever went to trial.

But the issue that angers gardaí most is the right of a murder suspect to refuse to give a blood sample. Obtaining such samples is critically important in solving cases of missing women who may have been raped and murdered. Detectives are acutely aware that if ever the bodies of these murder victims are discovered, there may still be evidence that could catch their killers. There is one case of a murdered woman in which the killer left a sample of his DNA at the murder scene, but this cannot be matched with the suspect because he cannot be compelled to give a blood sample.

Detective-Sergeant Pat Campbell, who has investigated many murder and other serious crime cases in south Co. Dublin, agrees that the Gardaí need more investigative tools.

> It's very frustrating that we could be sitting across a table from a man who we believe to be a cruel murderer and he has the right to silence and the right to refuse to give us a blood sample. It's absolute madness. You get a far greater penalty if you refuse to give a sample in a drink-driving case. I think a data-base of blood samples would help solve a lot of crimes, not just murders or rapes but even burglaries as well. If we do not get the powers to compel suspects to give a sample, I think more women will be abducted and murdered, other young women will go missing. It would also be a great preventive measure.

It is worth noting that, in relation to two women who were first classified as missing but whose bodies were later found, the killers were caught only because they volunteered a blood sample. If John Crerar had not volunteered a sample in 1980 he would not have been convicted twenty-two years later of the murder of Phyllis Murphy. If David Lawler had not volunteered a blood sample to detectives in Blanchardstown in 1996 he would not have been identified as the rapist and murderer of Marilyn Rynn, whose body lay undiscovered close to her home for seventeen days after she was attacked in December 1995. Lawler volunteered a blood sample only after reading on the internet that semen samples would not have survived intact by the time Marilyn's body was discovered. But he had not reckoned on the freezing temperatures that preserved the sample at the crime scene, and he is now serving a life sentence for murder. This was also one of the cases in which the Gardaí failed to find a body that lay close to where the victim was last seen alive. The public can breathe a sigh of relief that her body was discovered before the crucial evidence could be lost. It should also be noted that if John Crerar or David Lawler had declined to give a blood sample they would still be walking the streets, as other killers who have refused to give such samples do, free to attack other women.

The difficulties faced by detectives in finding the bodies of missing people is not confined to one police force. A case in which the body of a missing person in the United States lay undiscovered for more than a year involved the disappearance of Chandra Levy, a young woman who had a close relationship with Senator Gary Condit. She had been working in his Washington office, and after her disappearance it emerged that Condit had not at first admitted how close their relationship had been. Chandra Levy disappeared in May 2001, but it was more than a year before her body was found in a heavily wooded area in a park in Washington. The police had earlier said that Condit was not a suspect, and they had already searched more than 1,700 acres of Rock Creek Park following her disappearance. She was known to jog in the park, but for more than a year her body lay undiscovered in underbrush, and it was found only after a man who was looking for turtles while out walking his dog discovered her skull. The body was identified through dental records.

In recent years the police in England have been faced with a number of horrendous murders of girls whose bodies lay undiscovered for weeks or months, each case providing an example of how difficult it is to find a body if the killer goes to any lengths to hide his tracks. One of the biggest manhunts in English history was undertaken in August 2002 for the ten-year-old schoolgirls Holly Wells and Jessica Chapman, who disappeared from their home in the village of Soham, Cambridgeshire, on the evening of 4 August. For thirteen days the bodies of the two friends lay undiscovered off an isolated path in an area of countryside just a few miles away, despite the combing of the countryside by hundreds of police and hundreds of volunteers. Because the two bodies were exposed to the elements for so long, it was a number of days before they could be formally identified. Their school caretaker, Ian Huntley, was later charged with murdering the two girls; his girlfriend, Maxine Carr, a teaching assistant at the school, was also charged in connection with the killings.

For six months the body of fourteen-year-old Milly Dowler lay undiscovered twenty miles from where she disappeared near her home at Walton-on-Thames, Surrey, outside London. She was last seen walking from the local railway station on 21 March 2002. For six months she was classified as missing, but in September that year a man out walking his dog in a forested area made the shocking discovery that reclassified the case as a murder inquiry. The police believe the body lay undiscovered in the forest from soon after her disappearance in March. The six months before the discovery saw one of the most intensive police investigations in England, yet the body lay undiscovered in a forest only twenty miles from where she was last seen.

Other evil killers go to more extreme lengths to hide their crimes. In November 2000, 46-year-old John Taylor from Leeds abducted sixteen-year-old Leanne Tiernan as she was walking down a darkened alley on her way home from a Christmas shopping trip. He brought her to his house, where he blindfolded her, bound her hands with plastic ties, and sexually assaulted her. He also placed a dog collar around her neck, which was later to be of crucial value to the police investigation. Within hours of abducting the teenager he strangled her and placed her body in a freezer in his house. Some months later he removed the body and put it in a sleeping-bag and bin-liners bound with twine. Nine months after the girl's abduction and murder her body was found beneath a canopy of trees near Otley, Yorkshire, seventeen miles from where she was last seen alive. The police began an extensive investigation, part of which involved a scientific examination of the dog collar, which was still around the girl's neck when her body was found. They soon narrowed their list of suspects to a small number of people who had bought such a collar from a particular shop. One of those was John Taylor, who was later jailed for life after he admitted murdering Leanne Tiernan. It would later emerge that he had spent three weeks, under the pretext of walking his dog, roaming in a secluded wooded area in Leeds before selecting Leanne Tiernan for a random attack.

Another recent case of a teenage girl abducted and murdered in England is that of fifteen-year-old Danielle Jones, who was murdered in June 2001. Apart from the trauma of not knowing where the body of their daughter lies, her parents are faced with the awful reality that it was a close relative who abducted and murdered their daughter and hid her body in a secret place. In December 2002 Danielle Jones's 42-year-old uncle, Stuart Campbell, was convicted of murdering his niece. The police had earmarked him as a suspect within days of Danielle's disappearance from her home at East Tilbury, a few miles east of London, on 18 June 2001, after they had discovered indecent photographs of children during a search of his home. The murder trial heard that Campbell had a fascination with teenage girls and had become obsessed with his fifteen-year-old niece. The girl's father later revealed that he had suspected that his brother-in-law was indecently touching Danielle, but she was abducted and murdered before he could confront him. But despite initial optimism that Campbell might confess where he buried his niece's body, he has continued to protest his innocence since being jailed for life in December 2002. Despite hundreds of hours of searches of rivers, lakes and fields in Essex and Kent, Danielle Jones's unmarked grave has not been found. The awful reality that the killer of the fifteen-year-old was a close relative is a stark reminder that evil-minded people are not always strangers.

These and similar abductions and murders are ever-present in the thoughts of the Gardaí, who fear that similar killers may strike in Ireland. Detectives are extremely concerned about a number of abductions and attempted abductions of young children in recent years. In the summer of 2002 a man from Co. Tyrone living in Dublin tried to abduct two girls in Dundalk. The same man also tried to lure a boy and girl into his car in Coolmine, Co. Dublin, by asking them to help him look for his cat. In a separate investigation a man from Tullamore, Co. Offaly, was charged with abducting a girl in 2001 and another in 2002, both in the midlands. Both victims were found by the roadside some hours after they were allegedly abducted and subjected to physical assaults.

One idea that could help tackle such roadside abductions might be the placing of electronic warning notices along main roads throughout the country. These notices could alert motorists to the fact that a person had been abducted and could give a description of the car, the abductor, or the missing person. Such a concept would not have to be confined to missing people but could be used to trace cars used in bank robberies and other crimes in which criminals use motorways to make quick getaways. Such notices are a common feature of highways in America and have led to many killers and other criminals being caught through the quick actions of alert motorists.

The other common practice in the United States for helping to find missing people is for their photograph to be printed on milk cartons. Such appeals have been conducted in Ireland but not in a systematic manner. The families of missing people would dearly love to see such appeals printed on milk cartons or the packaging of other household items as part of an organised effort to find missing people.

A similar idea is for photographs of missing people to be featured on postage stamps or as part of the franking of envelopes. Fiona Pender's friend Emer Condron has already raised this question with An Post, and still hopes there may be a positive outcome. Such initiatives and ideas are the brainchild of relatives and friends of missing people. Emer Condron has also run a mini-marathon wearing a T-shirt bearing Fiona Pender's photograph to keep her memory alive, while Trevor Deely's family have arranged for his photograph to appear on milk cartons sold by the Iceland chain. Father Aquinas Duffy runs a web site to help families of missing people and to reach out to those missing people who have chosen to disappear.

Compared with many other countries, the number of people who disappear without trace in Ireland is low. However, the rate of such disappearances is increasing. Over the seventy-year period 1929–99, of the tens of thousands of people officially reported as missing only 298 cases were left unsolved; of this figure only eighteen would be categorised as suspicious. These include the six cases investigated by Operation Trace, the case of seven-year-old Mary Boyle, and the abducted thirteen-year-old schoolboy Philip Cairns. The fact that so many of the 'suspicious' unsolved disappearances were in the second half of the twentieth century suggests that potentially there are now more violent people at large than before who remain undetected. Operation Trace failed to clearly establish whether a serial killer was attacking women; but the alternative is equally disturbing. Despite the recent successes of the Gardaí in tackling drugs dealers, dissident republican organisations and organised criminal gangs, one thing remains clear: there remain up to ten murderers at large. These are killers who have left no crime scene, who have hidden the bodies of their victims, and who, if they are not caught, may kill again.

One detective who has worked on a number of investigations into the activities of suspected serial killers believes the Gardaí have done everything in their power to find any such killers, but he accepts that more must be done.

We have to work within the law, and sometimes the laws do not help us. Sometimes we cannot detain suspects long enough, and they do not have to account for their movements. We have looked high and low to try and catch those killers who may have killed someone in a crime of passion, and those who may have struck at random. Every single scrap of information that we get from the public is checked out. Yet still so many missing people who have been murdered remain untraced. Sometimes I wonder if the answer is staring us in the face: I wonder if maybe in ten or twelve years' time will we all have egg on our face if and when some house or field is found to contain the answer. But right now, we have done everything we are allowed to do.

The Gardaí have spent tens of thousands of hours trying to find missing people. Many detectives have worked on their days off to chase up leads in the hope that a crucial break might come. These gardaí have established strong relationships with many of the families of missing people, while some other families just do not see eye to eye with detectives. The dedication shown by the Gardaí cannot be questioned. The fact that one of the most senior detectives in Ireland is an uncle of one of the missing women shows that the families of gardaí can also suffer unexplained loss.

While the Gardaí have failed to come up with the answers that the public want and, more importantly, the families of missing people want, they remain dogged in their determination to find the answers, to find the missing people, and to find the invisible killers.

In years to come, advances in forensic science will see more and more killers taken off the streets. Murderers will be caught by anything from beads of sweat or tears to ear wax or mucus, which they will inadvertently leave at the scene of their crimes. But the advances that the laboratories will provide will need to be matched by legislation to allow for saliva or blood samples to be forcibly taken from murder suspects. Such advances will doubtless be of assistance in solving some of the missing persons cases, but very often in such cases there is no crime scene. The Gardaí would like to have more powers to compel suspects to account for their movements and more powers to hold suspects, to offer such suspects ample time in which to examine their conscience, instead of just picking a spot on a wall and staring at it for twelve hours.

In the cases of Fiona Pender, Ciara Breen and Fiona Sinnott there are suspects who may have information relating to what happened to the three young women. Suspicion alone does not make a case, and there is always the possibility that these suspects are not the guilty parties. Based on the powers the Gardaí have at present for arrest and detention, there is a converse argument that these suspects are in turn denied the opportunity to fully convince detectives of their innocence.

For more than a quarter of a century Ann and Charlie Boyle have wondered every day what happened to their seven-year-old daughter, Mary. Alice and Philip Cairns, the parents of thirteen-year-old Philip Cairns, who was abducted in 1986, have prayed every day for some news of their son. The same feeling of unrelenting anguish is felt by Annie McCarrick's parents, John and Nancy McCarrick, in New York. Eva Brennan's family have suffered her loss since she vanished, also in 1993. Jo Jo Dullard's three sisters and brother have constantly thought of their little sister since she was abducted and murdered in 1995. Josephine Pender and her son John continue to mourn the loss of Fiona Pender, who was seven months pregnant when she was murdered in 1996. Bernadette Breen lost her only child, and her best friend, when her seventeen-year-old daughter, Ciara, was abducted and murdered in Dundalk in 1997. Emma Rose Carroll lost her mother, Fiona Sinnott, when she vanished in Co. Wexford in 1998, leaving not only her young daughter but also her own parents and her two brothers and sisters.

And there are other missing people, some of whom have chosen to disappear because of depression, others perhaps because of amnesia. Each family continues to suffer an aching and unexplained loss. Despite the best efforts of the Gardaí, and despite the unique Operation Trace computer initiative, all these cases remain unsolved. Amid calls for more action to be taken by the state and the Gardaí, the devastating effects of the loss of a loved one are evident in the homes and the hearts of the families of Ireland's missing.